Lecture Notes in Computer Science 13586

Founding Editors

Gerhard Goos
Juris Hartmanis

Editorial Board Members

The series Lecture Notes in Computer Science (LNCS), including its subseries Lecture Notes in Artificial Intelligence (LNAI) and Lecture Notes in Bioinformatics (LNBI), has established itself as a medium for the publication of new developments in computer science and information technology research, teaching, and education.

LNCS enjoys close cooperation with the computer science R & D community, the series counts many renowned academics among its volume editors and paper authors, and collaborates with prestigious societies. Its mission is to serve this international community by providing an invaluable service, mainly focused on the publication of conference and workshop proceedings and postproceedings. LNCS commenced publication in 1973.

Xiahai Zhuang · Lei Li · Sihan Wang · Fuping Wu
Editors

Left Atrial and Scar Quantification and Segmentation

First Challenge, LAScarQS 2022
Held in Conjunction with MICCAI 2022
Singapore, September 18, 2022
Proceedings

Editors
Xiahai Zhuang (iD)
Fudan University
Shanghai, China

Lei Li
University of Oxford
Oxford, UK

Sihan Wang
Fudan University
Shanghai, China

Fuping Wu
University of Oxford
Oxford, UK

ISSN 0302-9743   ISSN 1611-3349 (electronic)
Lecture Notes in Computer Science
ISBN 978-3-031-31777-4   ISBN 978-3-031-31778-1 (eBook)
https://doi.org/10.1007/978-3-031-31778-1

This Springer imprint is published by the registered company Springer Nature Switzerland AG
The registered company address is: Gewerbestrasse 11, 6330 Cham, Switzerland

Preface

AF is the most common arrhythmia observed in clinical practice, occurring in up to 1% of the population and rising fast with advancing age. Radiofrequency catheter ablation using the pulmonary vein (PV) isolation technique has emerged as one of the most common methods for the treatment of AF patients. The position and extent of scars provide important information of the pathophysiology and progression of AF. Late gadolinium enhancement magnetic resonance imaging (LGE MRI) is a promising technique to visualize and quantify atrial scars. Many clinical studies mainly focus on the location and extent of scarring areas of the left atrium (LA) myocardium.

The Challenge provides 194 LGE MRIs acquired in real clinical environments from patients suffering atrial fibrillation (AF). It is aimed to create an open and fair competition for various research.

The target of this challenge is to automatically segment the LA cavity and quantify LA scars from LGE MRI. This is however still arduous. First, the image quality of LGE MRI could be poor. Second, the prior model of scars is hard to construct on account of the various LA shapes, the thin wall (mean thickness 1.89 ± 0.48 mm reported by Beinart et al), the surrounding enhanced regions and the complex patterns of scars in AF patients. To the best of our knowledge, little work has been reported in the literature to achieve the fully automatic segmentation and quantification of the LA cavity and scars from LGE MRI.

Note that the LA segmentation is normally required as an initialization for scar quantification. This is because atrial scars are located on the LA wall, and it is too hard to directly localize scars due to its small size. However, previous methods normally solved the two tasks independently and ignored the intrinsic spatial relationship between the LA and scars. Therefore, in this challenge, we encourage the participants to achieve joint segmentation. The challenge will provide 194 LGE MRIs globally, i.e., from multiple imaging centers around the world, for developing novel algorithms that can quantify or segment the LA cavity and scars. The challenge presents an open and fair platform for various research groups to test and validate their methods on these datasets acquired from the clinical environment. To ensure data privacy, the platform will enable remote training and testing on the dataset from different centers in local and the dataset can keep invisible. The aim of the challenge will not only be to benchmark various LA scar segmentation algorithms, but also to cover the topic of general cardiac image segmentation, quantification, joint optimization, and model generalization, and raise discussions for further technical development and clinical deployment. The readers

can find more information about LAScarQS on the website: https://zmiclab.github.io/
projects/lascarqs22/index.html.

October 2022   Xiahai Zhuang
Lei Li
Sihan Wang
Fuping Wu

Organization

General Chairs

Xiahai Zhuang   Fudan University, China
Lei Li   University of Oxford, UK
Sihan Wang   Fudan University, China
Fuping Wu   University of Oxford, UK

Program Committee

Byung-Woo Hong   Chung-Ang University, Seoul, South Korea
Chunna Jin   Zhejiang University Affiliated Second Hospital, China
Dana C. Peters   Yale University, USA
Guang Yang   Imperial College London, UK
Julia A. Schnabel   Technical University of Munich, Germany
Jichao Zhao   University of Auckland, New Zealand
Junseok Kwon   Chung-Ang University, Seoul, South Korea
Kawal Rhode   King's College London, UK
Linwei Wang   Rochester Institute of Technology, USA
Marco J. W. Gotte   Vrije Universiteit Amsterdam, The Netherlands
Oscar Camara   Universitat Pompeu Fabra, Spain
Rob S. MacLeod   University of Utah, USA
Shan Yang   Zhongshan Hospital, China

Technical Support Team

Chao Huang   Fudan University, China
Mian Jiang   Fudan University, China

Additional Reviewers

Boming Wang
Chenhao Pei
Hangqi Zhou

Jianhua Ji
Junyi Qiu
Kaiwen Wan
Ke Zhang
MenJun Wu
Wangbin Ding
Xinzhe Luo
Yuncheng Zhou
Zheyao Gao

Contents

LASSNet: A Four Steps Deep Neural Network for Left Atrial Segmentation and Scar Quantification

Arthur L. Lefebvre[1,2]( ), Carolyna A. P. Yamamoto[2,3], Julie K. Shade[2],
Ryan P. Bradley[2], Rebecca A. Yu[3], Rheeda L. Ali[2,3],
Dan M. Popescu[2], Adityo Prakosa[2], Eugene G. Kholmovski[2,3],
and Natalia A. Trayanova[2,3]

[1] Faculté polytechnique de Mons, UMONS, Mons, Belgium
lefearthur@gmail.com
[2] Alliance for Cardiovascular Diagnostic and Treatment Innovation (ADVANCE),
Johns Hopkins University, Baltimore, MD, USA
[3] Department of Biomedical Engineering, Johns Hopkins University School
of Medicine, Baltimore, MD, USA

Abstract. Accurate quantification of left atrium (LA) scar in patients
with atrial fibrillation is essential to guide successful ablation strategies. Prior to LA scar quantification, a proper LA cavity segmentation
is required to ensure exact location of scar. Both tasks can be extremely
time-consuming and are subject to inter-observer disagreements when
done manually. We developed and validated a deep neural network to
automatically segment the LA cavity and the LA scar. The global architecture uses a multi-network sequential approach in two stages which
segment the LA cavity and the LA Scar. Each stage has two steps: a
region of interest Neural Network and a refined segmentation network.
We analysed the performances of our network according to different
parameters and applied data triaging. 200+ late gadolinium enhancement magnetic resonance images were provided by the LAScarQS 2022
Challenge. Finally, we compared our performances for scar quantification
to the literature and demonstrated improved performances.

Keywords: Segmentation · Late gadolinium enhancement · Deep
learning · Atrial fibrillation · Left atrium

1 Introduction

Atrial fibrillation (AF) is the most prevalent sustained heart rhythm disorder,
contributing significantly to global health care costs and mortality and mor-
bidity rates [1]. Catheter ablation may offer a cure to AF in some patients.

N.T.
E. G. Kholmovski and N. A. Trayanova—Indicates equal contribution by senior
authors.

© The Author(s), under exclusive license to Springer Nature Switzerland AG 2023
X. Zhuang et al. (Eds.): LAScarQS 2022, LNCS 13586, pp. 1–15, 2023.
https://doi.org/10.1007/978-3-031-31778-1_1

However, AF ablation success rates are modest (50%) in patients with extensive structural remodeling (i.e., fibrosis infiltration, fat accumulation) of the left atrium (LA) [2]. Such structural remodeling is typically identified from pre-ablation late gadolinium-enhancement magnetic resonance imaging (LGE-MRI) [3]. Reconstruction of the atrial anatomy and quantification of the fibrotic substrate is clinically important for guiding catheter ablation [3]. The first step of anatomical reconstruction is the segmentation of the atrial myocardium from cardiac images. Generally, the LA endocardial walls [4] are manually segmented from the LGE-MRI to reconstruct the atrial anatomy. Location and segmentation of atrial structures such as the mitral valve, pulmonary veins, and atrial appendages are a challenge even with significant expertise. Variable left atrial anatomy and thin atrial walls, compounded with poor and inconsistent image quality, make segmentation time-consuming and challenging. Atrial segmentation is also hampered by partial volume effects as the LA is close in proximity to extra-cardiac structures [5]. Consequently, manual segmentation of the LA from LGE-MRI has high inter-operator variability even amongst experts [6]. Given the low reproducibility of existing LGE-MRI segmentation methods, a robust and fully automated LA segmentation method is critical for accurately reconstructing the atrium anatomy and identifying the structurally remodeled substrate. Recently, deep learning techniques have been applied to improve LA segmentation in LGE-MRI [7]. However, even the best networks struggle in segmenting regions with sudden changes in the LA anatomy like the pulmonary veins (PVs) [7]. Furthermore, while there has been increased development of machine learning techniques for LA segmentation in LGE-MRI, only a few methods propose segmentation of the scar [8–10]. We developed a deep learning approach to automatically segment both the LA and LA scar from LGE-MRI images. We term our network Left Atrium Scar Segmentation Network (LASSNet). LASSNet simultaneously segments the LA and LA scar and is robust to images collected by different clinical centers.

2   Methods

2.1   Training and Validation Data

The clinical data used for this work was provided by the LAScarQS 2022 Challenge [9,11,12]. All the data received institutional ethical approval and have been anonymized. The images and the corresponding ground truth (GT) segmentations were from four clinical centers and the images were acquired using 1.5 and 3 T MRI scanners.

LAScarQS 2022 Challenge was designed to solve two tasks: "LA Scar Quantification" and "Left Atrial Segmentation from Multi-Center LGE-MRIs". In order to solve the first task, 60 LGE-MRIs with the corresponding GT LA cavity segmentations and GT LA scars segmentations were accessible for training. 10 LGE-MRIs without the GT were used to validate the model through an online submission of the predictions. To solve the second task, 130 LGE-MRIs with the

GT left atrial cavity segmentations were made accessible for training. 20 LGE-MRIs without the corresponding GT were provided for validation of the model through an online submission of the predictions.

2.2 Data Inspection and Pre-processing

Segmentation performances of neural networks (NNs) are highly dependent on the quality of the input image data and ground truth annotation (segmentation) [13]. Therefore, data inspection was performed by a cardiac MRI expert in our team to identify image datasets of lower quality, which might have a detrimental effect on the training of LASSNet for both tasks (represented in Table 1).

Table 1. Analysis of the training data for Task 1 (LA Scar Quantification) and Task 2 (Left Atrial Segmentation from Multi-Center LGE-MRIs).

Analysis of the training data for Task 1	
Issue	*Dataset index*
Scans with poor fat suppression can create artifacts	28, 35, 49
Scans acquired too early after contrast injection result in poor contrast between blood pool and enhancement and therefore a low accuracy of scar detection	5, 12, 37, 49, 57, 59
Scans with poor image quality for accurate scar detection (severe blurring, very noisy, etc.)	7, 8, 19, 45, 47, 49, 50, 54
Analysis of the training data for Task 2	
Issue	*Dataset index*
Scans with poor fat suppression	70, 78, 85, 109, 111, 123
Scans with poor image quality	33, 39, 75, 129
Datasets with severe errors in LA cavity segmentation	19, 24, 45, 64, 74, 95, 100, 101, 112, 126, 130
Scans with partial coverage of left atrium appendage (LAA) and left superior pulmonary vein (LSPV)	97, 100, 129
Duplicate post-ablation scans of the same patient	51, 60

Figure 1 shows examples of the various quality LGE scans provided for LA scar segmentation. The expert indicated that significant discrepancies in LA cavity GT segmentations were observed in regions of pulmonary veins (PVs), mitral valve, LA floor and roof, and LA appendage. Furthermore, one of the right PVs was not segmented for patients with three right PVs. Poor training data represented 25% of the dataset for Task 1 and 18.46% for Task 2. We evaluated the performance of LASSNet with and without the low quality training data in Sect. 3.1.

Then before feeding the image volumes into the NN, the images were pre-processed to obtain the same voxel size and dimensions. Images and corresponding GT segmentations were pre-processed and normalized before training the

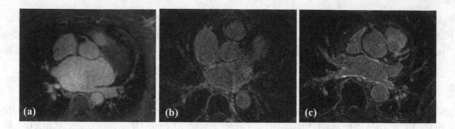

Fig. 1. Representative examples of various quality LGE scans for LA scar segmentation: (a) poor quality (very low contrast between scar and blood, sub-optimal inversion time (TI) value, bad signal-to-noise ratio (SNR)); (b) fair quality (good scar-blood contrast, optimal TI, low SNR, artifact in LA); (c) good quality (high scar-blood contrast, optimal TI, good SNR).

NN. Image augmentation was applied to the normalized images to increase the amount of data available for training and encourage generalizable performance.

During the scar GT inspection, mislabeled scar voxels were noticed: deep inside LA cavity (Fig. 2(a)), far outside LA wall (Fig. 2(b)) and enhanced voxels of anatomical structures adjacent to LA (Fig. 2(c)). Therefore, we constrained the scar GT voxels to be located into LA wall region of interest (ROI) masks.

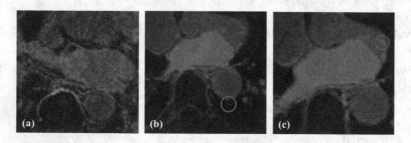

Fig. 2. Representative examples of various mislabeled scar voxels (red circles): (a) scar voxels deep inside LA cavity; (b) scar voxels far outside LA wall ROI; (c) enhanced voxels of the mitral valve were mislabeled as LA scar (Color figure online).

2.3   The Neural Network Architecture

The global architecture is presented in Fig. 3. It is composed of four NN models. LASSNet uses a multi-network sequential approach in two stages to segment the LA cavity and LA Scar. Each stage consists of two steps: (1) A ROI NN that first detects the anatomical location of the LA (or LA Scar) to be segmented, followed by (2) a LA (or LA Scar) segmentation (LA(S)SEG) NN that generates a refined LA cavity segmentation for the first stage or a refined LA Scar segmentation for the second stage.

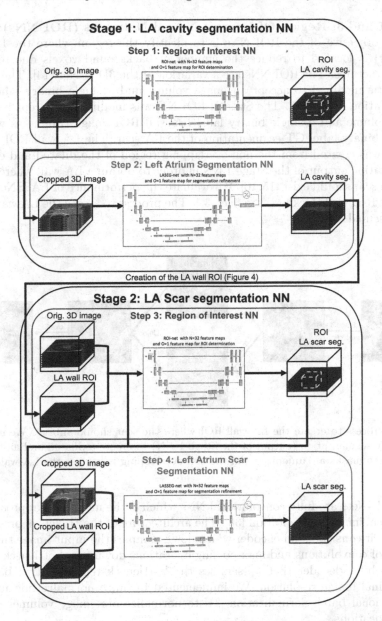

Fig. 3. LASSNet architecture. Step 1: LGE-MRI images are passed into ROI NN which identifies the region where the left atrium is located. The image volume is then cropped to the ROI and resampled. **Step 2:** The image is inputted into the Left Atrium Segmentation Network (LASEG NN) to perform the LA cavity segmentation. LASEG NN includes a discriminator for adversarial training. **Step 3:** LGE-MRI images and LA wall ROI masks are passed into ROI NN which identifies the region where the left atrium scar is located. The image volume and the LA wall ROI are then cropped to the identified ROI and resampled. **Step 4:** Cropped LGE-MRI images and LA wall ROI masks are then inputted into the Left Atrium Scar Segmentation Network (LASSEG NN) to refine the left atrium scar segmentation. LASSEG NN includes a discriminator for adversarial training.

Steps 1 and 3: Region Of Interest Neural Networks (ROI NNs):
The objective of the ROI NNs is to identify the region where the LA (or LA scar) is located to reduce the number of background voxels due to non-atrial structures. The ROI NNs are a variation of the 3D U-Net [14]. The Stage 1 NN was modified to accept an image volume and a single binary label GT segmentation of the LA. The Stage 2 ROI NN was modified to accept both an image volume and a single binary label LA wall ROI image volume as well as a single binary label GT segmentation of the LA scar. The LA wall ROI image volume was created from the non-overlapping region of the dilated and eroded segmentation output of the Stage 1 NN in order to obtain a LA wall where post-ablation scar should exist [15, 16]. We evaluate the performance of LASSNet with different ROI wall thicknesses in Sect. 3.1. The process to create the LA wall ROI is represented on Fig. 4.

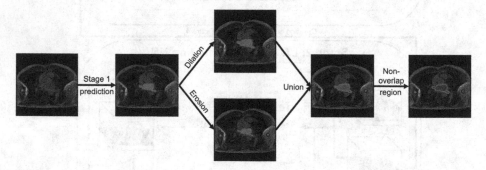

Fig. 4. Process to create the LA wall ROI where the scar should subsist. We use the LA cavity segmentation (output of the Stage 1 NN) to create a dilated and an eroded mask. Both masks are unionized and the non-overlapping is kept as the LA wall ROI.

The U-Nets are fully convolutional NNs which is the most used approach for biomedical image segmentation [30]. The architecture of the U-Nets is presented in Fig. 5; it consists of an encoder which down-samples the input image through a series of convolutions and max-pooling operations down to a bottleneck layer, followed by a decoder that up-samples the bottleneck representation back to the original image resolution. We implemented instance normalization instead of traditional batch normalization [31] to normalize our image volumes across spatial locations.

Predictions generated by the ROI NNs are activated by a sigmoid function to generate probabilities that a voxel is either ROI (voxel value 1) or background (voxel value 0). The predicted atrial (or atrial scar) ROI is then used to determine an appropriate bounding box by identifying the smallest rectangular prism containing all predicted ROI voxels. The prism is then padded with a 10-voxel buffer along all three dimensions. The original image is then cropped to the padded bounding box and converted to a volumetric array as input to the LA(S)SEG NN.

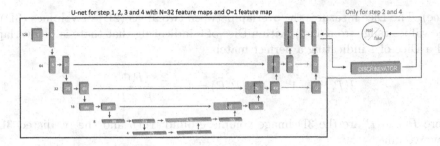

Fig. 5. U-Net model used for each step in LASSNet architecture.

Steps 2 and 4: Left Atrium (Scar) Segmentation Neural Networks (LA(S)SEG NNs)

The LA(S)SEG NNs are conditional generative adversarial network (GAN) combinations of a generator and a discriminator, and follow the PatchGan [17] framework. The generator of the LA(S)SEG NNs follows the same variant of the 3D U-Net used for the ROI NNs and generates the predicted segmentations. The architecture is presented in Fig. 5. The step 2 NN was modified to accept a cropped image volume and a cropped single binary label GT segmentation of the LA. The step 4 NN was modified to accept both a cropped image volume and a cropped single binary label LA wall ROI image volume as well as a single binary label GT segmentation of the LA scar. The discriminator is a deep convolutional NN that performs image classification. It accepts the GT segmentations and the predicted segmentation output from the generator as inputs and predicts the likelihood of the predicted segmentation being real (GT) or fake (generated). The discriminator is penalized if it misclassifies a predicted segmentation as GT or vice versa. The discriminator is then used to train the generator. Since the generator's output is connected directly to the discriminator's input, through backpropagation, the discriminator provides feedback to the generator so it can generate more realistic segmentation predictions. The goal of the generator is to encourage the discriminator to misclassify the predicted segmentations as the GT [18].

2.4 Implementation

Overall, 130 image volumes (LGE-MRI with LA cavity GT segmentations) were used in the training of Stage 1 and 60 image volumes (LGE-MRI with LA cavity and LA scar GT segmentations) were used in the training of Stage 2. To avoid overfitting, early stopping was implemented. Step 1 NNs ran on average for 205 epochs ($\approx$ 12 hours computation time), step 2 NNs for 148 epochs ($\approx$ 12 hours computation time), step 3 NNs for 175 epochs ($\approx$ 6 hours computation time) and step 4 NNs for 146 epochs ($\approx$ 6 hours computation time). All networks used the Adam optimizer [19] with an adaptive learning rate (LR) starting at 10^{-3}. The NNs were trained using Keras [20] and Tensorflow [21] on an Nvidia K80 GPU (24GB GDDR5). The loss function is based on the Sørensen-Dice Coefficient

(Dice). The Dice measures the overlap between two areas (2D) or volumes (3D). Dice values range from $[0, 1]$, with a Dice of 0 indicating that there is no overlap and a Dice of 1 indicating a perfect match.

$$l(P, \widehat{P}) = 1 - Dice(P, \widehat{P}) = 1 - \frac{2 * (P \cap \widehat{P})}{P + \widehat{P}} \tag{1}$$

where P and $\widehat{P}$ are the 3D image volume ground truth and the predicted 3D image volume.

3   Experimental Results

The LAScarQS 2022 Challenge was divided in three different phases: training phase, validation phase and test phase. We present the results obtained from the validation phase in the following section. To evaluate the performances of the LA segmentation network (Stage 1) of LASSNet, the Sørensen-Dice Coefficient (Dice) [22], the Average Surface Distance (ASD) [23,24] and Hausdorff distance (HD) [25] were used for each image volume as metrics. In addition to those metrics that focuses on the LA cavity; the accuracy, the specificity, the sensitivity, the Sørensen-Dice Coefficient and the Generalized Dice score (GDice) [26,27] were used to evaluate the performances of the LA scar segmentation (Stage 2).

3.1   Segmentation Performances and Discussion

We present a two stages deep learning (DL) approach to automatically segment both LA and LA scar from LGE-MRI. We show that LASSNet provides a continuous and realistic scar pattern and promising results for scar quantification.

First, we trained LASSNet with a ROI wall thickness of 2.5 mm and analyzed the performances depending on whether or not data quality selection was applied in Table 2. The LA cavity segmentation varied in Dice from 0.8659 to 0.8892, ASD from 2.59 to 2.179 mm and HD from 30.66 to 26.27 mm when changing the training data of Stage 1. Dice, ASD and HD were all improved when increasing the dataset from 46 to 130 scans; 46 scans is not enough data for LASSNet to learn to segment the LA cavity correctly. When data quality selection was applied to the 130 scans dataset by removing the 24 worst quality scans, it further increased all Stage 1 performances, showing how important it is to have a high quality training dataset.

For Stage 2, the LA scar segmentation averaged the same accuracy and specificity (0.99993 and 0.99996) throughout the different LASSNet trainings. The sensitivity varied from 0.576 to 0.624, scar Dice from 0.559 to 0.591 and GDice from 0.8942 to 0.9004. Since fewer scans were available, using the full dataset achieved better results than when quality selection was used. Therefore, it is preferable to train the model over the 60 scans available with scar GT than over the 46 higher quality scans only.

Then we analyzed how the Stage 2 segmentation performance changed depending on the LA wall ROI thickness (2.5 mm or 5 mm). Since Stage 1 was

Table 2. LASSNet average segmentation performances depending on the data quality selection. Left atrium cavity Dice coefficient (LA$_{cav}$ Dice), Left atrium cavity average surface distance (LA$_{cav}$ ASD), Left atrium cavity Hausdorff distance (LA$_{cav}$ HD), Left atrium scar accuracy (LA$_{scar}$ Acc), Left atrium scar specificity (LA$_{scar}$ Spe), Left atrium scar sensitivity (LA$_{scar}$ Sen), Left atrium scar Dice coefficient (LA$_{scar}$ Dice), Left atrium scar generalized Dice coefficient (LA$_{scar}$ GDice) are shown for 4 LASSNet trainings with the Dice as loss function and a ROI wall thickness of 2.5 mm and depending on whether data quality selection was applied (green if applied and red if not): LASSNet$_1$ both stages were trained on the Task 1 selected data (46 LGE scans), LASSNet$_2$ Stage 1 was trained on the Task 2 full data (130 LGE scans) and Stage 2 was trained on the Task 1 full data (60 LGE scans), LASSNet$_3$ Stage 1 was trained on the Task 2 selected data (106 LGE scans) and Stage 2 was trained on the Task 1 selected data (46 LGE scans), LASSNet$_4$ Stage 1 was trained on the Task 2 selected data (106 LGE scans) and Stage 2 was trained on the Task 1 full data (60 LGE scans). Acc, Spe and Sen are expressed in percentage terms, Dice and GDice are adimensional, and HD and ASD are in millimeters. The best performing model is written in bold.

NNs	LA$_{cav}$ Dice	LA$_{cav}$ ASD	LA$_{cav}$ HD	LA$_{scar}$ Acc	LA$_{scar}$ Spe	LA$_{scar}$ Sen	LA$_{scar}$ Dice	LA$_{scar}$ GDice
LASSNet$_1$	0.8659	2.59	30.66	0.9999246	0.9999627	0.576	0.559	0.8953
Stage 1	± 0.0751	± 1.31	± 8.01	±2.23×10^{-5}	±1.05×10^{-5}	± 0.137	± 0.160	± 0.0229
LASSNet$_2$	0.8737	2.44	27.14	0.9999258	0,9999603	0.621	0.586	0.8987
Stage 1 & 2	± 0.0648	± 1.33	± 8.77	±2.39×10^{-5}	±1.38×10^{-5}	± 0.116	± 0.134	± 0.0237
LASSNet$_3$	0.8892	2.179	26.27	0.9999231	0.9999596	0.588	0.563	0.8942
Stage 1 & 2	± 0.0432	± 0.950	± 11.24	±2.65×10^{-5}	±1.32×10^{-5}	± 0.136	± 0.151	± 0.0281
LASSNet$_4$	**0.8892**	**2.179**	**26.27**	**0.9999273**	**0.9999616**	**0.624**	**0.591**	**0.9004**
Stage 1 & 2	**± 0.0432**	**± 0.950**	**± 11.24**	**±2.38×10^{-5}**	**±1.22×10^{-5}**	**± 0.124**	**± 0.137**	**± 0.0241**

identical for each LASSNet, all models obtained the same LA cavity segmentation performances: 0.8892 for Dice, 2.179 mm for ASD and 26.27 mm for HD. The LA scar segmentation averages the same accuracy and specificity (0.99992 and 0.99996). Sensitivity varied between 0.588 and 0.680, Dice between 0.563 and 0.588 and GDice from 0.8942 to 0.8948. We obtain very similar performance for the GDice but better results for the Dice and sensitivity when trained on a thicker LA wall ROI; LASSNet segments more scar and overlaps more with the GT. Figure 7 provides visualizations for the scar segmentation results of LASSNet trained on 5 mm ROI wall thickness and 2.5 mm ROI wall thickness compared to the ground truth. Both LASSNet predicted scar distributions agree better with typical ablation locations than the scar GT. Figure 6 shows a representative example of the two different thicknesses used for training (5 mm and 2.5 mm) and illustrates the area each LA wall ROI covers. It shows that the definition of the LA wall ROI used for this study includes too much blood pool assuming perfect LA cavity segmentation. Typical LA wall thicknesses range from 0.5 to 3.5 mm [16]. The LA wall ROI of 5 mm thickness generates better results because the majority of LA wall voxels are included in the LA wall ROI. On the other hand, for the LA wall ROI of 2.5 mm, only part of LA wall is included and some scar voxels are situated outside the LA wall ROI. To prevent this, a more realistic definition of LA wall thickness can be used to retrain the NN. The 2.5 mm LA wall ROI was created through an erosion and dilation process with the identical kernel size. To get a more realistic definition of the LA wall ROI and keep a thickness of 2.5 mm, we need to apply a smaller kernel size for the erosion and a larger kernel size for the dilation.

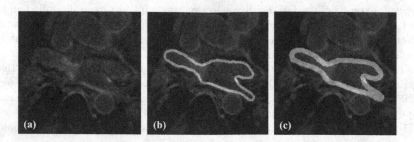

Fig. 6. Representative example of the two different thicknesses used for training: (a) LGE-MRI; (b) 2.5 mm LA wall ROI thickness; (c) 5 mm LA wall ROI thickness.

Table 3 shows how the best GDice performing LASSNet behaves for every scan in the testing dataset. Three scans (Test 1, 5 and 8) failed to achieve a LA cavity Dice above 0.86. This is because Stage 1 creates artifacts for some scans when segmenting the LA cavity. Those artifacts are easily noticeable and quick to correct manually. When excluded, the LA cavity Dice changes to 0.9129 which correspond to the values obtained in the literature. For scar segmentation, Test 5 and 7 get very low Dice scores (under 0.5) because both have low contrast between scar (enhancement) and blood pool. GT and LASSNet predictions are non-accurate for such scans; they are shown on Fig. 8 and Fig. 9. Figure 10 illustrates LASSNet results with the best scar Dice and scar GDice scores for testing dataset (Test 9). LASSNet segments more realistic continuous fully connected scar on the posterior LA wall compared to the GT. Figure 7 also shows more continuous scar on the posterior LA wall and around the right superior

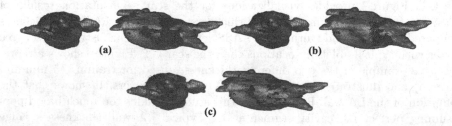

Fig. 7. Comparison of the LA scar prediction depending on the ROI wall thickness to the ground truth on Test 3: (a) LA scar prediction of LASSNet trained on 5 mm ROI wall thickness; (b) LA scar prediction of LASSNet trained on 2.5 mm ROI wall thickness; (c) LA scar ground truth.

pulmonary vein compare to the GT. Figure 10 demonstrates obvious inconsistencies through slice direction in scar GT. Multiple scans in the testing set have similar GT scar appearance with obvious scar discontinuities in slice direction. Such post-ablation LA scar distributions are not realistic and are caused by scar segmentation methods without scar contiguity constraint in slice direction (e.g. 2D slice-by-slice segmentation) [28, 29]. Scar discontinuities in slice direction can be easily seen in coronal or sagittal view of scar GT segmentations. Figure 10(b) shows a comparison between scar GT and LASSNet prediction in coronal view.

Table 3. Detailed segmentation performances of LASSNet $_4$ on the testing set. Left atrium scar accuracy (LA$_{scar}$ Acc), Left atrium scar specificity (LA$_{scar}$ Spe), Left atrium scar sensitivity (LA$_{scar}$ Sen), Left atrium scar Dice coefficient (LA$_{scar}$ Dice), Left atrium scar generalized Dice score (LA$_{scar}$ GDice) are shown for each LGE scan from the testing set. Acc, Spe and Sen are expressed in percentage terms, Dice and GDice are adimensional, and HD and ASD are in millimeters. Worst scar Dice is written in red and the best is written in green.

NNs	LA$_{cav}$ Dice	LA$_{cav}$ ASD	LA$_{cav}$ HD	LA$_{scar}$ Acc	LA$_{scar}$ Spe	LA$_{scar}$ Sen	LA$_{scar}$ Dice	LA$_{scar}$ GDice
Test$_0$	0.9135	1.871	28.16	0.9998893	0.9999653	0.573	0.648	0.8665
Test$_1$	0.8005	3.925	36.52	0.9999533	0.9999693	0.704	0.620	0.9121
Test$_2$	0.8931	1.755	15.33	0.9999294	0.9999622	0.686	0.671	0.8858
Test$_3$	0.9382	1.150	16.91	0.9998901	0.9999459	0.643	0.647	0.8968
Test$_4$	0.8871	2.697	29.02	0.9999296	0.9999574	0.681	0.628	0.8997
Test$_5$	0.8530	2.310	18.87	0.9999459	0.9999580	0.622	0.425	0.9110
Test$_6$	0.9176	1.472	26.12	0.9999270	0.9999529	0.701	0.625	0.8807
Test$_7$	0.9316	1.543	16.00	0.9999362	0.9999663	0.288	0.277	0.9353
Test$_8$	0.8487	3.608	51.75	0.9999137	0.9999494	0.665	0.621	0.8776
Test$_9$	0.9089	1.460	24.04	0.9999587	0.9999889	0.673	0.751	0.9388

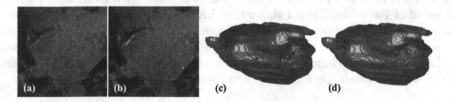

Fig. 8. LASSNet result with the worst Dice score and scar detection sensitivity for testing dataset (Test 7 - scan with low contrast between scar and blood pool): (a) LGE-MRI; (b) Scar GT (red) and scar prediction (green); (c) 3D view of the LA cavity with scar GT (red); (d) 3D view of the LA cavity with scar prediction (green) (Color figure online).

Fig. 9. LASSNet result for LGE scan with low contrast between scar (enhancement) and blood pool (Test 5): (a) LGE-MRI, (b) Scar GT (red) and scar prediction (green), (c) 3D view of the LA cavity with corresponding scar GT (red) and (d) 3D view of the LA cavity with corresponding scar prediction (green) (Color figure online).

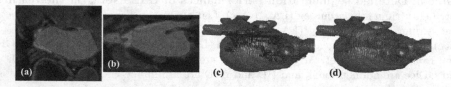

Fig. 10. LASSNet result with the best Dice and GDice scores for Testing dataset (Test 9): (a) LGE-MRI with scar GT (red) and scar prediction (green) in the axial view; (b) LGE-MRI with scar GT (red) and scar prediction (green) in the coronal view; (c) 3D view of the LA cavity with scar GT (red); (d) 3D view of the LA cavity with scar prediction (green) (Color figure online).

Table 4 further demonstrates the performances of LASSNet by comparing it with the previously published methods. For the segmentations of LA and LA scars, we compared the segmentation performances of LASSNet to the JAS-GAN model of Jun Chen et al. [8], AtrialJSQnet NN of Lei Li et al. [9], and a multiview two-task (MVTT) method proposed by Guang Yang et al. [10]. Each method used different datasets or additional cardiac magnetic resonance (CMR) scans. Jun Chen et al. and Lei Li et al. results come from the MICCAI 2018 Atrial Segmentation Challenge dataset which provided 100 scans with labels of LA wall and LA endocardium. Guang Yang et al. used their own dataset which consisted of 190 scans. Table 4 shows that LASSNet achieves the highest GDice among those LA scar segmentation methods. LASSNet also achieves the best LA scar Dice when Test 5 and Test 7 (scans with poor contrast between blood pool and scar) are excluded. The LA cavity Dice score is slightly lower, compare to the other methods' performances and could be further improve.

Table 4. Comparison of combined LA and LA scar average segmentation NNs performances. Left atrium cavity Dice coefficient (LA$_{cav}$ Dice), Left atrium scar sensitivity (LA$_{scar}$ Sen), Left atrium scar Dice coefficient (LA$_{scar}$ Dice), Left atrium scar generalized Dice score (LA$_{scar}$ GDice) are shown for 5 NNs: LASSNet$_4$, LASSNet$_{4BIS}$ without Test 5&7, Jun Chen et al. [8] Lei Li et al. [9] and Guang Yang et al. [10]. Sen is expressed in percentage terms, Dice and GDice are adimensional. The best scores are written in bold. Note: As the cited sources use different data sets or additional cardiac magnetic resonance scans, an exact comparison with our results cannot be made. The benchmarks are thus provided solely as information.

Method	LA$_{cav}$ Dice	LA$_{scar}$ Sen	LA$_{scar}$ Dice	LA$_{scar}$ GDice
LASSNet$_4$	0.8892 ±0.0432	0.624±0.124	0.591±0.137	**0.9004 ±0.0241**
LASSNet$_{4BIS}$	0.8885 ±0.0443	**0.6647 ±0.0422**	**0.6515 ±0.0438**	0.8947 ±0.0241
Jun Chen [8]	0.913 ±0.027	-	0.621 ±0.0110	-
Lei Li [9]	0.913 ±0.032	-	0.543±0.097	0.872 ±0.024
Guang Yang [10]	**0.931 ±0.018**	0.8677 ±0.0464	-	0.8659 ±0.0560

Accurate and reproducible segmentation of the atrial anatomy and quantification of the fibrotic substrate is clinically important for guiding catheter ablation in AF patients. However, this clinically essential information is only available to clinicians in a few research centers because manual segmentation of LA and LA scar is time-consuming (30-60 mins), challenging and requires very specific expertise. We have developed deep neural network LASSNet to drastically speedup and simplify segmentation of LA anatomy and LA scar from atrial LGE-MRI. Once the model is trained, it takes only a couple of minutes to predict the segmentations. The network was validated on LGE scans acquired at 4 clinical centers using 1.5 and 3 T MRI scanners. LASSNet demonstrated excellent performance in LA and LA scar segmentation making it a viable tool for use in wide clinical practice.

4   Conclusion

In this work, we proposed a deep learning approach to automatically segment both the LA cavity and LA scar which proved to be robust to atrial LGE-MRI collected by different clinical centers. Although, the LA cavity segmentation could be further improved, LASSNet achieves superior scar segmentation performances over previously published methods and shows promising results for scar segmentation with realistic scar pattern in agreement with typical ablation locations. Limitations to this work are the limited number of adequate quality LGE-MRI scans in training and validation datasets, inconsistencies in LA cavity GT and scar GT segmentations, and LGE-MRI scans from only 4 clinical centers. The LASSNet framework could easily be applied to other segmentation tasks that demand a two stages refined segmentation task.

References

1. Stewart, S., et al.: Cost of an emerging epidemic: an economic analysis of atrial fibrillation in the UK. Heart **90**(3), 286–292 (2004)
2. Burstein, B., Nattel, S.: Atrial fibrosis: mechanisms and clinical relevance in atrial fibrillation. J. Am. College Cardiol. **51**(8), 802–809 (2008)
3. Marrouche, N.F., et al.: Association of atrial tissue fibrosis identified by delayed enhancement MRI and atrial fibrillation catheter ablation: the DECAAF study. In: Jama **311**(5), 498–506 (2014)
4. Karim, R., Mohiaddin, R., Rueckert, D.: Left atrium segmentation for atrial fibrillation ablation. In: Medical Imaging 2008: Visualization, Image-Guided Procedures, and Modeling, vol. 6918. SPIE, pp. 941–948 (2008)
5. Ho, S.Y., McCarthy, K.P., Faletra, F.F.: Anatomy of the left atrium for interventional echocardiography. Eur. J. Echocardiography **12**(10), i11–i15 (2011)
6. Mohrs, O.K., et al.: Thrombus detection in the left atrial appendage using contrast-enhanced MRI: a pilot study. Am. J. Roentgenol. **186**(1), 198–205 (2006)
7. Xiong, Z., et al.: A global benchmark of algorithms for segmenting the left atrium from late gadolinium-enhanced cardiac magnetic resonance imaging. Med. Image Anal. **67**, 101832 (2021)
8. Chen, J., et al.: JAS-GAN: generative adversarial network based joint atrium and scar segmentations on unbalanced atrial targets. IEEE J. Biomed. Health Inf. **26**(1), 103–114 (2022)
9. Li, L., et al.: AtrialJSQnet: a New framework for joint segmentation and quantification of left atrium and scars incorporating spatial and shape information. Med. Image Analys. **76**, 102303 (2022). issn: 1361–8415
10. Yang, G., et al.: Simultaneous left atrium anatomy and scar segmentations via deep learning in multiview information with attention. Futur. Gener. Comput. Syst. **107**, 215–228 (2020)
11. Li, L., et al.: Medical image analysis on left atrial LGE-MRI for atrial fibrillation studies: a review. Med. Image Anal. **77**, 102360 (2022). issn: 1361–8415
12. Li, L., Zimmer, V.A., Schnabel, J.A., Zhuang, X.: AtrialGeneral: domain generalization for left atrial segmentation of multi-center LGE MRIs. In: de Bruijne, M., Cattin, P.C., Cotin, S., Padoy, N., Speidel, S., Zheng, Y., Essert, C. (eds.) MICCAI 2021. LNCS, vol. 12906, pp. 557–566. Springer, Cham (2021). https://doi.org/10.1007/978-3-030-87231-1_54
13. Li, L., Zimmer, V.A., Schnabel, J.A., Zhuang, X.: AtrialGeneral: domain generalization for left atrial segmentation of multi-center LGE MRIs. In: de Bruijne, M., Cattin, P.C., Cotin, S., Padoy, N., Speidel, S., Zheng, Y., Essert, C. (eds.) MICCAI 2021. LNCS, vol. 12906, pp. 557–566. Springer, Cham (2021). https://doi.org/10.1007/978-3-030-87231-1_54
14. Ronneberger, O., Fischer, P., Brox, T.: U-Net: convolutional networks for biomedical image segmentation. In: Navab, N., Hornegger, J., Wells, W.M., Frangi, A.F. (eds.) MICCAI 2015. LNCS, vol. 9351, pp. 234–241. Springer, Cham (2015). https://doi.org/10.1007/978-3-319-24574-4_28
15. Karim, R., et al.: Evaluation of current algorithms for segmentation of scar tissue from late gadolinium enhancement cardiovascular magnetic resonance of the left atrium: an open-access grand challenge. J. Cardiovascular Magnetic Resonance **15**(1), 1–17 (2013)
16. Roy, B., et al.: Left atrial wall thickness variability measured by CT scans in patients undergoing pulmonary vein isolation. J. Cardiovascular Electrophysiology **22**(11), 1232–1236 (2011)

17. Chen, C., et al.: Deep learning for cardiac image segmentation: a review. Front. Cardiovascular Med. **7**, 25 (2020)
18. Isola, P., et al.: Image-to-image translation with conditional adversarial networks. In: Proceedings of the IEEE Conference on Computer Vision and Pattern Recognition, pp. 1125–1134 (2017)
19. Kingma, D.P., Ba, J.: Adam: a method for stochastic optimization. In: arXiv preprint arXiv:1412.6980 (2014)
20. Chollet, F., et al.: Keras (2015). https://keras.io
21. Abadi, M., et al.: TensorFlow: Large-Scale Machine Learning on Heterogeneous Systems. Software available from tensorflow.org (2015). https://www.tensorflow.org/
22. Dice, L.R.: Measures of the amount of ecologic association between species. Ecology **26**(3), 297–302 (1945)
23. Teguh, D.N., et al.: Clinical validation of atlas-based auto-segmentation of multiple target volumes and normal tissue (swallowing/mastication) structures in the head and neck. Int. J. Radiation Oncology* Biology* Phys. **81**(4), 950–957 (2011)
24. Kiser, K.J., et al.: Novel autosegmentation spatial similarity metrics capture the time required to correct segmentations better than traditional metrics in a thoracic cavity segmentation workflow. J. Digital Imaging **34**(3), 541–553 (2021)
25. Birsan, T., Tiba, D.: One hundred years since the introduction of the set distance by Dimitrie Pompeiu. In: IFIP Conference on System Modeling and Optimization, pp. 35–39. Springer (2005)
26. Sudre, C.H., Li, W., Vercauteren, T., Ourselin, S., Jorge Cardoso, M.: Generalised dice overlap as a deep learning loss function for highly unbalanced segmentations. In: Cardoso, M.J., Arbel, T., Carneiro, G., Syeda-Mahmood, T., Tavares, J.M.R.S., Moradi, M., Bradley, A., Greenspan, H., Papa, J.P., Madabhushi, A., Nascimento, J.C., Cardoso, J.S., Belagiannis, V., Lu, Z. (eds.) DLMIA/ML-CDS -2017. LNCS, vol. 10553, pp. 240–248. Springer, Cham (2017). https://doi.org/10.1007/978-3-319-67558-9_28
27. Crum, W.R., Camara, O., Hill, D.L.G.: Generalized overlap measures for evaluation and validation in medical image analysis. IEEE Trans. Med. Imaging **25**(11, 1451–1461 (2006)
28. Badger, T.J., et al.: Evaluation of left atrial lesions after initial and repeat atrial fibrillation ablation: lessons learned from delayed-enhancement MRI in repeat ablation procedures. Circulation: Arrhythmia Electrophysiology **3**(3), 249–259 (2010)
29. McGann, C.J., et al.: New magnetic resonance imaging-based method for defining the extent of left atrial wall injury after the ablation of atrial fibrillation. J. Am. Coll. Cardiol. **52**(15), 1263–1271 (2008)
30. Asgari Taghanaki, Saeid, et al.: Deep semantic segmentation of natural and medical images: a review. Artif. Intell. Rev. **54**(1), 137–178 (2021)
31. Ulyanov, D., Vedaldi, A., Lempitsky, V.: Instance normalization: the missing ingredient for fast stylization. arXiv preprint arXiv:1607.08022 (2016)

Multi-depth Boundary-Aware Left Atrial Scar Segmentation Network

Mengjun Wu[ID], Wangbin Ding[ID], Mingjing Yang[✉], and Liqin Huang

College of Physics and Information Engineering, Fuzhou University, Fuzhou, China
yangmj5@fzu.edu.cn

Abstract. Automatic segmentation of left atrial (LA) scars from late gadolinium enhanced CMR images is a crucial step for atrial fibrillation (AF) recurrence analysis. However, delineating LA scars is tedious and error-prone due to the variation of scar shapes. In this work, we propose a boundary-aware LA scar segmentation network, which is composed of two branches to segment LA and LA scars, respectively. We explore the inherent spatial relationship between LA and LA scars. By introducing a Sobel fusion module between the two segmentation branches, the spatial information of LA boundaries can be propagated from the LA branch to the scar branch. Thus, LA scar segmentation can be performed condition on the LA boundaries regions. In our experiments, 40 labeled images were used to train the proposed network, and the remaining 20 labeled images were used for evaluation. The network achieved an average Dice score of 0.608 for LA scar segmentation.

Keywords: Left Atrial Scar · Multi-depth Segmentation · Boundary-Aware

1 Introduction

Atrial fibrillation (AF) is the most common arrhythmia, occurring at any age, from children to the elderly [3]. Clinically, catheter ablation (CA) [8] is a widely used invasive procedure for AF treatment, but with a 45% recurrence rate [1]. Recent studies demonstrated the relationship between the recurrence of AF and left atrial (LA) scars after CA [5,15]. Late gadolinium enhanced (LGE) cardiac MR has emerged as one of the promising techniques for imaging LA scars [14]. Delineating scarring regions from LGE images could analyze the formation of LA scars, and benefit the monitoring and management of AF patients.

Conventional scar segmentation methods are mainly based on thresholding, region-growing and graph-cut algorithms [7]. Deep-learning (DL) based methods have recently been widely studied for LA scar segmentation tasks. Most DL-based methods explore employing LA or LA walls to improve the scar segmentation. For instance, Chen *et al.* [2] presented a multi-task segmentation

---

M. Wu and W. Ding—The two authors have equal contributions to the paper.

X. Zhuang et al. (Eds.): LAScarQS 2022, LNCS 13586, pp. 16–23, 2023.
https://doi.org/10.1007/978-3-031-31778-1_2

methods, where LA and scars were jointly predicted with an attention model; Li *et al.* [9,11] formulated the spatial relationship between LA walls and scars as loss function, which could force the network to focus on objective regions during inference.

Generally, the size of LA scars is varied largely. In the training dataset of LAscarQS 2022 [10–12], each LGE image contains average 41.17 scars, and the size of scars are ranged from $0.98\,mm^3$ to $7545.89\,mm^3$. Table 1 presents the statistical information of the scars in LAscarQS 2022. One can observe, 76.1% of scars sizes are within $50\,mm^3$, and they occupy 16.17% of total scars volume; whereas only 2.8% of scars sizes are larger than $500\,mm^3$, but they cover 48% of total scars volume in the whole dataset. For the tiny objects, a shallower network could outperform the deep U-Net; For the large objects, a deeper network could outperform the shallower network [16]. The optimal depth of a segmentation network can vary due to the variety of sizes, which poses an additional challenge in performing scar segmentation.

Table 1. Statistical information of scarring regions in the training dataset of LAScarQS2022

Range (mm^3)	0–50	50–100	100–150	150–200	200–250	250–300	300–350	350–400	400–450	450–500	>500
Number of Scar	1881	262	121	39	24	17	20	14	14	7	71
Percentage (%)	76.15	10.61	4.89	1.58	0.97	0.69	0.809	0.566	0.566	0.28	2.87
Total Number	2470										
Scar Volume	33014	18624	14981	6778	5237	4632	6510	5273	5898	3321	99918
Percentage (%)	16.17	9.12	7.34	3.32	2.56	2.27	3.19	2.58	2.89	1.626	48.93
Total Scar Volume	204191										

As shown in Fig. 1, we propose a multi-depth boundary-aware network, namely MDBAnet, to segment different sizes of LA scars. The main contribution of this work includes: (1) We present a multi-depth segmentation network to segment multiple sizes of scars. (2) We propose a plug-and-play Sobel [13] fusion module, which aims to extract LA boundary information to improve scar segmentation.

2   Method

2.1   Network Architecture

MDBAnet comprises two branches, which segment LA and LA scars, respectively. Scars are distributed on the LA wall, and the size of scars varies largely, as seen from our statistical information (Table 1). In order to achieve scar segmentation of different sizes, the scar branch is stacked with multiple U-Nets that share the same encoder but with different decoder depths. We expect that the shallow networks will focus on segmenting small-size scars, while the deep networks will focus on segmenting large-size scars. Finally, we fuse segmentation results of each U-Net as follows:

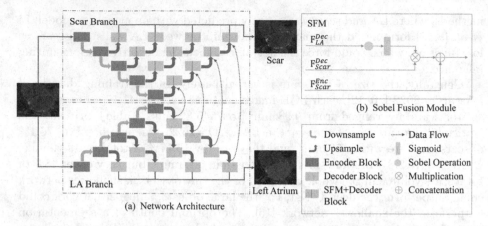

(a) Network Architecture

(b) Sobel Fusion Module

Fig. 1. The architecture of multi-depth boundary-aware network (MDBAnet). It consists of two segmentation branches, i.e., the scar branch and the left atrial (LA) branch. In both branches, we introduce multiple U-Nets with different depths to perform scar and LA segmentation. Furthermore, we propose a Sobel fusion module to extract and propagate LA boundaries information from the LA branch to the scar branch. For conciseness, we only reserve the data flow between the deepest LA decoder path and scar decoder, and all skip connections are omitted.

$$\hat{Y}_{Scar} = \frac{1}{N} \sum_{n=1}^{N} \hat{Y}_n, \tag{1}$$

where N is the number of U-Nets with different depths, and $\hat{Y}_n$ is the output of the corresponding U-Net.

Furthermore, we aim to improve the performance of scar segmentation by jointly performing LA segmentation. Thus, as shown in Fig. 1, we introduce the LA branch for LA segmentation. The network architecture of the LA branch is symmetric to the scar branch, which is stacked with multiple U-Nets. It outputs LA regions for LGE images.

2.2 Sobel Fusion Module

We explore the inherent spatial relationship between LA and LA scars. Generally, LA scars are distributed around LA boundaries. We introduce a Sobel [6] operator to extract the boundary information of feature maps. Then a Sobel fusion module (SFM) is proposed to take full advantage of the spatial relationship between boundary information and LA scars. The input of SFM includes the feature maps of LA decoder, the previous layer of scar decoder and scar encoder. The output of SFM can be calculated as follows:

$$F^{out} = \left(F_{Scar}^{Dec} \otimes S \left(F_{LA}^{Dec} \right) \right) \oplus F_{Scar}^{Enc}, \tag{2}$$

where $\otimes$ and $\oplus$ represent element-wise multiplication and concatenation, respectively, S represents 3D Sobel operation, F^{Enc} and F^{Dec} are the feature map from the encoder path and decoder path, respectively. Here, Sobel operation is implemented by a fixed kernel convolution layer, which consists of three 3D Sobel kernels. Following Xu *et al.* [13], each 3D Sobel Kernel can be described as a 3×3×3 matrix, as shown in Fig. 2. They can be used to extract the boundary information from the axial, sagittal and coronal views of image.

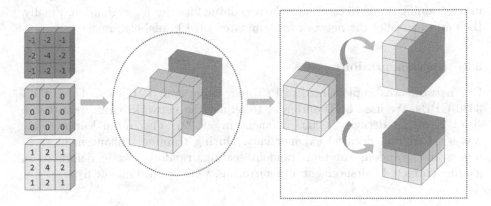

Fig. 2. Our 3D Sobel kernel

Based on the SFM, the feature map from the decoder path of the LA branch could be passed to the 3D Sobel Kernel to get the boundary information of LA. Then we re-calibrate the feature map of the scar branch with the boundary information, which provides spatial attention and forces the network to focus on the LA boundaries region.

2.3 Loss Function

We employ Dice loss and cross-entropy loss to jointly optimize the segmentation results of the network. The total loss of our network is:

$$\mathcal{L} = - DCS(\hat{Y}_{Scar}, Y_{Scar}) + CE(\hat{Y}_{Scar}, Y_{Scar}) \\ - DCS(\hat{Y}_{LA}, Y_{LA}) + CE(\hat{Y}_{LA}, Y_{LA}), \tag{3}$$

where $\hat{Y}_{\{Scar,LA\}}$ and $Y_{\{Scar,LA\}}$ are the predicted and gold standard labels, respectively; $DCS(a,b)$ calculate the Dice score (DS) between a and b; and $CE(a,b)$ calculate the cross-entropy loss.

3   Experiment

3.1   Dataset

We trained and evaluated our method on the Left Atrial and Scar Quantification & Segmentation Challenge 2022 (LAScarQS 2022) dataset, which aimed to segment LA and LA scars from LGE CMR images. The challenge dataset provides a total of 60 labeled and 10 unlabeled LGE CMR images, and gold standard labels include: LA and LA scars. In our experiment, we split the labeled images into a training set of 40 cases, and the remaining 20 cases for evaluation. Finally, the performance of the network was evaluated on 10 unlabeled images.

3.2   Implementations

Our network was implemented in PyTorch, using two NVIDIA GeForce RTX 3080 GPUs. We used SGD optimizer to adjust the network parameters (batch size $= 2$, weight decay $= 0.00003$, momentum $= 0.99$). The initial learning rate was set 0.01 and decayed exponentially. During training, enhancement techniques, i.e., random rotation, random scaling, random elastic deformation, gamma-corrected enhancement and mirroring, were applied on the fly.

3.3   Result

We compared our method to three different segmentation methods:

- nnU-Net [4]: One of the state-of-the-art segmentation networks. We trained it with 3D LGE images as well as corresponding scar or LA labels.
- MDnet: A multi-depth segmentation network based on U-Net. which is the scar or LA branch of MDBAnet.
- MDBAnet$_{mul}$: A variation of MDBAnet. We implement a multiplication fusion module to propagate information from the LA branch to the scar branch.
- MDBAnet: The proposed network. It consists two branches with multi-depth network to segment LA and scars. We implement a Sobel fusion module to propagate information from the LA branch to the scar branch.

To evaluate methods, DS, Hausdorff distance (HD), sensitivity (Sen) and specificity (Spe) were calculated between the prediction results and the gold standard label.

Table 2 shows the segmentation performance of different methods. Methods using a multi-depth strategy (i.e., MDBAnet, MDBAnet$_{mul}$ and MDnet) had obtained better segmentation performance compared to single-depth network, i.e., nnU-Net. Particularly, MDnet improved Dice and HD by 0.01 and 1 for scar segmentation, respectively. It proves the effectiveness of using multi-depth strategy. Meanwhile, scar segmentation could be further improved by jointly performing LA segmentation. One can see that both MDBAnet$_{mul}$ and MDBAnet improve the scar segmentation results by utilizing information from

Table 2. The performance of different methods. DS: Dice score; HD: Hausdorff distance; Sen: Sensitivity; Spe: Specificity. Note that MDBAnet and MDBAnet$_{mul}$ jointly produce scar and LA segmentation, while nnU-Net and MDnet independently produce scar or LA segmentation.

Methods	LA			
	DS	HD (mm)	Sen	Spe
nnU-Net	0.903 (0.032)	20.99 (9.08)	0.926 (0.045)	0.999 (0.001)
MDnet	0.906 (0.032)	22.41 (9.35)	0.918 (0.048)	**0.999 (0.001)**
MDBAnet$_{mul}$	**0.926 (0.021)**	**17.83 (11.33)**	**0.934 (0.037)**	0.991 (0.004)
MDBAnet	0.923 (0.027)	19.18 (11.10)	0.933 (0.038)	0.990 (0.005)
	Scar			
nnU-Net	0.488 (0.090)	39.62 (12.81)	0.418 (0.111)	**0.999 (0.001)**
MDnet	0.501(0.085)	40.66 (12.88)	0.450 (0.101)	0.999 (0.001)
MDBAnet$_{mul}$	0.504 (0.087)	33.21 (10.43)	0.459 (0.120)	0.999 (0.001)
MDBAnet	**0.512 (0.083)**	**31.67 (10.86)**	**0.475 (0.122)**	0.999 (0.001)

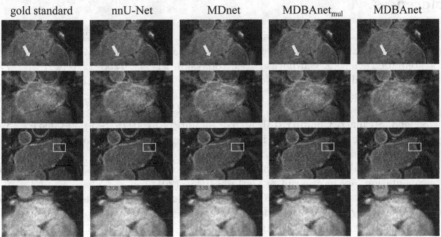

Fig. 3. Visualization of different scar segmentation methods. Yellow Arrows mark the advantage of MDBAnet, while yellow Boxes denote the tiny scars. (Color figure online)

the LA branch. For example, MDBAnet achieved an improvement DS by 1.3% (p = 0.125), and significantly reduced HD from 40.66 to 31.67 (p < 0.05) against MDnet. Besides, MDBAnet$_{mul}$ propagated the entire feature maps of the LA branch, while the MDBAnet extracted the boundary information via SFM. MDBAnet could obtain better DS and HD for scar segmentation. This implied the benefit of SFM.

In Fig. 3, we showed four typical cases for visualization. nnU-Net may failed to perform segmentation for tiny scars (yellow Boxes), which is consist to the quantanity result of Table 2. Moreover, MDBAnet achieved better results for some difficult cases, such as ambiguity scars (yellow Arrows). This was probably due to the usage of SFM, which could force the scar branch to focus on boundary regions.

4   Conclusion

In this work, we have proposed a multi-depth boundary-aware LA scar segmentation network. It consists of two segmentation branches based on multi-depth strategy. Meanwhile, we implemented a SFM to propagate information from LA branch to scar branch. The experimental results showed that multi-depth network has a positive effect on scar segmentation, and SFM was capable of further improving scar segmentation performance. The network achieved a DS of 0.608 on validation data of LAScarQS 2022.

References

1. Balk, E.M., Garlitski, A.C., Alsheikh-Ali, A.A., Terasawa, T., Chung, M., Ip, S.: Predictors of atrial fibrillation recurrence after radiofrequency catheter ablation: a systematic review. J. Cardiovasc. Electrophysiol. **21**(11), 1208–1216 (2010)
2. Chen, J., et al.: Multiview two-task recursive attention model for left atrium and atrial scars segmentation. In: Frangi, A.F., Schnabel, J.A., Davatzikos, C., Alberola-López, C., Fichtinger, G. (eds.) MICCAI 2018. LNCS, vol. 11071, pp. 455–463. Springer, Cham (2018). https://doi.org/10.1007/978-3-030-00934-2_51
3. Heeringa, J., et al.: Prevalence, incidence and lifetime risk of atrial fibrillation: the Rotterdam study. Eur. Heart J. **27**(8), 949–953 (2006)
4. Isensee, F., et al.: nnu-net: Self-adapting framework for U-net-based medical image segmentation. arXiv preprint arXiv:1809.10486 (2018)
5. Jefairi, N.A., et al.: Relationship between atrial scar on cardiac magnetic resonance and pulmonary vein reconnection after catheter ablation for paroxysmal atrial fibrillation. J. Cardiovasc. Electrophysiol. **30**(5), 727–740 (2019)
6. Kanopoulos, N., Vasanthavada, N., Baker, R.L.: Design of an image edge detection filter using the Sobel operator. IEEE J. Solid-State Circuits **23**(2), 358–367 (1988)
7. Karim, R., et al.: Evaluation of current algorithms for segmentation of scar tissue from late gadolinium enhancement cardiovascular magnetic resonance of the left atrium: an open-access grand challenge. J. Cardiovasc. Magn. Reson. **15**(1), 1–17 (2013)
8. Kirchhof, P., Calkins, H.: Catheter ablation in patients with persistent atrial fibrillation. Eur. Heart J. **38**(1), 20–26 (2017)
9. Li, L., Weng, X., Schnabel, J.A., Zhuang, X.: Joint left atrial segmentation and scar quantification based on a DNN with spatial encoding and shape attention. In: Martel, A.L., et al. (eds.) MICCAI 2020. LNCS, vol. 12264, pp. 118–127. Springer, Cham (2020). https://doi.org/10.1007/978-3-030-59719-1_12

10. Li, L., Zimmer, V.A., Schnabel, J.A., Zhuang, X.: AtrialGeneral: domain general-ization for left atrial segmentation of multi-center LGE MRIs. In: de Bruijne, M., et al. (eds.) MICCAI 2021. LNCS, vol. 12906, pp. 557–566. Springer, Cham (2021). https://doi.org/10.1007/978-3-030-87231-1_54

11. Li, L., Zimmer, V.A., Schnabel, J.A., Zhuang, X.: Atrialjsqnet: a new framework for joint segmentation and quantification of left atrium and scars incorporating spatial and shape information. Med. Image Anal. **76**, 102303 (2022)

12. Li, L., Zimmer, V.A., Schnabel, J.A., Zhuang, X.: Medical image analysis on left atrial LGE MRI for atrial fibrillation studies: a review. Med. Image Anal. 102360 (2022)

13. Xu, Z., Wu, Z., Feng, J.: CFUN: combining faster R-CNN and U-net network for efficient whole heart segmentation. arXiv preprint arXiv:1812.04914 (2018)

14. Yang, G., et al.: Simultaneous left atrium anatomy and scar segmentations via deep learning in multiview information with attention. Futur. Gener. Comput. Syst. **107**, 215–228 (2020)

15. Zghaib, T., Nazarian, S.: New insights into the use of cardiac magnetic resonance imaging to guide decision making in atrial fibrillation management. Can. J. Cardiol. **34**(11), 1461–1470 (2018)

16. Zhou, Z., Siddiquee, M.M.R., Tajbakhsh, N., Liang, J.: Unet++: redesigning skip connections to exploit multiscale features in image segmentation. IEEE Trans. Med. Imaging **39**(6), 1856–1867 (2019)

Self Pre-training with Single-Scale Adapter for Left Atrial Segmentation

Can Tu[1,2], Ziyan Huang[1,2], Zhongying Deng[3], Yuncheng Yang[1,2], Chenglong Ma[4], Junjun He[2], Jin Ye[2], Haoyu Wang[1,2], and Xiaowei Ding[1(✉)]

[1] Shanghai Jiao Tong University, Shanghai, China
{13262638253,ziyanhuang,dingxiaowei}@sjtu.edu.cn
[2] Shanghai AI Lab, Shanghai, China
[3] University of Surrey, Guildford GU2 7XH, UK
[4] Fudan University, Shanghai, China

Abstract. Accurate Left Atrial (LA) segmentation from Late Gadolinium Enhancement Magnetic Resonance Imaging (LGE MRI) is fundamental to the diagnosis of Atrial Fibrillation (AF). Previous approaches tended to solve this problem by refining network architecture to leverage spatial priors in medical imaging. However, the priors modeling can hardly be achieved due to low image quality and various shapes of LA. In this paper, we try to learn the priors from generation. The motivation is simple: if a model can generate or recover image content well, it possibly has learned the priors well. With the priors built in, such a model can better segment LA. Specifically, we investigate the self pre-training paradigm, i.e., models are pre-trained and fine-tuned on the same LGE-MRI dataset, based on Mask Autoencoder (MAE). In the pre-training stage, we utilize Vision Transformers (ViT) based auto-encoders to perform the pretext task of reconstructing the original MRI images from only partial patches, where the ViT encoder is encouraged to learn contextual information as priors by aggregating global information to recover the contents in masked patches. In the fine-tuning process, we further propose an single-scale adaptor for downstream task. The adapter first has different branches with different numbers of upsampling blocks to remedy the plain, non-hierarchical property of the ViT. This can better adapt ViT to dense prediction task. Then, it constructs a feature pyramid directly from the single-scale feature map of ViT using the multi-scale features from different branches. Finally, the adapter incorporates a decoder to predict the segmentation results based on the feature pyramid. The proposed model (called ViTUNet) outperforms baseline trained from scratch and widely used nnUNet model. The final trained model shows a validation score of 0.89013, 1.70567 and 17.12375 for Dice coefficient, ASD and HD metric, respectively.

Keywords: Left Atrial Segmentation · Masked Autoencoder · Self-supervised Learning · Vision Transformer Adapter

© The Author(s), under exclusive license to Springer Nature Switzerland AG 2023
X. Zhuang et al. (Eds.): LAScarQS 2022, LNCS 13586, pp. 24–35, 2023.
https://doi.org/10.1007/978-3-031-31778-1_3

1   Introduction

Left Atrium (LA) myocardium segmentation with high anatomical variability using Cardiac Magnetic Resonance (CMR) imaging can assist doctors in accurately assessing Atrial Fibrillation (AF), which is the most common arrhythmia observed in clinical practice [1]. CMR imaging uses magnetic resonance imaging technology to diagnose heart and prominent blood vessel diseases. It has good soft tissue contrast resolution, a large scanning field, and can obtain oblique cross-sectional images in various directions and angles. Non-invasive CMR examination is currently the gold standard for evaluating cardiac structure and function. Combined with Late Gadolinium Enhancement Magnetic Resonance Imaging (LGE MRI), it can comprehensively evaluate cardiac structure and morphology, cardiac function, myocardial perfusion and myocardial activity. Histopathologically, the degree of LGE-MRI is consistent with the extent of myocardial necrosis or fibrosis. Therefore, LGE MRI has important clinical significance.

Left Atrial and Scar Quantification & Segmentation (LAScarQS 2022) Challenge[1] [2–4] aims to automatically segment LA cavity and quantify LA scars from LGE MRI. It provides 200+ LGE MRIs acquired from patients suffering from AF. The challenge is arduous because the image quality of MRI could be poor and various shapes of LA and scar make the model hard to aggregate the spatial information. By investigating the leading methods in previous CMR segmentation challenge, we find that all these methods refine network architecture [5] or adopt a coarse-to-fine segmentation paradigm [6,7]. Zhang et al. [5] refines both encoder and decoder. It employs EfficientNet [8] for better representation ability and a weighted bi-directional feature pyramid network as the decoder. Another method [6] proposes a two-staged method: firstly detecting a small ROI pathological region and then performing pathological region segmentation. Liu et al. [7] also firstly locates the rough position of segmentation target, then predicts accurate masks in the second stage. Despite the improved performance, these methods can hardly adapt to various LA shapes, which require the networks to capture both global and local context priors *in an adaptive way*. Since these methods use heuristically- and artificially-designed networks, they cannot adaptively capture optimal global and local context for each shape.

Vision Transformer (ViT) [9] based masked image modeling (MIM) [10–12] pre-training is a good alternative to tackle the drawback of the above methods. This is because MIM can adaptively aggregate global context to recover the contents in masked local patches. When the MIM can generate local patches well, it possibly have learnt both the global and local context very well for generating various LA shapes in different local patches. The basic idea of MIM is *masking* random patches from the input image and *reconstructing* these patches from other visible patches. Usually, MIM is pre-trained on a large-scale pretext dataset, then fine-tuned on downstream tasks. However, due to the prohibition of using external datasets in the LAScarQS 2022 challenge, we conduct MAE pre-training on the same downstream task dataset, which is termed as *self pre-*

---

[1] https://zmiclab.github.io/projects/lascarqs22/.

training. MIM approach randomly samples patches from images to construct masked and visible patches for the training of a global self-attention-based ViT backbone, thus encouraging the network to aggregate global context for better representative features. The ViT is adopted as the backbone for MIM pre-training because it does not introduce vision-specific inductive biases. This means that ViT can be applied to deal with multi-modal data (such as image and text) and multiple tasks (supervised or unsupervised detection/segmentation). Thus, our ultimate goal is to pre-train ViT on large-scale multi-modal datasets to better learn prior knowledge for a variety of downstream tasks. Particularly, ViT pre-trained with MIM has demonstrated good performance for segmentation [13], with a potential application for segmenting multi-modal medical images such as CT and MRI.

The concept of *adapter* was proposed in the natural language processing (NLP) field. Adapters are introduced in pre-trained encoders for task-specific fine-tuning, facilitating the pre-trained model to adapt to the downstream task. Current state-of-the-art ViT models for dense prediction tasks are the variants of ViT that are combined with convolutional inductive bias. The vanilla ViT architecture lacks prior information of images—hierarchical features, which are essential for dense prediction tasks. Thus a pre-trained ViT is not competitive with other transformer architectures combined with inductive bias when transferred to downstream segmentation task. In conclusion, designing an adapter that constructs hierarchical features for pre-trained ViT is essential for downstream segmentation tasks.

Following [14], we propose to utilize Masked Autoencoder (MAE) based self pre-training paradigm for LGE MRI. To avoid using external datasets in the LAScarQS 2022 challenge, we first conduct *self pre-training* on the same downstream task dataset. This is achieved by using MAE training strategy to pre-train a ViT encoder. For downstream segmentation task, we design an adaptor that comprises a modified backbone encoder, a feature pyramid and a decoder. Due to the plain, non-hierarchical property of ViT, we need to redesign a hierarchical backbone as the encoder for efficient training and better performance. We achieve this goal by a single-scale adapter, i.e., constructing a feature pyramid from the last single-scale feature map of ViT as in [15]. This enables the pre-trained ViT model to be fine-tuned for segmentation tasks without the need to modify the hierarchical backbone or extract features from different layers and upsample for different times. Then the feature pyramid is input to a UNETER decoder to obtain the segmentation results. The results demonstrate that the proposed fine-tuned model, termed as ViTUNet, outperforms ViTUNet trained from scratch and other competitive models such as nnUNet.

2   Dataset

The LAScarQS 2022 dataset provides 200 cases of LGE MRI acquired from patients suffering AF in the validation phase. All these clinical data have gotten institutional ethic approval and have been anonymized. The challenge involves two tasks, i.e., "LA Scar Quantification" and "Left Atrial Segmentation from Multi-Center LGE MRIs". The LA segmentation is typically utilized as a prior for scar quantification as atrial scars are located on the LA wall.

We mainly participate in the "Left Atrial Segmentation from Multi-Center LGE MRIs" task, which contains 130 LGE MRIs collected from different institutions. The spatial resolutions of 3D LGE MRI scan from different institutions are different, i.e., $1.25 \times 1.25 \times 2.5$ mm, $1.4 \times 1.4 \times 1.4$ mm and $1.3 \times 1.3 \times 4.0$ mm, which reveals the difficulty of the task.

3   Method

Our proposed method pre-trains the ViT encoder by solving the masked image modeling pretext task so that global and local contexts are adaptively learned as priors for downstream tasks. For downstream segmentation tasks, we initialize the ViT encoder with the pre-trained weights and construct a feature pyramid from the last single-scale feature map of the non-hierarchical ViT backbone. Then we input the feature pyramid into a decoder to obtain segmentation results. An overview of the proposed segmentation method is presented in Fig. 1.

3.1   Self Pre-training with Masked Autoencoders

The input LGE MRI volume is firstly randomly split into two sets of patches: visible patches and masked patches. The pretext task in MIM methods is to reconstruct the masked patches with the context information from unmasked patches.

Encoder: The ViT encoder only handles the visible patches and embeds these visible patches to the latent features. The encoder first maps unmasked patches to token embeddings by linear projections. Combined with position embedding, the tokens are then fed into a sequence of transformer blocks which consist of self-attention modules.

Decoder: The decoder maps the embedding latent tokens from the encoder and learnable mask tokens to the original images. With additional position embeddings, the decoder can reconstruct each patch in specific position. The decoder also stacks several transformer blocks, but more lightweight than the encoder to reduce the training budget. The decoder is abandoned after pre-training phase and will not appear in the downstream fine-tuning stage.

Loss Function: The MSE loss is conducted between the raw voxel values of the original images and reconstructed voxel values.

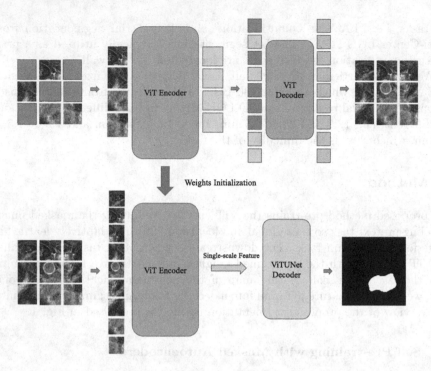

Fig. 1. Our pre-training and fine-tuning architecture. In the pre-training phase, random patches are masked and only the unmasked patches are input to the encoder to obtain unmasked tokens. The unmasked tokens and learnable mask tokens are processed by a decoder which reconstructs the image. During fine-tuning, the pre-trained decoder is discarded and a new ViTUNet decoder is used for segmentation task.

3.2 Adapter for Downstream Segmentation Task

Considering the non-hierarchical property of ViT, an adapter is necessary to better adapt the pre-trained ViT encoder to segmentation tasks. The adapter has a modified backbone encoder, a feature pyramid and a decoder. Firstly, the pre-trained ViT backbone is modified to better adapt to the segmentation task during fine-tuning stage. In previous method [12], all the transformer blocks are divided into 4 subsets and interact with different convolution layers to extract features of different scales (downsample 4, 8, 16, 32 compared to the original image). These multi-scale features are then used to construct feature pyramid, which is input to a decoder to obtain segmentation results. Our proposed adapter is compatible with the single-scale feature map of pre-trained ViT.

Feature Pyramid: Due to the plain, non-hierarchical property of ViT, we need to modify the pre-trained ViT to make it a hierarchical backbone for efficient training and better performance. We achieve this goal by designing a single-scale

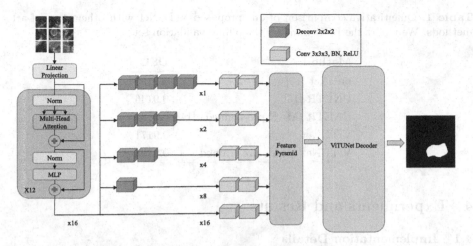

Fig. 2. During fine-tuning, the last single-scale feature map from the ViT encoder is applied with different convolutions or deconvolutions to construct multi-scale features or feature pyramid. Then the feature pyramid is input to a UNTER decoder to output the segmentation map.

adapter. We construct a feature pyramid based on the modified backbone. We follow [15] to relax the hierarchical constraint on the ViT backbone and explore the single-scale backbone for dense prediction tasks. This leads to a single-scale adapter. In our method, the last feature map from the ViT encoder is applied with different convolutions or deconvolutions to construct multi-scale features. Taking stride of patch embedding as 16 for an example, feature maps of different scales $\{\frac{1}{32}, \frac{1}{16}, \frac{1}{8}, \frac{1}{4}\}$ are processed with convolutions of stride $\{2, 1, \frac{1}{2}, \frac{1}{4}\}$ ($\frac{1}{2}, \frac{1}{4}$ means deconvolution). The detailed operations are displayed in Fig. 2.

Segmentation Decoder: After constructing the feature pyramid, we utilize UNETR [16] decoder, which is randomly initialized, as our segmentation decoder. The sequential input of our constructed feature pyramid, i.e., $\{h_1, h_2, h_3, h_4, h_5\}$ (the index represents the downsample scale compared to the original resolution), is input to the UNETR decoder.

Starting from the feature h_5, a $2 \times 2 \times 2$ deconvolution layer is inserted to increase the resolution to fit with h_4, then h_5 and h_4 are concatenated and upsampled to match the resolution of larger feature. Such operations are conducted until the concatenation of h_2 and h_3 are upsampled to the original size. Then the output layer takes the upsampled features and h_1 to output the segmentation results.

Table 1. Quantitative comparison of our proposed ViTUNet with other state-of-art methods. We report the DSC value on the offline validation set.

Method	DSC
nnUNet [17]	0.9190
UNETR [16]	0.9146
UNETR (MAE pre-trained) [14]	0.9181
ViTUNet	0.9171
ViTUNet (MAE pre-trained)	0.9193

4   Experiments and Results

4.1   Implementation Details

All experiments are conducted with CUDA 11.3, Pytorch 1.12 on NVIDIA Tesla A100 with 80 GB VRAM. We implement our method in the nnU-Net framework and we adopt the default pre-processing, data augmentation, and post-processing procedure as in nnU-Net. We adopt data augmentation of additive brightness, gamma, rotation, scaling, elastic deformation on the fly during training. In all our experiments, we set the batch size to 2 and use AdamW optimizer with weight decay 0.1. We train the models for 1000 epochs, with each epoch having 250 iterations. In the first 50 epochs, we warm-up the learning rate from 0 to $2e-4$, then the learning rate decayed following the cosine schedule. During MAE pre-training, we randomly crop a $96 \times 96 \times 96$ volume as the input, the patch size is $16 \times 16 \times 16$ and the mask ratio is 0.75.

4.2   Quantitative Results on Validation Set

Due to the restricted online submission times, we split the provided training data into training and validation sets with a ratio of 80%:20%. For a fair comparison, we train all the models on only 80% training data and report the quantitative results on the offline validation set. All the results are experimented on Task 2 "Left Atrial Segmentation from Multi-Center LGE MRIs".

We report our results on our split validation set in Table 1, our proposed ViTUNet can outperform UNETR in terms of DSC when they are trained from scratch. Note that our ViTUNet only uses single-scale feature from ViT backbone while UNETR uses multi-scale features. Our ViTUNet also achieves competitive performance to nnUNet. Moreover, with MAE self pre-training, ViTUNet can achieve even better performance than nnUNet. In Fig. 3, we visualize the segmentation results of our ViTUNet and nnUNet on the offline split validation set. It is obvious that the segmentation results of our ViTUNet outperforms the results of nnUNet in keeping details.

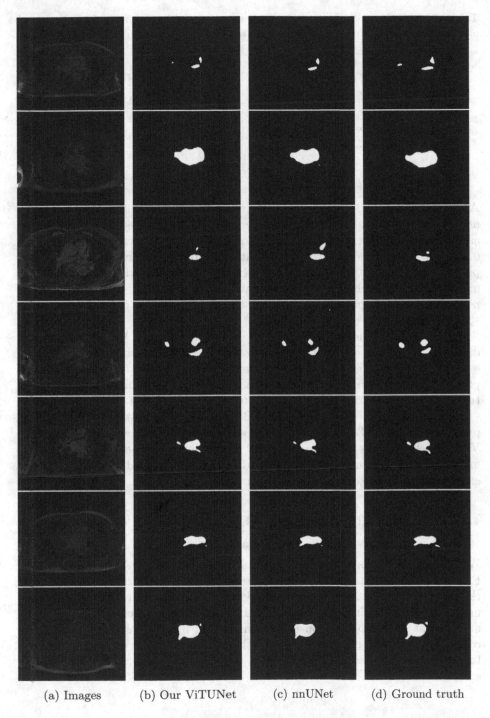

(a) Images   (b) Our ViTUNet   (c) nnUNet   (d) Ground truth

Fig. 3. The segmentation results. The first column is original image, the second and third columns are the segmentation results of out pre-trained ViTUNet and nnUNet, and the last column represents the ground truth.

Table 2. Ablations. We study the effectiveness of each component of our proposed pipeline on offline splited validation set and report DSC. Last row: Our default setting.

Self Pre-train	Adapter	Normed	DSC
✗	✗	\	0.9146
✗	✔	\	0.9171
✔	✗	✗	0.9181
✔	✔	✗	0.9193
✔	✔	✔	0.9194

Ablation Study. In Table 2, we conduct ablation experiments on each component of our pipeline. Firstly, the effectiveness of the self pre-train is confirmed as this method outperforms the method of training from scratch by 0.35% and 0.22% for the setting of without and with adapter, respectively. Secondly, our proposed single-scale adapter improves the segmentation performance by 0.25% and 0.12% for models trained from scratch and fine-tuned. Lastly, setting the normalized value in patches as the reconstruction target also outperforms reconstructing raw pixels.

Moreover, we conduct ablation study on mask ratio and ViT scale. Figure 5 displays the influence of the masking ratio. The optimal ratios is 75% in our setting. Masking 75% patches in the input images provides a sufficiently hard pretext task for the auto-encoder and encourages the pre-trained model to capture context information, which contributes to the learning of downstream tasks.

Figure 5 also demonstrates that ViT-Base achieves the best performance compared with other ViT models. Due to the lack of inductive bias in self-attention, ViT model tends to converge better in larger dataset, especially for big ViT models, so there is an experimental trade-off of the optimal ViT scale. In our experiment, ViT-Base outperforms other ViT scales (Fig. 4).

4.3 Qualitative Results from MAE Reconstruction on Validation Set

We display the reconstruction results of MAE with a mask ratio of 75% in Fig. 5. The three columns represent the original images, the masked images and the reconstructed images. The visualization indicates that our MAE pre-training model is capable of inferring the masked information from context. It is worth noting that visible patches in the reconstructed images are blurrier, and the contrast of restored pixels differs from the overall image as our reconstruction target is the normalized value of patches.

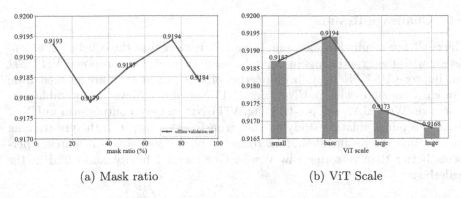

(a) Mask ratio   (b) ViT Scale

Fig. 4. MAE setting ablations. The left figure displays the final results of 10%, 30%, 50%, 75%, 90% mask ratio, and the right figure represents the segmentation results of different ViT scale. The conclusion is consistent with our setting that the 75% mask ratio and ViT-Base encoder achieve best performance in the challenge.

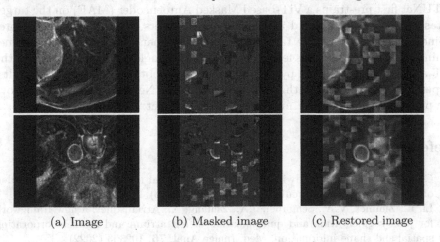

(a) Image   (b) Masked image   (c) Restored image

Fig. 5. MAE reconstruction visualization. The first column is the original image, the second column represents the masked images and masked patches are replaced with gray blocks, the third column shows the MAE reconstruction results. (Color figure online)

Table 3. Quantitative comparison of our proposed ViTUNet with other state-of-art methods. We report the DSC, NSD and HD value on the online validation leaderboard.

Method	DSC	NSD	HD
nnUNet [17]	0.8875	1.7664	17.5357
UNETR [16]	0.8728	2.2195	22.0160
ViTUNet	0.8864	1.7582	16.7074
ViTUNet (MAE pre-trained w/o norm)	0.8888	1.7100	16.5931
ViTUNet (MAE pre-trained w/norm)	0.8901	1.7057	17.1238

4.4 Challenge Results

The challenge results are shown in Table 3. It is clear that the conclusion is consistent with the experiments in our split validation set. Our proposed ViTUNet can improve UNETR by 1.36% in terms of DSC when they are trained from scratch. Compared with nnUNet, our ViTUNet also achieves comparable performance. With MAE self pre-training, ViTUNet can even outperform nnUNet. We also conduct ablation study on the reconstruction target in the pre-training process, and the results show that restoring normalized voxels in patches performs better than restoring raw voxels. Our method finally ranks 2nd in the leaderboard.

5 Conclusion

In this paper, we propose a ViTUNet for Left Atrial (LA) segmentation. The ViTUNet first pre-trains a ViT-based Masked Autoencoder (MAE) on the target dataset to learn both global and local context priors, then fine-tunes the pre-trained model on the same target dataset for segmentation task. During fine-tuning, ViTUNet constructs feature pyramid from single-scale feature map of the ViT and inputs the feature pyramid to decoder to obtain segmentation results. Experimental results show that our proposed ViTUNet can effectively improve the performance of baseline models and beat nnUNet.

References

1. Chugh, S.S., et al.: Worldwide epidemiology of atrial fibrillation: a global burden of disease 2010 study. Circulation **129**(8), 837 (2013)
2. Li, L., Zimmer, V.A., Schnabel, J.A., Zhuang, X.: Atrialjsqnet: a new framework for joint segmentation and quantification of left atrium and scars incorporating spatial and shape information. Med. Image Anal. **76**, 102303 (2022)
3. Li, L., Zimmer, V.A., Schnabel, J.A., Zhuang, X.: Medical image analysis on left atrial lge mri for atrial fibrillation studies: a review. Med. Image Anal., 102360 (2022)
4. Li, L., Zimmer, V.A., Schnabel, J.A., Zhuang, X.: AtrialGeneral: domain generalization for left atrial segmentation of multi-center LGE MRIs. In: de Bruijne, M., Cattin, P.C., Cotin, S., Padoy, N., Speidel, S., Zheng, Y., Essert, C. (eds.) MICCAI 2021. LNCS, vol. 12906, pp. 557–566. Springer, Cham (2021). https://doi.org/10.1007/978-3-030-87231-1_54
5. Zhang, J., Xie, Y., Liao, Z., Verjans, J., Xia, Y.: EfficientSeg: a simple but efficient solution to myocardial pathology segmentation challenge. In: Zhuang, X., Li, L. (eds.) MyoPS 2020. LNCS, vol. 12554, pp. 17–25. Springer, Cham (2020). https://doi.org/10.1007/978-3-030-65651-5_2
6. Martín-Isla, C., Asadi-Aghbolaghi, M., Gkontra, P., Campello, V.M., Escalera, S., Lekadir, K.: Stacked BCDU-net with semantic CMR synthesis: application to myocardial pathology segmentation challenge. In: Zhuang, X., Li, L. (eds.) MyoPS 2020. LNCS, vol. 12554, pp. 1–16. Springer, Cham (2020). https://doi.org/10.1007/978-3-030-65651-5_1

7. Liu, Y., Zhang, M., Zhan, Q., Gu, D., Liu, G.: Two-stage method for segmentation of the myocardial scars and edema on multi-sequence cardiac magnetic resonance. In: Zhuang, X., Li, L. (eds.) MyoPS 2020. LNCS, vol. 12554, pp. 26–36. Springer, Cham (2020). https://doi.org/10.1007/978-3-030-65651-5_3

8. Tan, M., Le, Q.: Efficientnet: rethinking model scaling for convolutional neural networks. In: International conference on machine learning, pp. 6105–6114, PMLR (2019)

9. Dosovitskiy, A., et al.: An image is worth 16×16 words: Transformers for image recognition at scale, arXiv preprint arXiv:2010.11929 (2020)

10. Bao, H., Dong, L., Wei, F.: Beit: Bert pre-training of image transformers, arXiv preprint arXiv:2106.08254 (2021)

11. Xie, Z., et al.: Simmim: a simple framework for masked image modeling. In: Proceedings of the IEEE/CVF Conference on Computer Vision and Pattern Recognition, pp. 9653–9663 (2022)

12. He, K., Chen, X., Xie, S., Li, Y., Dollár, P., Girshick, R.: Masked autoencoders are scalable vision learners. In: Proceedings of the IEEE/CVF Conference on Computer Vision and Pattern Recognition, pp. 16000–16009 (2022)

13. Chen, Z., Duan, Y., Wang, W., He, J., Lu, T., Dai, J., Qiao, Y.: Vision transformer adapter for dense predictions. arXiv preprint arXiv:2205.08534 (2022)

14. Zhou, L., Liu, H., Bae, J., He, J., Samaras, D., Prasanna, P.: Self pre-training with masked autoencoders for medical image analysis. arXiv preprint arXiv:2203.05573 (2022)

15. Li, Y., Mao, H., Girshick, R., He, K.: Exploring plain vision transformer backbones for object detection. arXiv preprint arXiv:2203.16527 (2022)

16. Hatamizadeh, A., et al.: Unetr: transformers for 3d medical image segmentation. In: Proceedings of the IEEE/CVF Winter Conference on Applications of Computer Vision, pp. 574–584, (2022)

17. Isensee, F., Jaeger, P.F., Kohl, S.A., Petersen, J., Maier-Hein, K.H.: nnu-net: a self-configuring method for deep learning-based biomedical image segmentation. Nat. Methods 18(2), 203–211 (2021)

UGformer for Robust Left Atrium and Scar Segmentation Across Scanners

Tianyi Liu[1], Size Hou[3], Jiayuan Zhu[2], Zilong Zhao[1], and Haochuan Jiang[1(✉)]

[1] School of Robotics, XJTLU Entrepreneur College (Taicang), Xi'an
Jiaotong-Liverpool University, Taicang, Suzhou, Jiangsu 215412, P.R. China
H.Jiang@xjtlu.edu.cn
[2] School of Artificial Intelligence and Advanced Computing, XJTLU Entrepreneur
College (Taicang), Xi'an Jiaotong-Liverpool University, Taicang, Suzhou, Jiangsu
215412, P.R. China
[3] School of Science, Xi'an Jiaotong-Liverpool University,
SIP, Suzhou, Jiangsu 215123, P.R. China

Abstract. Thanks to the capacity for long-range dependencies and robustness to irregular shapes, vision transformers and deformable convolutions are emerging as powerful vision techniques of segmentation. Meanwhile, Graph Convolution Networks (GCN) optimize local features based on global topological relationship modeling. Particularly, they have been proved to be effective in addressing issues in medical imaging segmentation tasks including multi-domain generalization for low-quality images. In this paper, we present a novel, effective, and robust framework for medical image segmentation, namely, UGformer. It unifies novel transformer blocks, GCN bridges, and convolution decoders originating from U-Net to predict left atriums (LAs) and LA scars. We have identified two appealing findings of the proposed UGformer: 1). an enhanced transformer module with deformable convolutions to improve the blending of the transformer information with convolutional information and help predict irregular LAs and scar shapes. 2). Using a bridge incorporating GCN to further overcome the difficulty of capturing condition inconsistency across different Magnetic Resonance Images scanners with various inconsistent domain information. The proposed UGformer model exhibits outstanding ability to segment the left atrium and scar on the LAScarQS 2022 dataset, outperforming several recent state-of-the-arts.

Keywords: Left atrium segmentation · Scar prediction ·
Transformer · Graph convolution model

1 Introduction

Late gadolinium enhancement magnetic resonance imaging (LGE-MRI) is typically used to provide quantitative information on atrial scars [25]. In this mea-

---

This research is funded by XJTLU Research Development Funding 20-02-60. Computational resources used in this research are provided by the School of Robotics, XJTLU Entrepreneur College (Taicang), Xi'an Jiaotong-Liverpool University.

X. Zhuang et al. (Eds.): LAScarQS 2022, LNCS 13586, pp. 36–48, 2023.
https://doi.org/10.1007/978-3-031-31778-1_4

surement, location and size in the left atrium (LA) indicate pathology (i.e., LA scars) and progression of atrial fibrillation [12].

Nowadays, deep learning models have been widely used to segment LA cavities and quantify LA scars from LGE-MRIs [3] to help radiologists with initial screening for quick pathology detection. Meanwhile, LGE-MRIs are often collected by multiple scanners and possibly in low imaging quality. Each of them produces inconsistent domain information [14], including different contrast and spatial resolutions. (1) Promoting the generalization of a segmentation model against domain inconsistency becomes another challenge (Fig. 1).

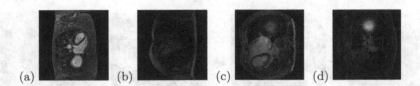

(a)   (b)   (c)   (d)

Fig. 1. Typical examples of LAScarQS Dataset [14–16] in various contrast: (a) Proper contrast, (b) low contrast, and different spatial resolution (c) 886×864, (d) 480×480.

Essentially, semantic segmentation is a mapping from input images to output pixel labels through an empirically designed segmentation model. Recent computer vision research communities have witnessed great achievements brought by the Convolutional Neural Network (CNN) and Vision Transformers (ViT) [4,10]. However, there is a lack of theoretical explanations to guarantee prediction and generalization performance [2]. Besides, there is no fixed shape in human anatomies (i.e., LAs) and pathologies (i.e., LA scars). Atlas-based segmentation strategy cannot be utilized ideally [13,30], while normal CNNs are not good at predicting deformable objects either [22].

Conventional CNN-based segmentation models only take care of local dependencies since the convolutional kernel only sees visual information in closing pixels within the receptive field. It leads to ignoring the full picture as a whole [21]. Common pooling layers in CNN will also degrade spatial information since it regards neighboring pixels as one single pixel. Losses in spatial information restrict the prediction performance of conventional CNN models [26].

Fortunately, Graph Convolutional Networks (GCN) are promised to address those challenges effectively by leveraging the robustness brought by the topological properties [11]. The topological relationship extracted by GCN while performing representation learning has been proved more stable against various application scenarios than that of the geometric relationship of general vision models, i.e., CNNs and ViTs [1]. In addition to the local features extracted by CNNs, GCN also provides an approach to model the relationship among different local features. It optimizes local features of low-quality images by Laplacian smoothing to a certain extent [9], beneficial to promoting generation across data from different domains.

Meanwhile, recently ViT models are becoming popular in semantic segmentations in handling long-range dependencies. It models spatial image information by engaging the self-attention mechanism [24]. Swin Transformer [17] and Seg-Former [27] are two pioneering approaches to engaging ViTs in segmentation tasks. Swin Transformer engages sliding window operation. It fulfills the localization of convolutional operations while saving time consumption in computation. SegFormer connects the transformer to lightweight multi-layer perception decoders, allowing it to combine local and global attention. In medical image segmentations, TransUnet [4], UTnet [7], and LeViT-Unet [28] are the first few trials to integrate ViT modules in the U-Net [22] architecture. All of them achieve state-of-the-art segmentation performance on the Synapse dataset [23].

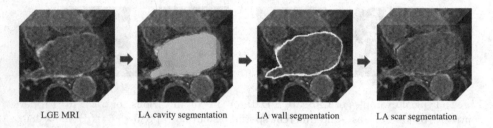

LGE MRI   LA cavity segmentation   LA wall segmentation   LA scar segmentation

Fig. 2. Positions of LA and LA scars [16]

In terms of LA scar prediction, prior work predicts LA and LA scars separately without considering the relationship between them [16]. Meanwhile, the size of the scars is relatively insignificant, bringing difficulties in the prediction. Fortunately, LAs are much easier to be predicted, while LA scars are often detected near identified LA boundaries Fig. 2. Inspired by [29], we believe that combining the prediction of LAs and LA scars can be expected to improve scar segmentation performance.

In this paper, we propose a novel U-shaped GCN with Enhanced Transformer module (UGformer). It is a two-stage segmentation model by segmenting the LA before quantifying the irregularly shaped LA scars. It consists of a novel transformer block as the encoder, convolution blocks as the decoder, and skip-connections with a GCN as the bridge.

In the encoder, the novel transformer block, namely, enhanced transformer block (ETB), is built by replacing the single multi-head self-attention module with paralleling the multi-head self-attention module (MHSA) and deformable convolutions (DCs). It models global spatial attention while dealing with irregular shape information by leveraging advantages in both convolutions and transformers, i.e., proper generalization ability and sufficient model capacity [26]. The bridge with GCN connection optimizes the fusion of long-range information and context information between the encoder and the decoder [9]. It continuously strengthens the representation of intermediate feature maps to find a low-dimensional invariant topology, improving the extrapolation of segmentation models.

The major contributions of this paper are summarized as follows:

- We proposed the UGformer, a novel two-stage segmentation model for LA and LA scar segmentation.
- In the encoder, we designed a novel enhanced transformer block combining multi-head self-attention and deformable convolutions to model global attention and address irregular shapes of LA scars.
- In the bridge, we proposed a novel GCN-based structure to optimize the global space of intermediate feature layers.
- Compared to other state-of-the-art baselines, the predicting performance of the proposed model on LAScarQS dataset [14–16] demonstrates the effectiveness and generalizability of the proposed UGformer.

2 Methodology

As depicted in Fig. 3, the proposed UGformer consists of an encoder, a U-Net decoder [22], and a bridge. Specifically, the encoder is constructed by ETB, while deconvolutions are used to build the decoder. They are connected by the bridge with GCN.

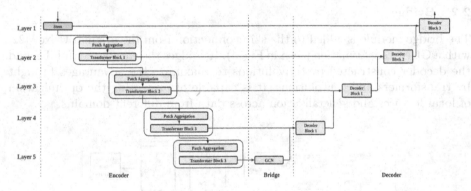

Fig. 3. UGformer Structure

2.1 Encoder Block

In the encoder, the convolutional STEM module [8], including a convolution module, a GELU module, and a batchnorm to vectorize the input features with down-sampling, was employed. It promotes quick convergence and robustness during training.

Each encoding layer (seen in Fig. 3) is constructed by a Patch Aggregation Block. Be noted that the transformer operation is not designed to downsample the feature dimension. Instead, it is constructed by the Patch Aggregation Block, including a 2×2 kernel and a stride operation with two steps to fulfill the hierarchy structure.

Besides, each layer also contains an ETB (seen in Fig. 4) to enable the UGformer to obtain both long-range dependencies and local context.

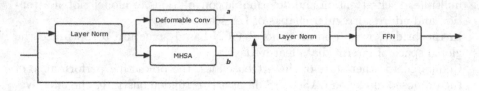

Fig. 4. EBT in UGformer

Inspired from [24], a single MHSA block is involved in ETB to extract long-range relationships and spatial dependencies. We engage DCs [5] parallel to MHSA to improve segmenting irregular LAs and quantifying LA scars. To make ETB adapt to both MHSA and deformable convolutions, a set of learnable parameters (a and b see Fig. 4) are set to leverage both paralleling parts [19].

2.2 Bridge

The bridge module is added to the skip connection from the original U-Net [22] with a GCN transformation (seen in Fig. 5). It bridges the encoder with ETB and the decoder constructed by convolutions to maximize the advantages brought by transformers and convolutions. It is capable of promoting the optimization of local features and generalization across data from different domains.

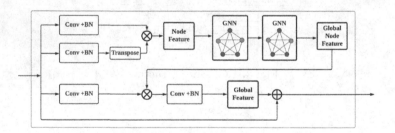

Fig. 5. The GCN Architecture in Fig. 3

GCN in Fig. 5 (see detail structure in Fig. 7) is to extract the spatial features of topological graphs by using the topologically-stable relationship information. Meanwhile, after convolutional graph operation, pixels feature belonging to the same class in semantic segmentation will be close to each other in the feature manifold (see Fig. 6).

We multiplied the feature map with the corresponding transpose as input of the GCN block. Global features will be generated by two layers of GCN blocks

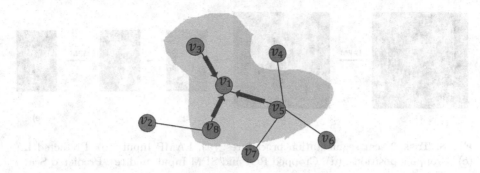

Fig. 6. GCN Topology: the global relationship of graph-based feature structure. The arrows represent the closer relationship by GCN operations in the graph. The shadow represents the topology composed of the neighbors of node v1.

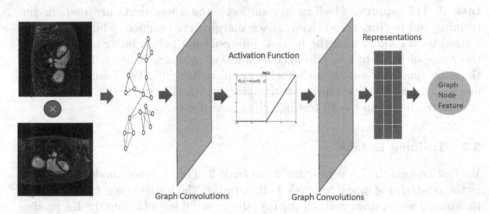

Fig. 7. Two Layers of GCN Blocks: Input feature map multiplies its transpose and update by aggregation rules in GCN block [11].

(see Fig. 7), while the global topological relationship of graph structure-based features (see Fig. 6) is obtained. The final feature map is fused by adding (see Fig. 5) the encoder output and the global relationship node feature together.

3 Implementation

3.1 Dataset and Pre-processing

The LAScarQS dataset includes two tasks: 1). LA and LA Scar segmentation (**task 1**), and 2). LA Segmentation across scanners (**task 2**). The first task contains 60 3D LGE-MRIs with labels containing LAs and LA scars, while the second consists of 130 3D LGE-MRIs from multiple medical centers with labels containing only LAs [12].

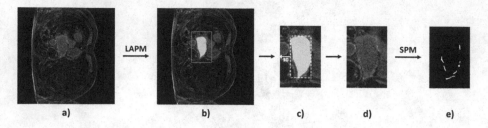

Fig. 8. Task 2 scar segmentation procedures: (a). LAMP Input, (b), Predicted LA, (c). Cropping positions, (d). Cropped ROI and SPM Input, and (e). Predicted Scar

In **task 1**, 54 subjects (approx. 44 slices per subject) are involved in the training test, while the remaining 6 subjects are used in the validation set. In **task 2**, 117 (approx. 44 slices per subject) and 13 subjects are used in the training and testing, respectively. Black margins are cropped, while images are resized to 224 × 224 with the bilinear interpolation before being normailzed to the range of [0, 1] by the min-max normalization. Each image is augmented 4 times by random rotation with angles sampled from [0°, 180°] and translation less than $0.1 \cdot w$, where w represents the image width. The prediction performance is reported based on the 10 testing subjects available.

3.2 Training Details

We first trained the LA segmentation on **task 2**. The obtained model was loaded as the pre-training model for **task 1**. In detail, in the initial stage, the segmentation model was trained with all the LA labels available, obtaining the LA prediction model (LAPM). Then, we used the LAPM to roughly segment the targetted LA region, according to which images in the training set were cropped to train the scar prediction model (SPM). Specifically, the cropping region of interest (ROI) was implemented via $((x_{min} - 30, y_{min} - 30), (x_{max} + 30, y_{max} + 30))$, while x_{min}, x_{max}, y_{min}, y_{max} were boundary pixels of the predicted LA region, 30 was an empirically-selected tolerance of LA prediction (Fig. 8). Finally, the prediction map was restored to its original size using zero padding.

We implemented our network with the PyTorch library [20]. We ran 30 epochs on one NVIDIA Geforce RTX 3080Ti GPU. The batch size was 8, and the SGD optimizer was used. The initial learning rate was set as 10^{-4}, which would be decayed to the previous 0.1 times when the validation dice records were updated.

4   Experiment

On both tasks, we compared our UGformer with other SOTA models, including U-Net [22], Res-U-Net [6], Attention-U-Net [18]. We also performed ablation studies to demonstrate the effectiveness of our EBT and GCN bridge modules. From obtained results demonstrated in Table 1, Table 2, and Table 3, we found that in both **task 1** and **task 2**, the proposed UGformer outperforms other baselines where transformers are engaged when evaluated by the Dice Score (DS).

4.1 Comparison to the State-of-the-art Methods (SOTA)

LA on Task 1 and Task 2: In Table 1, the dice scores outside before parentheses are performance by the model trained only with **task 1** LA dataset, while the numbers in brackets present results of models pre-trained by **task 2** dataset. We can clearly obverse that UGformer presents better prediction accuracy when predicting the LAs. Specifically, the proposed UGformer achieves the highest dice in **task 2**, outperforming all involved baselines. As shown in Fig. 9, the proposed UGformer is capable of predicting small pathological areas. At the same time, unlike Res-U-Net, UGformer is able to avoid most false detection. We believe that such an appealing factor is brought by the fact that transformers are more sensitive to irregularly shaped pathological regions [26], while the GCN module further enhances the predictive power to small regions.

We can also find from Table 1 that the Attention-U-Net performs the best no matter whether the pre-training stages are presented or not. In the meanwhile, if initialized by the pre-trained model, the DS of all the involved approaches is approx. 92 and 93. It is because that LA segmentation of **task 1** is a relatively simple assignment with consistent style information since they are generated from one single scanner.

Scar on Task 1: The proposed UGformer performs the best in this scenario by at least 2.5% compared to other baselines. It demonstrates that it is particularly useful in quantifying irregular and scattered LA scars. As shown in Fig. 10, UGformer clearly identifies more pathological regions and contributes to fewer false detections.

Table 1. Comparison between SOTA models.

Method	Task 1-LA	Task 1-Scar	Task 2-LA
	DS↑	DS↑	DS↑
U-Net	85.95 (92.24)	67.76	84.42
Res-U-Net	85.26 (92.28)	62.61	83.74
Attention-U-Net	87.40 (**93.22**)	70.11	85.37
UGformer	85.49 (92.36)	**72.66**	**86.59**

4.2 Ablation Studies

Influence of ETB Module: In Table 2, ablations of MHSAs and DCs in the ETB are presented. We can conclude that both MHSAs and DCs are essential to

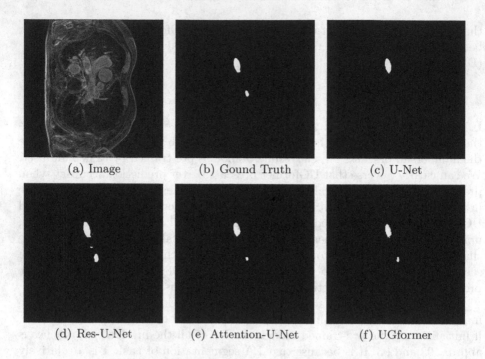

(a) Image   (b) Gound Truth   (c) U-Net

(d) Res-U-Net   (e) Attention-U-Net   (f) UGformer

Fig. 9. Prediction results on task 2 LA.

achieve the best segmentation performance at 85.49%, 72.66%, and 86.59% on DS on **task 1-LA**, **task 1-Scar**, and **task 2-LA**, respectively. Particularly, the combination of MHSAs and DCs module makes the greatest significant improvement on **task 2-LA** by 7%. It proves that the two modules contribute to each other and help the prediction of the model.

Table 2. Comparison of ETB module.

MHSA	DC	Task 1-LA	Task 1-Scar	Task 2-LA
		DS	DS	DS
✓		85.06	69.65	78.67
	✓	85.26	70.50	80.66
✓	✓	**85.49**	**72.66**	**86.59**

Influence of GCN: Table 3 enumerates the results of ablations of GCN block when the proposed UGformer and U-Net are used as backbones. From there, we can find that GCN improves the prediction performance of U-Net in **task 1-LA** and **task 2-LA**. However, the improvement in scar prediction in **task 1-Scar** with U-Net is insignificant. When GCN is implemented in the UGformer

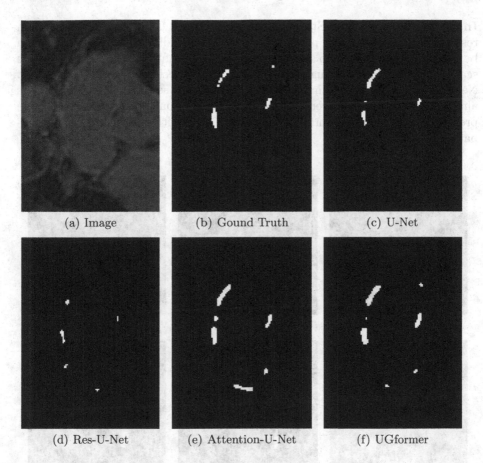

(a) Image   (b) Gound Truth   (c) U-Net

(d) Res-U-Net   (e) Attention-U-Net   (f) UGformer

Fig. 10. Prediction results on task 1 Scar. Res-U-Net can not predict the pathology. U-Net and Attention-U-Net can predict a certain part of the pathology. Nevertheless, we can also obverse worse false detection than that predicted by the proposed UGformer.

architecture, it improves the prediction performance in all settings. Particularly, when predicting scars, GCN module improves the transformer performance from 70.82% to 72.66% by 2.6%.

Table 3. Comparison of different bridge module.

Architecture	GCN	Task 1-LA DS	Task 1-Scar DS	Task 2-LA DS
U-Net		85.95	**67.76**	84.42
	✓	**87.93**	67.72	**86.79**
UGformer		84.47	70.82	85.44
	✓	**85.49**	**72.66**	**86.59**

Influence of the Two-Stage Method: Figure 11 displays the prediction results with the two-stage prediction approaches and the normal ones. It can be clearly seen that the two stage method has successfully predicted most of the scars (see Fig. 11(c)), although some kind of false detection can still be observed. Nevertheless, with the common prediction method (see Fig. 11(f)), the scar is almost impossible to be predicted. We can hereby conclude that the two-stage prediction approach is essential in quantifying scars with irregular and tiny occupations on the picture.

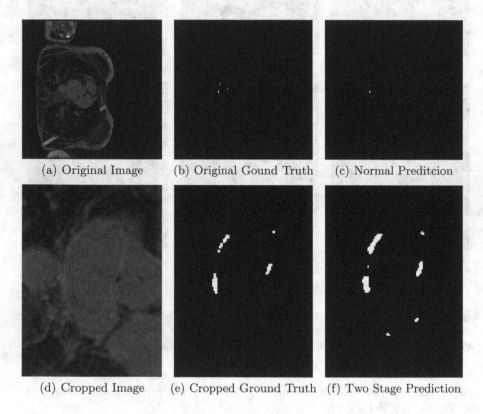

(a) Original Image   (b) Original Gound Truth   (c) Normal Preditcion

(d) Cropped Image   (e) Cropped Ground Truth   (f) Two Stage Prediction

Fig. 11. Prediction results on original images and cropped images

5   Conclusions

In this paper, we proposed the UGformer, a novel U-shaped transformer architecture with a GCN bridge. It is capable of segmenting the left atrium (LA) across different scanners and quantifying LA scars with a two-stage predicting strategy given late gadolinium enhancement magnetic resonance images. Specifically, an enhanced transformer block combining multi-head self-attention and deformable convolutions is introduced to model global attention and overcome degradation in quantifying scars with irregular shapes. We also employ a graph convolution network (GCN), a novel GCN-based bridge, to optimize the global space of intermediate feature layers. Extensive empirical experiments on the LAScarQS 2022 challenge dataset have demonstrated the effectiveness and robustness of the proposed UGformer architecture in LA prediction and scar quantification.

References

1. Carlsson, G., Gabrielsson, R.B.: Topological approaches to deep learning. In: Baas, N.A., Carlsson, G.E., Quick, G., Szymik, M., Thaule, M. (eds.) Topological Data Analysis. AS, vol. 15, pp. 119–146. Springer, Cham (2020). https://doi.org/10.1007/978-3-030-43408-3_5
2. Chan, K.H.R., Yu, Y., You, C., Qi, H., Wright, J., Ma, Y.: Redunet: a white-box deep network from the principle of maximizing rate reduction. J. Mach. Learn. Res. **23**(114), 1–103 (2022). http://jmlr.org/papers/v23/21-0631.html
3. Chen, C., Bai, W., Rueckert, D.: Multi-task learning for left atrial segmentation on GE-MRI. In: Pop, M., Sermesant, M., Zhao, J., Li, S., McLeod, K., Young, A., Rhode, K., Mansi, T. (eds.) STACOM 2018. LNCS, vol. 11395, pp. 292–301. Springer, Cham (2019). https://doi.org/10.1007/978-3-030-12029-0_32
4. Chen, J., et al.: Transunet: transformers make strong encoders for medical image segmentation. arXiv preprint arXiv:2102.04306 (2021)
5. Dai, J., et al.: Deformable convolutional networks. In: Proceedings of the IEEE International Conference on Computer Vision, pp. 764–773 (2017)
6. Diakogiannis, F.I., Waldner, F., Caccetta, P., Wu, C.: Resunet-a: a deep learning framework for semantic segmentation of remotely sensed data. ISPRS J. Photogramm. Remote. Sens. **162**, 94–114 (2020)
7. Gao, Y., Zhou, M., Metaxas, D.N.: UTNet: a hybrid transformer architecture for medical image segmentation. In: de Bruijne, M., Cattin, P.C., Cotin, S., Padoy, N., Speidel, S., Zheng, Y., Essert, C. (eds.) MICCAI 2021. LNCS, vol. 12903, pp. 61–71. Springer, Cham (2021). https://doi.org/10.1007/978-3-030-87199-4_6
8. Guo, J., Han, K., Wu, H., Tang, Y., Chen, X., Wang, Y., Xu, C.: Cmt: convolutional neural networks meet vision transformers. In: Proceedings of the IEEE/CVF Conference on Computer Vision and Pattern Recognition, pp. 12175–12185 (2022)
9. Han, K., Wang, Y., Guo, J., Tang, Y., Wu, E.: Vision gnn: an image is worth graph of nodes. arXiv preprint arXiv:2206.00272 (2022)
10. Huang, X., Deng, Z., Li, D., Yuan, X.: Missformer: an effective medical image segmentation transformer. arXiv preprint arXiv:2109.07162 (2021)
11. Kipf, T.N., Welling, M.: Semi-supervised classification with graph convolutional networks. arXiv preprint arXiv:1609.02907 (2016)
12. Lab, F.Z.: Lascarqs 2022: Left atrial and scar quantification & segmentation challenge. [EB/OL]. https://zmic.fudan.edu.cn/lascarqs22/. Accessed June 30, 2022
13. Li, L., Wu, F., Yang, G., Xu, L., Wong, T., Mohiaddin, R., Firmin, D., Keegan, J., Zhuang, X.: Atrial scar quantification via multi-scale cnn in the graph-cuts framework. Med. Image Anal. **60**, 101595 (2020)
14. Li, L., Zimmer, V.A., Schnabel, J.A., Zhuang, X.: AtrialGeneral: domain generalization for left atrial segmentation of multi-center LGE MRIs. In: de Bruijne, M., Cattin, P.C., Cotin, S., Padoy, N., Speidel, S., Zheng, Y., Essert, C. (eds.) MICCAI 2021. LNCS, vol. 12906, pp. 557–566. Springer, Cham (2021). https://doi.org/10.1007/978-3-030-87231-1_54

15. Li, L., Zimmer, V.A., Schnabel, J.A., Zhuang, X.: Atrialjsqnet: a new framework for joint segmentation and quantification of left atrium and scars incorporating spatial and shape information. Med. Image Anal. **76**, 102303 (2022)
16. Li, L., Zimmer, V.A., Schnabel, J.A., Zhuang, X.: Medical image analysis on left atrial lge mri for atrial fibrillation studies: a review. Medical Image Analysis, p. 102360 (2022)
17. Liu, Z., et al.: Swin transformer: hierarchical vision transformer using shifted windows. In: Proceedings of the IEEE/CVF International Conference on Computer Vision, pp. 10012–10022 (2021)
18. Oktay, O., et al.: Attention u-net: Learning where to look for the pancreas. arXiv preprint arXiv:1804.03999 (2018)
19. Pan, X., et al.: On the integration of self-attention and convolution. In: Proceedings of the IEEE/CVF Conference on Computer Vision and Pattern Recognition, pp. 815–825 (2022)
20. Paszke, A., et al.: Pytorch: an imperative style, high-performance deep learning library. In: Wallach, H., Larochelle, H., Beygelzimer, A., d'Alché-Buc, F., Fox, E., Garnett, R. (eds.) Advances in Neural Information Processing Systems 32, pp. 8024–8035. Curran Associates, Inc. (2019). http://papers.neurips.cc/paper/9015-pytorch-an-imperative-style-high-performance-deep-learning-library.pdf
21. Raghu, M., Unterthiner, T., Kornblith, S., Zhang, C., Dosovitskiy, A.: Do vision transformers see like convolutional neural networks? Adv. Neural. Inf. Process. Syst. **34**, 12116–12128 (2021)
22. Ronneberger, O., Fischer, P., Brox, T.: U-Net: convolutional networks for biomedical image segmentation. In: Navab, N., Hornegger, J., Wells, W.M., Frangi, A.F. (eds.) MICCAI 2015. LNCS, vol. 9351, pp. 234–241. Springer, Cham (2015). https://doi.org/10.1007/978-3-319-24574-4_28
23. Synapse, M.: Multi-atlas labeling beyond the cranial vault - workshop and challenge. [EB/OL]. https://www.synapse.org/#!Synapse:syn3193805/wiki/89480. Accessed June 30, 2022
24. Vaswani, A., et al.: Attention is all you need. Advances in neural information processing systems 30 (2017)
25. Vergara, G.R., Marrouche, N.F.: Tailored management of atrial fibrillation using a lge-mri based model: from the clinic to the electrophysiology laboratory. J. Cardiovasc. Electrophysiol. **22**(4), 481–487 (2011)
26. Xiao, T., Singh, M., Mintun, E., Darrell, T., Dollár, P., Girshick, R.: Early convolutions help transformers see better. Adv. Neural. Inf. Process. Syst. **34**, 30392–30400 (2021)
27. Xie, E., Wang, W., Yu, Z., Anandkumar, A., Alvarez, J.M., Luo, P.: Segformer: simple and efficient design for semantic segmentation with transformers. Adv. Neural. Inf. Process. Syst. **34**, 12077–12090 (2021)
28. Xu, G., Wu, X., Zhang, X., He, X.: Levit-unet: make faster encoders with transformer for medical image segmentation. arXiv preprint arXiv:2107.08623 (2021)
29. Zhou, X., Koltun, V., Krähenbühl, P.: Probabilistic two-stage detection. arXiv preprint arXiv:2103.07461 (2021)
30. Zhu, L., Gao, Y., Yezzi, A., Tannenbaum, A.: Automatic segmentation of the left atrium from mr images via variational region growing with a moments-based shape prior. IEEE Trans. Image Process. **22**(12), 5111–5122 (2013)

Automatically Segment the Left Atrium and Scars from LGE-MRIs Using a Boundary-Focused nnU-Net

Yuchen Zhang[1], Yanda Meng[2], and Yalin Zheng[2,3](✉)

[1] Center for Bioinformatics, Peking University, Beijing, China
[2] Department of Eye and Vision Science, University of Liverpool, Liverpool, UK
yalin.zheng@liverpool.ac.uk
[3] Liverpool Centre for Cardiovascular Science, University of Liverpool and Liverpool Heart and Chest Hospital, Liverpool, UK

Abstract. Atrial fibrillation (AF) is the most common cardiac arrhythmia. Accurate segmentation of the left atrial (LA) and LA scars can provide valuable information to predict treatment outcomes in AF. In this paper, we proposed to automatically segment LA cavity and quantify LA scars with late gadolinium enhancement Magnetic Resonance Imagings (LGE-MRIs). We adopted nnU-Net as the baseline model and exploited the importance of LA boundary characteristics with the TopK loss as the loss function. Specifically, a focus on LA boundary pixels is achieved during training, which provides a more accurate boundary prediction. On the other hand, a distance map transformation of the predicted LA boundary is regarded as an additional input for the LA scar prediction, which provides marginal constraint on scar locations. We further designed a novel uncertainty-aware module (UAM) to produce better results for predictions with high uncertainty. Experiments on the LAScarQS 2022 dataset demonstrated our model's superior performance on the LA cavity and LA scar segmentation. Specifically, we achieved 88.98% and 64.08% Dice coefficient for LA cavity and scar segmentation, respectively. We will make our implementation code public available at https://github.com/level6626/Boundary-focused-nnU-Net.

Keywords: 3D U-Net · Segmentation · Left atrium · Boundary focused · Distance map

1 Introduction

Atrial fibrillation (AF) is the most common heart rhythm disturbance worldwide, affecting over 33 million people as of 2020 [3]. The shape and distribution of LA scars due to AF ablation treatments are established indicators of treatment outcome and long term prognosis [20]. Thus, the accurate segmentation

Supplementary Information The online version contains supplementary material available at https://doi.org/10.1007/978-3-031-31778-1_5.

of the LA region and scars in MRI images is essential for ablation planning and the post-operation care. In recent years, late gadolinium enhancement magnetic resonance imaging (LGE-MRI) has proved to be a promising tool for scar visualization and evaluation. In LGE-MRI, scar regions are enhanced with high intensity compared with healthy tissues nearby [23]. However, manual annotation of the LA region and scars is a time-consuming and subjective task. Hence, developing an automatic segmentation algorithm for the LA region and scars in LGE-MRI images is vital. To this end, we developed an accurate LA region and scar segmentation framework with precise objects boundaries.

Related Works. The development of deep learning methods has recently led to great improvements in biomedical segmentation tasks [13, 14]. For example, the popular U-Net [21] backbone used a u-shaped architecture consisting of a contracting path and an expansive path to extract features from multi-scales and recovered them to precise localization. It was the most commonly used backbone for LGE-MRI LA Segmentation Challenge in MICCAI 2018 [10]. Dozens of variations of U-Net were proposed to boost its performance, such as residual connections [1] and attention modules [19]. Specifically, *Fabian et al.* [5] believed that fine-tuning a plain U-Net is more worthwhile than adding various architecture modifications. They proposed nnU-Net [5], which explores the inherent properties of datasets to achieve automatic parameter configuration. Their framework facilitates and enables data preprocessing, network architecture selection, network training, and predictions post-processing without the need of detailed domain knowledge.

The use of loss functions is of importance for segmentation tasks. For example, *Cheng et al.* [2] proposed a boundary IoU metrics, which has been widely adopted by previous segmentation methods [12, 15, 16, 18]. *Kervadec et al.* [6] designed a novel integral way to compute the distance between two boundaries, avoiding differential computations of boundary locations. In the field of LA segmentation, *Zhao et al.* [28] proposed a boundary loss on the distance between the predicted boundary·and ground truth to optimize the segmentation results. *Li et al.* [9] employed a spatial encoding loss based on the distance probability map to introduce a regularization term for the LA segmentation.

On the other hand, the limited number of works [7, 9, 25, 26] reporting LA scar segmentation performance implies its challenging nature. The small size and discrete distribution of scars make it hard to achieve a high region-based evaluation score. In the related works [7, 9, 25, 26], the predicted LA regions have been used to provide constraints for the scar segmentation to coerce the predicted scars located near the LA boundary. For example, *Li et al.* [9] designed a shape attention mechanism channeling the distance probability map of LA prediction to the scar predicting module, which is proved to be effective.

Our Contributions. Inspired by the importance of the object boundary in the LA scar segmentation, we developed a boundary-based framework upon nnU-Net [5] for LAScarQS 2022 challenge [8–10]. Our framework consists of two

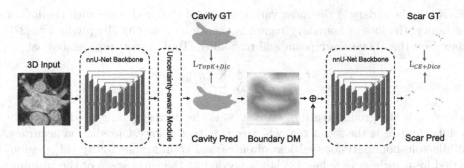

Fig. 1. Illustration of our proposed framework. GT means ground truth; Pred means prediction; DM means signed distance map; CE means cross entropy. The 3D input image is cropped for better visualization.

stages: (1) For LA cavity segmentation, we adopted TopK [24] in conjunction with Dice [4] as the loss function, because TopK loss [24] could automatically pay close attention to the boundary regions during the training process. (2) For LA scar quantification, we exploited the underlying spatial coherence between the LA cavities and the scars by directly concatenating the signed distance maps of the boundaries of the predicted LA cavities to the raw LGE-MRI images as the input. Notably, the outputs of the first stage were post-processed by our proposed novel uncertainty-aware module (UAM) to improve the final results of high-uncertainty predictions.

2   Methods

The framework of our method is shown in Fig. 1. We adopted nnU-Net [5] as the backbone for segmenting both the LA cavities and scars. A combined loss function of TopK [24] and Dice [4] is adopted in the first stage. The predicted probability maps of the LA cavities are processed by UAM to achieve better results. After that, the predicted results of the LA cavities are transformed to a signed distance map of the LA boundaries. The inputs of the second stage are constructed by concatenating the raw LGE-MRI and the signed distance map of boundaries. Cross entropy and Dice [4] loss are combined in the second stage.

TopK Loss for LA Segmentation. Widely-used region-based losses, such as Dice [4], can usually lead to high accurate segmentations. However, it tends to overlook the sophisticated boundary shape because a large number of voxels inside the target shadow the significance of those on the boundary [6,17]. This may lead to a relatively inaccurate LA boundary segmentation and in turn an inaccurate scar segmentation. To address this, we adopted TopK loss (1) [24] to introduce attention to the LA boundary during the training. Boundary-focus methods [7,9] of LA segmentation attempt to give attention to the boundary. Actually, for objects that are not too small compared to the receptive field of

CNN, the boundary is the most variable part of the prediction with the lowest certainty, the loss of boundary region is the highest among the prediction [27]. Based on the above assumption and reasoning, TopK loss is represented as:

$$L_{TopK} = -\frac{1}{N} \sum_{i \in K} g_i \log s_i \tag{1}$$

where g_i is the ground truth of voxel i, s_i is the corresponding predicted probability, and K is the set of the $k\%$ voxels with the lowest prediction accuracy. While sole boundary-focused loss often causes training instability [11], region-based loss, such as Dice loss (2) [4], is needed at the early stage of the training. We represent Dice loss as follow:

$$L_{Dice} = 1 - \frac{2|V_s \cap V_g|}{|V_s| + |V_g|} \tag{2}$$

where V_g is the ground truth label and V_s is the prediction result of segmentation. we coupled TopK with region-based Dice loss as our final loss function (3) for the LA segmentation.

$$L = L_{TopK} + L_{Dice} \tag{3}$$

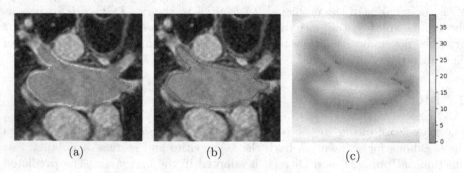

Fig. 2. Boundary constraint: (a) overlap of the LA cavity label (green) and the scar label (red); (b) overlap of the the extracted boundary mask from the LA cavity ground truth (blue), LA cavity label (green) and the scar label (red); (c) overlap of the signed distance map of the boundary mask using Euclidean distance transformation and the scar label (red). (Color figure online)

Boundary Constraints for Scar Segmentation. Anatomically LA scars should be exactly located at the surface of the LA cavity. However, we found that LA scars were located in the adjacent area of the LA boundary. It is inaccurate to restrict the scars on the hard mask of the LA boundary. To address this, instead of a hard boundary mask, we adopted a soft boundary distance map to guide the prediction of LA scars.

To calculate the distance map of the LA boundary, we generated a mask of the boundary shown in Fig. 2(b). In detail, we substitute the max-pooling for the erosion operation as follows.

$$M_b = Pool_d(V_g) + Pool_e(-V_g) \qquad (4)$$

where $Pool_d$ and $Pool_e$ denote the 2D max pooling operation for mask dilation and erosion respectively. $Pool_d$ uses a kernel with size 5 * 5 and stride 1, while $Pool_e$ uses a kernel with size 3 * 3 and stride 1. The width of the boundary mask is 3 pixels, consisting of 2 pixels out of the exact boundary and 1 pixel inside. The results finely cover scar labels from the training data.

Given the boundary mask, the distance map of the LA boundary (shown in Fig. 2(c)) was calculated using Euclidean distance transformation as follows,

$$E(M) = [d(M_{ijk}, b_{ijk})_{ijk}] \qquad (5)$$

$$D = E(-M) \cdot (-M) - (E(M) - 1) \cdot M \qquad (6)$$

where $d(\cdot)$ calculates the Euclidean distance between two voxels; M_{ijk} denotes the voxels on the input mask; b_{ijk} denotes the background voxel with the smallest Euclidean distance to the corresponding input point; n is the number of dimensions. The original voxel spacing is taken into account in the transformation instead of assuming equal spacing along axes. The masked distance map of the boundary is then subtracted from its negated counterpart in 6, giving the final signed distance map. The signed distance map will be concatenated to the corresponding raw LGE-MRI image as the input of the network of the second stage.

Highly Uncertain Prediction. To boost the robustness of our framework, we designed an uncertainty-aware module (UAM) to detect the highly uncertain predictions. For these predictions, automatically lowering the threshold of the probability maps to the final mask outputs proves to be effective in improving the prediction results. After training each fold of the five-fold cross-validation, we computed the sum of Shannon entropy [22] for the output probability of each validation case. The mean and standard deviation was further calculated for all the cases after the training of all the folds is completed. When doing inference, the Shannon entropy [22] of the output probability is compared to the population mean and deviation. We defined an outlier as three standard deviations away from the population mean. For outliers, the threshold of probability is lower to 0.2 rather than 0.5 to confirm a voxel as foreground.

3   Experiments

Dataset and Preprocessing. The public dataset used in this study is from the MICCAI 2022 Left Atrial and Scar Quantification & Segmentation Challenge [8–10]. Task 1 "LA Scar Quantification" provides 60 post-ablation LGE-MRI training data with manual segmentation of LA and LA scars. Task 2 "Left Atrial Segmentation from Multi-Center LGE MRIs" provides 100 LGE-MRI training data with manual segmentations of the LA from three medical centers. Both pre-ablation and post-ablation images were included in this task. Images in the training dataset have two different sizes: 576 * 576 * 44 voxels and 640 * 640 * 44 voxels but with the same voxel dimension of 0.625 * 0.625 * 2.5 mm^3. We used the Task 2 dataset only for the LA segmentation whilst used the Task 1 dataset for the joint segmentation of LA and LA scars. For testing, Task 1 provides 10 LGE-MRI images and Task 2 provides 20 LGE-MRI images. Images in the testing dataset have two different sizes: 576 * 576 * 88 voxels and 640 * 640 * 88 voxels with the same voxel dimension of 1.0 * 1.0 * 1.0 mm^3. All the input images were normalized by subtracting their mean and dividing by their standard deviation. Then, the input images were resampled by third-order spline interpolation and labels were resampled by one-order spline interpolation. Data augmentation was performed with the batchgenerators module, including Gaussian noise, gamma correction, random scaling, random rotations, and mirroring.

Implementation Details. For the baseline, We implemented the original nnU-Net [5] for the LA cavity and scar segmentation using Dice [4] and cross-entropy as the loss function. All the inputs are original LGE-MRI images. We used stochastic gradient descent (SGD) with an initial learning rate of 0.01 and a momentum of 0.99 as the default settings. For the LA segmentation and LA scar segmentation on the Task 1 dataset, we ran training for 500 epochs and 130 epochs, respectively. For the LA segmentation on the Task 2 dataset, we ran training for 1000 epochs. Each epoch consists of 250 iterations. The learning rate was decayed in a polynomial style. If the average of the training loss does not improve during the previous 30 epochs, the learning rate will be divided by 5. No further uncertainty postprocessing was performed.

We implemented our framework in PyTorch with the same optimizer, learning rate scheduler and maximum epochs as the baseline. It takes 30 s per image to calculate the distance map of the LA boundary. We proposed the UAM only for LA segmentation. Because the scar segmentation is inherent uncertainty [8], we set the softmax threshold for scar segmentation as 0.2 for all cases. We used 5 NVIDIA GeForce GTX3090 GPUs to train all the 5 folds with a batch size of 2. On the Task 1 dataset, it took 9.5 h to train the LA segmentation model and another 2.5 h to train the LA scar segmentation model. On the Task 2 dataset, it took 21.5 h to train the LA segmentation model.

4   Results

Comparison Between Models. The performance of our framework is compared to the baseline (original nnU-Net [5]). For the LA segmentation, Dice coefficient (Dice [4]), Hausdorff distance (HD), and Average surface distance (ASD) were used to evaluate the results. For the LA scar segmentation, the Dice was used to evaluate the segmentation performance.

We conducted thorough experiments to validate the effectiveness of the value K in the TopK loss. The testing results with different K values for the LA segmentation are shown in Table 1. When $K = 10$, substitution of TopK for cross-entropy reduces Hausdorff distance (HD) by 3.5% and Average surface

Table 1. LA segmentation with different K values. When $K = 100$, TopK is the same as the cross-entropy. When $K = 5$, it appears that the network cannot be trained because 5% area is relative small for the network to learn the general region leading to the highly unstable training process.

K	Dice (%)		HD		ASD	
	Mean	Std	Mean	Std	Mean	Std
100	88.78	5.72	16.94	5.27	1.749	0.804
20	88.87	5.66	17.05	5.23	1.735	0.796
10	**88.96**	5.60	**16.45**	5.16	**1.715**	0.784
5	-	-	-	-	-	-

distance by 2.5%, while Dice score is improved slightly by 0.2%. We visualized the area of highest 10% cross-entropy loss, i.e., TopK ($K = 10$) focused area, during the training process in Supplementary Fig. 1. At the initial training steps, TopK focused areas are rather scattered when the network is learning the overall region of the target. While as the training goes on, these areas become more confined to the boundary area of the LA. When K equals to 5, the training process is highly unstable, because the 5% area is relative small for the network to learn the overall region. When K becomes bigger, however, the boundary focusing ability is gradually lost as shown by larger ASD and HD values.

Table 2. Results of the LA cavity prediction in the ablation study of the LA scar segmentation. UAM denotes uncertainty-aware module.

Method	cavity Dice (%)		cavity HD		cavity ASD	
LA cavity	Mean	Std	Mean	Std	Mean	Std
U-Net	85.77	18.47	50.74	65.57	2.201	2.607
U-Net+TopK	88.09	11.67	25.86	15.51	2.110	2.386
U-Net+TopK+UAM	**90.51**	4.53	**23.32**	8.32	**1.64**	0.987

Table 3. Results of the LA scar prediction in the ablation study of the LA scar segmentation. DM denotes distance map; UAM denotes uncertainty-aware module.

Method		scar Dice (%)	
LA cavity	LA scar	Mean	Std
U-Net	U-Net	60.46	18.32
U-Net+TopK	U-Net+DM	61.45	15.59
U-Net+TopK+UAM	U-Net+DM	**64.08**	**13.40**

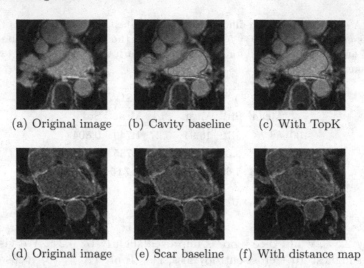

(a) Original image   (b) Cavity baseline   (c) With TopK

(d) Original image   (e) Scar baseline   (f) With distance map

Fig. 3. Visualisation of Segmentation Results. (a)–(c) show the segmentation results of the LA cavity, (d)–(f) show the segmentation results of the LA scars. The ground truth of the LA cavity is labelled with a red line, while the segmentation boundary from each model is in green. The ground truth of the LA scars is labelled in red, while the segmentation result from each model is in yellow. (Color figure online)

The testing results of the joint LA and LA scar segmentation are shown in Table 2, Table 3 and Fig. 3. We conducted ablation studies on the TopK loss function, distance map of boundary (DM), and UAM. There is a significant 4.7 % improvement in Dice, 27 mm reduction in HD, and 0.56 mm reduction in ASD of LA cavity segmentation when the TopK loss function was applied and the uncertainty-aware module was in action. In the scar segmentation, the distance map concatenated with TopK and UAM brings a 4% improvement in Dice over our baseline. The reason might be that the additional LA boundary information helps to constrain and locate scar predictions. The improved LA cavity prediction for the uncertainty cases also provides more accurate location guidance for scar predictions.

5   Conclusion

In this paper, we proposed a nnU-Net based approach to segment the LA cavity and LA scars from LGE-MRI images. Given the importance of the shape characteristics of the LA, we substituted the TopK loss function for the default cross-entropy, which automatically focuses on the LA boundary. To take into account the LA boundary in the scar prediction, we proposed to include distance information by concatenating the distance map of the LA boundary to raw LGE-MRI images. An uncertainty-aware module was designed for post-processing prediction results of poor-quality LGE-MRI images. Our proposed method has been evaluated on the LAScarQS 2022 dataset and the results have demonstrated its high accuracy on the LA and LA scar segmentation. In the future, Our proposed method can be used as a promising tool to support the managements of cardiovascular diseases.

References

1. Alom, M.Z., Yakopcic, C., Hasan, M., Taha, T.M., Asari, V.K.: Recurrent residual U-Net for medical image segmentation. J. Med. Imaging 6(1), 014006 (2019)
2. Cheng, B., Girshick, R., Dollár, P., Berg, A.C., Kirillov, A.: Boundary IoU: improving object-centric image segmentation evaluation. In: Proceedings of the IEEE/CVF Conference on Computer Vision and Pattern Recognition, pp. 15334–15342 (2021)
3. Chung, M.K., Eckhardt, L.L., Chen, L.Y., Ahmed, H.M., Gopinathannair, R., Joglar, J.A., Noseworthy, P.A., Pack, Q.R., Sanders, P., Trulock, K.M., et al.: Lifestyle and risk factor modification for reduction of atrial fibrillation: a scientific statement from the American heart association. Circulation 141(16), e750–e772 (2020)
4. Drozdzal, M., Vorontsov, E., Chartrand, G., Kadoury, S., Pal, C.: The importance of skip connections in biomedical image segmentation. In: Carneiro, G., Mateus, D., Peter, L., Bradley, A., Tavares, J.M.R.S., Belagiannis, V., Papa, J.P., Nascimento, J.C., Loog, M., Lu, Z., Cardoso, J.S., Cornebise, J. (eds.) LABELS/DLMIA -2016. LNCS, vol. 10008, pp. 179–187. Springer, Cham (2016). https://doi.org/10.1007/978-3-319-46976-8_19
5. Isensee, F., et al.: nnu-net: self-adapting framework for u-net-based medical image segmentation. arXiv preprint arXiv:1809.10486 (2018)
6. Kervadec, H., Bouchtiba, J., Desrosiers, C., Granger, E., Dolz, J., Ayed, I.B.: Boundary loss for highly unbalanced segmentation. In: International Conference on Medical Imaging with Deep Learning, pp. 285–296. PMLR (2019)
7. Li, L., Wu, F., Yang, G., Xu, L., Wong, T., Mohiaddin, R., Firmin, D., Keegan, J., Zhuang, X.: Atrial scar quantification via multi-scale CNN in the graph-cuts framework. Med. Image Anal. 60, 101595 (2020)
8. Li, L., Zimmer, V.A., Schnabel, J.A., Zhuang, X.: AtrialGeneral: domain generalization for left atrial segmentation of multi-center LGE MRIs. In: de Bruijne, M., Cattin, P.C., Cotin, S., Padoy, N., Speidel, S., Zheng, Y., Essert, C. (eds.) MICCAI 2021. LNCS, vol. 12906, pp. 557–566. Springer, Cham (2021). https://doi.org/10.1007/978-3-030-87231-1_54
9. Li, L., Zimmer, V.A., Schnabel, J.A., Zhuang, X.: Atrialjsqnet: a new framework for joint segmentation and quantification of left atrium and scars incorporating spatial and shape information. Med. Image Anal. 76, 102303 (2022)
10. Li, L., Zimmer, V.A., Schnabel, J.A., Zhuang, X.: Medical image analysis on left atrial LGE MRI for atrial fibrillation studies: a review. Medical Image Analysis, p. 102360 (2022)

11. Ma, J., Chen, J., Ng, M., Huang, R., Li, Y., Li, C., Yang, X., Martel, A.L.: Loss odyssey in medical image segmentation. Med. Image Anal. **71**, 102035 (2021)
12. Meng, Y., et al.: Shape-aware weakly/semi-supervised optic disc and cup segmentation with regional/marginal consistency. In: Wang, L., Dou, Q., Fletcher, P.T., Speidel, S., Li, S. (eds.) MICCAI 2022. LNCS, vol. 13434. Springer, Cham (2022). https://doi.org/10.1007/978-3-031-16440-8_50
13. Meng, Y., Meng, W., Gao, D., Zhao, Y., Yang, X., Huang, X., Zheng, Y.: Regression of instance boundary by aggregated CNN and GCN. In: Vedaldi, A., Bischof, H., Brox, T., Frahm, J.-M. (eds.) ECCV 2020. LNCS, vol. 12353, pp. 190–207. Springer, Cham (2020). https://doi.org/10.1007/978-3-030-58598-3_12
14. Meng, Y., Wei, M., Gao, D., Zhao, Y., Yang, X., Huang, X., Zheng, Y.: CNN-GCN aggregation enabled boundary regression for biomedical image segmentation. In: Martel, A.L., Abolmaesumi, P., Stoyanov, D., Mateus, D., Zuluaga, M.A., Zhou, S.K., Racoceanu, D., Joskowicz, L. (eds.) MICCAI 2020. LNCS, vol. 12264, pp. 352–362. Springer, Cham (2020). https://doi.org/10.1007/978-3-030-59719-1_35
15. Meng, Y., et al.: BI-GCN: boundary-aware input-dependent graph convolution network for biomedical image segmentation. In: 32nd British Machine Vision Conference: BMVC 2021. British Machine Vision Association (2021)
16. Meng, Y., et al.: Dual consistency enabled weakly and semi-supervised optic disc and cup segmentation with dual adaptive graph convolutional networks. IEEE Trans. Med. Imaging in press (2022)
17. Meng, Y., Zhang, H., Zhao, Y., Yang, X., Qian, X., Huang, X., Zheng, Y.: Spatial uncertainty-aware semi-supervised crowd counting. In: Proceedings of the IEEE/CVF International Conference on Computer Vision, pp. 15549–15559 (2021)
18. Meng, Y., Zhang, H., Zhao, Y., Yang, X., Qiao, Y., MacCormick, I.J., Huang, X., Zheng, Y.: Graph-based region and boundary aggregation for biomedical image segmentation. IEEE Trans. Med. Imaging **41**(3), 690–701 (2021)
19. Oktay, O., et al.: Attention U-net: learning where to look for the pancreas. arXiv preprint arXiv:1804.03999 (2018)
20. Ranjan, R., et al.: Gaps in the ablation line as a potential cause of recovery from electrical isolation and their visualization using MRI. Circulation: Arrhythmia Electrophysiology **4**(3), 279–286 (2011)
21. Ronneberger, O., Fischer, P., Brox, T.: U-Net: convolutional networks for biomedical image segmentation. In: Navab, N., Hornegger, J., Wells, W.M., Frangi, A.F. (eds.) MICCAI 2015. LNCS, vol. 9351, pp. 234–241. Springer, Cham (2015). https://doi.org/10.1007/978-3-319-24574-4_28
22. Shannon, C.E.: A mathematical theory of communication. ACM SIGMOBILE Mobile Comput. Commun. Rev. **5**(1), 3–55 (2001)
23. Siebermair, J., Kholmovski, E.G., Marrouche, N.: Assessment of left atrial fibrosis by late gadolinium enhancement magnetic resonance imaging: methodology and clinical implications. JACC: Clin. Electrophysiology **3**(8), 791–802 (2017)
24. Wu, Z., Shen, C., Hengel, A.v.d.: Bridging category-level and instance-level semantic image segmentation. arXiv preprint arXiv:1605.06885 (2016)
25. Yang, G., Chen, J., Gao, Z., Li, S., Ni, H., Angelini, E., Wong, T., Mohiaddin, R., Nyktari, E., Wage, R., et al.: Simultaneous left atrium anatomy and scar segmentations via deep learning in multiview information with attention. Futur. Gener. Comput. Syst. **107**, 215–228 (2020)
26. Yang, G., et al.: A fully automatic deep learning method for atrial scarring segmentation from late gadolinium-enhanced mri images. In: 2017 IEEE 14th International Symposium on Biomedical Imaging (ISBI 2017), pp. 844–848. IEEE (2017)

27. Yang, X., Wang, N., Wang, Y., Wang, X., Nezafat, R., Ni, D., Heng, P.-A.: Combating uncertainty with novel losses for automatic left atrium segmentation. In: Pop, M., Sermesant, M., Zhao, J., Li, S., McLeod, K., Young, A., Rhode, K., Mansi, T. (eds.) STACOM 2018. LNCS, vol. 11395, pp. 246–254. Springer, Cham (2019). https://doi.org/10.1007/978-3-030-12029-0_27
28. Zhao, Z., Puybareau, E., Boutry, N., Géraud, T.: Do not treat boundaries and regions differently: An example on heart left atrial segmentation. In: 2020 25th International Conference on Pattern Recognition (ICPR), pp. 7447–7453. IEEE (2021)

Two Stage of Histogram Matching Augmentation for Domain Generalization: Application to Left Atrial Segmentation

Xuru Zhang⑩, Xinye Yang, Lihua Huang, and Liqin Huang⁽✉⁾

College of Physics and Information Engineering, Fuzhou University, Fuzhou, China
hlq@fzu.edu.cn

Abstract. Convolutions neural networks have obtained promising results in various medical image segmentation tasks. However, these methods ignore the problem of domain shift, which will lead to a model trained in a source domain performing poorly when applied to different target domains. In this work, we propose a two-stage segmentation network, and utilize histogram matching to eliminate domain shift. Specifically, the first stage obtains the region of interest by performing coarsely segmentation on down-sample images. Then the second stage segments the left atrium (LA) based on the region of interest. The method is evaluated on LAScarQS 2022 data-set, acquiring average Dice of 0.87790 for LA segmentation. Besides, the two-stage network is about four times faster against a single-stage network in the test phase.

Keywords: Deep Learning · Left Atrial Segmentation · Histogram Matching Augmentation · Domain Shift

1 Introduction

Cardiovascular disease is an important factor causing high mortality in the world. Previous studies on cardiac images relay on manual delineation and analysis of cardiac tissue structures such as the bi-ventricular and left atrium [1]. In clinical application, manually depict the contour of the double ventricle and left atrium of the heart is time-consuming and inefficient. Utilizing computer-aided methods could rapidly process large amounts of cardiac image data, and benefit clinical diagnosis procedures [2].

Traditional atrial segmentation methods include Hough Transform, super-pixel segmentation, and threshold algorithm [3]. In recent years, deep learning based methods have been extensively studied in left atrium segmentation. Xia *et al.* [4] designed two networks based on V-Net for GE-MRI three-dimensional

---

X. Zhang and X. Yang—The two authors have equal contributions to the paper.

X. Zhuang et al. (Eds.): LAScarQS 2022, LNCS 13586, pp. 60–68, 2023.
https://doi.org/10.1007/978-3-031-31778-1_6

automatic segmentation of atrium. The first network locates the position of the atrium, and simultaneous coarse segmentation of the atrium. Then the second network precisely splits the results obtained in the first network. This will reduces memory costs. Chen *et al.*. [5] proposed shape-aware multi-view auto-encoder(Shape MAE), learn anatomical shape priors from cardiac short-axis and long-axis views, then fuse the anatomical priors learned by Shape MAE into an improved U-Net architecture for cardiac short-axis image segmentation. The model keeps the compute ascendancy of 2D networks and uses fewer parameters during training than 3D U-Net, which improves the computational efficiency.

However, these methods ignore the problem of domain shift, which can make a model trained in a source domain performing poorly when applied to different target domains. The difference between various collection protocols or instrument, even the tiny distinction among the location of patients' hearts will lead to a result in domain shift problem.

In the LAScarQS2022, the data-set consists of LGE MRI images of the heart provided by multiple centers. Because of the different acquisition devices or acquisition protocols used by each center, the quality of these LGE MRI images is very different. As shown in Fig. 1, The intensity distribution of the reference domain image is quite different from the seen domain image. These differences bring great challenges to the segmentation of the left atrium, mainly reflected in the problem of domain shift, which leads to the poor robustness of the model.

Nowadays, a number of researches have put forward to solve the issue of domain shift, such as domain adaptation [6] and domain generalization [7]. Domain generalization technology attempts to design a model that can be well applied to new test domains. It is assumed that any domain is composed of a underlying sharing factor and a domain-specific component, by decomposing these during the training of the source domain, a domain-independent component can be extracted as a model which also performs well in the new domain. Domain adaptation is to map the data of different distribution sources and target domains into a feature space, so that the distance between the two in space is as close as possible. That is, the objective function trained in the source domain can be migrated to the target domain.

However, for different applications, it requires to modify the network architecture or the loss function, which leads to less practicability. So Jun ma [8] introduced the method of histogram matching to solve this problem. However, during the training and testing, it was found that simply using the histogram matching with nnU-Net is time consuming. In addition, performing image-level HM will leads to an unsatisfactory result, as shown in Fig. 1 (image-level HM).

To address the mentioned limitation, we propose a two-stage method as shown in Fig. 2. A two-stage method combined with ROI-Level histogram matching, which can not only deal with the domain shift but also solve the problem of too long training time and reduce the influence of surrounding on histogram matching effect. Our approach performs well in segmentation tasks and simple to operate.

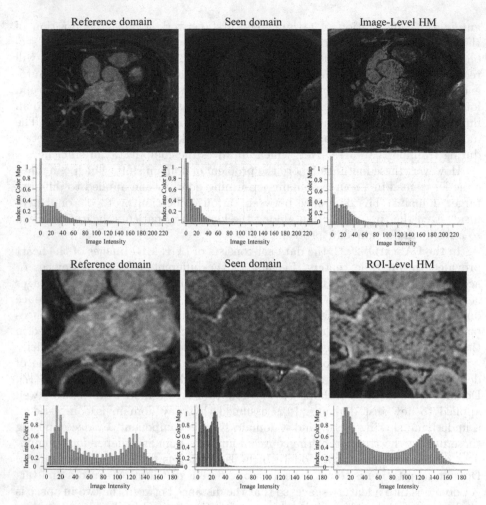

Fig. 1. There are various of intensity distribution among LGE-MRI images from different centers. The effect of ROI-Level is significantly better than Image-Level HM

2   Proposed Method

As shown in Fig. 2, we divide the segmentation process into two stages. In the first stage, the original image is reduced to 44×120×120 and then the performs histogram matching. And next, it is put into nnU-Net for rough segmentation to get a rough segmentation result. In the second stage, regions of interest are extracted from the original image according to the rough segmentation results of the first stage, and these regions of interest are histogram matched, then put into nnU-Net for segmentation. The final results are pasted back to the original image to get the final segmentation image.

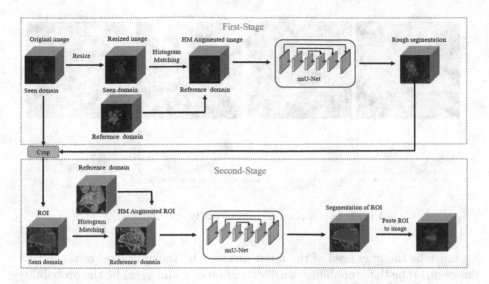

Fig. 2. schematic of the workflow of the proposed two stage segmentation framework.

2.1   ROI-Level Histogram Matching

Histogram matching, also known as histogram specification, refers to an image enhancement algorithm that converts the histogram of an image into a histogram of a specified shape, that is to match the histogram of an image to another image. Because the histogram reflects the distribution of the global pixel gray value of the image, histogram matching can adjust the global brightness and contrast [9].

As shown in Fig. 1 (Image-Level HM), in the right area of the left atrium. Due to the interference of the surrounding background, after the histogram matching, some areas are still similar to the background, and the difference between the left atrium and the reference domain is still obvious.

In order to reduce the influence of the surrounding on the left atrium during histogram matching. We specifically perform histogram matching on the ROI. First, the compressed image is roughly segmented to obtain the approximate area of the left atrium, this area is the ROI. Then select an image as a reference, and the rest of the images are histogram matched according to this image. If ROI-Level HM is performed, the effect will be significantly improved. Figure 3 shows intensity distribution of the reference domain, seen domain, ROI-Level HM and Image-Level HM of LA. We can see that the intensity distribution using ROI-Level HM is closer to the intensity distribution of the reference domain. Then introduce the principle of histogram matching.

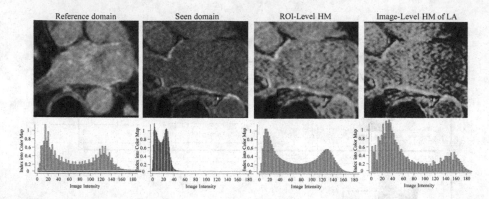

Fig. 3. Left atrium and its intensity distribution.

Let r be the gray level of the input image, z be the gray level of the output image, $p_s(s)$ be the probability density function of s, and $p_z(z)$ be the probability density function of z. The goal is to estimate $p_r(r)$ from the given input image, and then get $p_z(z)$ from $p_r(r)$, that is, to get the image we want to output with the specified probability density function.

First, in histogram equalization, s is the gray level of the image after r is equalized, and its conversion expression is:

$$s = T(r) = (L-1) \int_0^r p_r(w)\mathrm{d}w \tag{1}$$

where L is a power function of 2, if 8-bit gray level, L=256. This formula shows that r is mapped to s through the transformation function T.

On this basis, a random variable z is defined:

$$G(z) = (L-1) \int_0^z p_z(t)\mathrm{d}t = s \tag{2}$$

The expression is that z is mapped to s through the transformation function G, so we can get $G(z) = T(r)$, so z must satisfy the following equation:

$$z = G^{-1}[T(r)] = G^{-1}(s) \tag{3}$$

From a given image, getting an image whose gray level has a specified probability density function should follow the following steps:

- The probability density function is obtained from the input image $P_r(r)$, then the value of histogram equalization $s = T(r)$ can be obtained according to equation(3), and round S_k to $[0, L-1]$. Where S_k is the value after histogram matching;
- Solve inverse transformation function $z = G^{-1}(s)$. Because z is obtained by s, this step is the mapping from s to z, and z is the value we expect;
- Since there is also a mapping from r to s, we can replace s with r, and replace the expression obtained in the second step with the mapping from r to z.

2.2   nnU-Net

The network structure used in our method is nnU-Net. Because too much artificial adjustment of the network structure will lead to over-fitting of specific data sets. The impact of a non-network structure may have a greater impact on task segmentation. nnU-Net is based on the original U-Net network structure, will automatically select the optimal pre-processing, training, inference, and post-processing stages. In many segmentation tasks, nnU-Net has achieved very jelly results [10].

3   Experiment and Results

3.1   Dataset and Training Protocols

The training set in the LAScarQS challenge has a total of 130 images, and the test set has 20 images. These images are from three different centers of cardiac LGE MRI images. These centers are the University of Utah, Beth Israel Deaconess Medical Center, and King's College London. The equipment used came from two different MRI scanner suppliers (Siemens and Philips). The spatial resolution of the images provided by each center is also different, which is $1.25 \times 1.25 \times 2.5$ mm, $1.4 \times 1.4 \times 1.4$ mm, $1.3 \times 1.3 \times 4.0$ mm. Among the 130 training set images, the contours of the left atrium were manually segmented by clinically experienced physicians [11–13].

In the process of image preprocessing at each stage, all images are histogram-matched according to a certain image. Then nnU-Net is used for training, and the batch size is set to 2. Finally, the images with histogram matching operation or not are compared respectively. For each experiment, 100 epochs are carried on the GPU of GTX2080, and the best epoch model is saved to predict.

3.2   Result

As mentioned above, directly matching the histogram of the image will influence the surrounding, resulting in a result that is not so great. So we first roughly segment the image and then extract the region of interest according to the former segmentation result. Then do the histogram matching with these regions, which

Table 1. Segmentation and quantification results of histogram matched and unprocessed datasets.

Method	Dice	Jaccard	95%HD	ASSD	Time
SU-Net	0.8998	0.8203	4.968	1.283	30 min
HSU-Net	0.9172	0.8483	10.5807	2.3286	45 min
TU-Net	0.9229	0.8662	2.7045	0.7525	3 min
HTU-Net	0.9328	0.8749	2.4788	0.7095	10 min

can reduce the influence of the surrounding on the region to be segmented. The result of histogram matching is shown in the Fig. 1.

In the process of image pre-processing at each stage, we divided 130 images into 90 training images and 40 verification images, and do four groups of comparative tests.

- SU-Net: A single stage nnU-Net without histogram matching.
- HSU-Net: A single stage nnU-Net with histogram matching.
- TU-Net: Two stages nnU-Net without histogram matching.
- HTU-Net: Two stages nnU-Net with histogram matching.

The results of each group of comparative tests in the validation image are shown in Table 1. Dice, Jaccard, 95% Hausdorff distance (95%HD) and Mean surface distance (ASSD) are given in the table. It can be seen that the Dice coefficient of HTU-Net is larger. From these evaluation indicators, we can see that the accuracy of HTU-Net is higher. Figure 4 shows the visualization of segmentation results. From left to right are the original images, ground truth, the result of SU-Net, the result of HSU-Net, the result of TU-Net, and the result of HTU-Net.

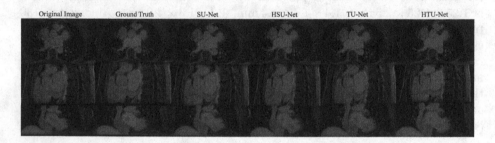

Fig. 4. Visualization of segmentation results

At the same time, in the verification stage, the speed of the two stages is much faster than that of the single stage. Because of the two stages, the first stage uses downsampling, which avoids semantic segmentation in a high-resolution image. In the second stage, we only segment the ROI area, which greatly reduces the area that needs to be segmented. Therefore, in the verification process, the speed of the two-stage is much faster than the speed of the single-stage. As shown in Table 1. It takes about 30 min to verify 40 images in SU-Net, 45 min to verify 40 images in HSU-Net, 3 min to verify 40 images in TU-Net, and 10 min to verify 40 images in HTU-Net. It can be seen that the speed of the two stages is much faster than that of the single stage. Although HTU-Net takes a little more time than TU-Net, it improves the accuracy. In general, HTU-Net is better than TU-Net.

4 Conclusion

In this paper, in order to solve the problem of large differences in intensity distribution between different images caused by multi-center data-sets, we use histogram matching to solve this problem. In order to speed up the time in the test phase and improve the effect of histogram matching, we use a two-stage nnU-Net, in which the first stage performs coarse segmentation, and the second stage is further divided according to the results of the coarse segmentation. In LAScarQS 2022, our method achieved satisfactory results. And through four sets of comparative experiments, it can be proved that our method has improved a lot of accuracy compared with the case without histogram matching, and the test speed is nearly four times faster. However, in some small areas, the segmentation effect is not very satisfactory. Subsequent work can improve the network by imposing size constraints, such as adding unit vector normalization.

References

1. Li, S., Zhang, C., He, X.: Shape-aware semi-supervised 3D semantic segmentation for medical images. In: Martel, A.L., Abolmaesumi, P., Stoyanov, D., Mateus, D., Zuluaga, M.A., Zhou, S.K., Racoceanu, D., Joskowicz, L. (eds.) MICCAI 2020. LNCS, vol. 12261, pp. 552–561. Springer, Cham (2020). https://doi.org/10.1007/978-3-030-59710-8_54
2. Yu, L., Wang, S., Li, X., Fu, C.-W., Heng, P.-A.: Uncertainty-aware self-ensembling model for semi-supervised 3D left atrium segmentation. In: Shen, D., et al. (eds.) MICCAI 2019. LNCS, vol. 11765, pp. 605–613. Springer, Cham (2019). https://doi.org/10.1007/978-3-030-32245-8_67
3. Habijan, M., et al.: Overview of the whole heart and heart chamber segmentation methods. Cardiovasc. Eng. Technol. **11**(6), 725–747 (2020)
4. Xia, Q., Yao, Y., Hu, Z., Hao, A.: Automatic 3D atrial segmentation from GE-MRIs using volumetric fully convolutional networks. In: Pop, M., et al. (eds.) STACOM 2018. LNCS, vol. 11395, pp. 211–220. Springer, Automatic 3d atrial segmentation from ge-mris using volumetric fully convolutional networks (2019). https://doi.org/10.1007/978-3-030-12029-0_23
5. Chen, C., Biffi, C., Tarroni, G., Petersen, S., Bai, W., Rueckert, D.: Learning shape priors for robust cardiac MR segmentation from multi-view images. In: Shen, D., et al. (eds.) MICCAI 2019. LNCS, vol. 11765, pp. 523–531. Springer, Cham (2019). https://doi.org/10.1007/978-3-030-32245-8_58
6. Chen, C., Dou, Q., Jin, Y., Chen, H., Qin, J., Heng, P.-A.: Robust multimodal brain tumor segmentation via feature disentanglement and gated fusion. In: Shen, D., et al. (eds.) MICCAI 2019. LNCS, vol. 11766, pp. 447–456. Springer, Cham (2019). https://doi.org/10.1007/978-3-030-32248-9_50
7. Dou, D., de Castro, D.C., Kamnitsas, K., Glocker, B.: Domain generalization via model-agnostic learning of semantic features. Advances in Neural Information Processing Systems, 32 (2019)
8. Ma, J.: Histogram matching augmentation for domain adaptation with application to multi-centre, multi-vendor and multi-disease cardiac image segmentation. In: Puyol Anton, E., et al. (eds.) STACOM 2020. LNCS, vol. 12592, pp. 177–186. Springer, Cham (2021). https://doi.org/10.1007/978-3-030-68107-4_18

9. Shapira, D., Avidan, S., Hel-Or, Y.: Multiple histogram matching. In: 2013 IEEE international conference on image processing, pp. 2269–2273. IEEE (2013)

10. Isensee, F., et al.: nnu-net: self-adapting framework for u-net-based medical image segmentation. arXiv preprint arXiv:1809.10486 (2018)

11. Li, L., Zimmer, V.A., Schnabel, J.A., Zhuang, X.: Atrialjsqnet: a new framework for joint segmentation and quantification of left atrium and scars incorporating spatial and shape information. Med. Image Anal. **76**, 102303 (2022)

12. Li, L., Zimmer, V.A., Schnabel, J.A., Zhuang, X.: Medical image analysis on left atrial lge mri for atrial fibrillation studies: a review. Med. Image Anal., p. 102360 (2022)

13. Li, L., Zimmer, V.A., Schnabel, J.A., Zhuang, X.: AtrialGeneral: domain generalization for left atrial segmentation of multi-center LGE MRIs. In: de Bruijne, M., et al. (eds.) MICCAI 2021. LNCS, vol. 12906, pp. 557–566. Springer, Cham (2021). https://doi.org/10.1007/978-3-030-87231-1_54

Sequential Segmentation of the Left Atrium and Atrial Scars Using a Multi-scale Weight Sharing Network and Boundary-Based Processing

Abbas Khan[1,2], Omnia Alwazzan[1,2], Martin Benning[2,3],
and Greg Slabaugh[1,2(✉)]

[1] School of Electronic Engineering and Computer Science,
Queen Mary University of London, London, UK
{a.rayabatkhan,g.slabaugh}@qmul.ac.uk
[2] Queen Mary's Digital Environment Research Institute (DERI), London, UK
[3] School of Mathematical Sciences, Queen Mary University of London, London, UK

Abstract. Left atrial (LA) segmentation and quantification of atrial scars have opened a path to automating Atrial Fibrillation (AF) diagnosis. This paper proposes a two-stage approach for sequential segmentation of the LA cavity and scars. Our Multi-scale Weight Sharing (MSWS) Network extracts features at multiple scales and is used for LA cavity segmentation. We also propose a Boundary2Patches method which performs segmentation of scars around the detected LA cavity boundary. The MSWS network learns a better representation of features through sharing weights across scales, and the Boundary2Patches method focuses on smaller scars constrained in the region around the LA cavity wall. On the challenge cohort (validation set), our method achieves an average Dice score of 0.938 and 0.558 for the LA cavity and scars segmentation of task 1, and a Dice score of 0.846 for LA cavity segmentation of task 2. The pre-trained models, source code, and implementation details are available at https://github.com/kabbas570/LAScarQS2022.

Keywords: Left Atrial segmentation · Scar quantification · Atrial fibrillation (AF) · Multi-scale Weight Sharing Network · Boundary2patches

1 Introduction

Atrial Fibrillation (AF) is a condition that produces an irregular, fast or sluggish heartbeat in the upper chamber of the heart. According to the US Centers for Disease Control and Prevention (CDC) [5], AF is one of the most prevalent forms of cardiac arrhythmia that increases the risk of ischemic stroke. Strokes resulting from AF complications are typically more severe than strokes due to other underlying causes [6]. Treatment and diagnosis of AF remain a concern. The assessment of AF patients may depend on the position and size of scars

© The Author(s), under exclusive license to Springer Nature Switzerland AG 2023
X. Zhuang et al. (Eds.): LAScarQS 2022, LNCS 13586, pp. 69–82, 2023.
https://doi.org/10.1007/978-3-031-31778-1_7

which could provide vital information about the onset of AF. Late gadolinium enhancement magnetic resonance imaging (LGE MRI) has evolved to assess the extent of scars and the Left Atrial (LA) cavity [10]. The LGE MRI has allowed scientists to automate the time-consuming diagnosis of AF. However, such automation requires LA cavity segmentation and scars quantification.

Analyzing the LGE MRI scans could provide valuable insight for AF diagnosis and treatment stratification [18]; however, the manual delineation of LA scarring and cavities for quantification is laborious and highly subjective [16]; therefore, it is desirable to automate the process. This challenge has attracted considerable research interest even before the era of deep learning. Intensity-based thresholding [12], clustering methods [7], and graph-cuts [17] were popular traditional methods. However, these methods have limitations of computational costs and manual selection for the areas of interest to be segmented.

With the advent of deep learning, LA segmentation and scars quantification have attracted additional research. Several fully automated methods have been proposed in this field. One of the most recent methods by Li et al. [15] utilized shape attention (SA) through a surface projection of the LA cavity and achieved higher performance for scar quantification. The authors used the inherent correlation between the LA cavity and scars, and trained a joint segmentation architecture. A hybrid method based on graph cuts and CNNs was used by [13] for the automatic scar segmentation. A multi-scale three-stage network was used to learn both local and global features. Vesal et al. [20] employed a UNet [19] based model with dilated convolutions in the bottleneck to segment 3D volumetric scans. Each volume is centre-cropped to remove over-represented backgrounds and to learn only a particular region of interest to improve LA segmentation. Bian et al. [3] used a pyramid pooling module to extract the features at different scales and improved the robustness of the model against various shapes of the LA. They also implemented an Online Hard Negative Example Mining strategy to classify a voxel with low certainty. A contour loss is introduced by [9] to provide spatial distance information during training and used in a two-stage, three-dimensional UNet-based architecture. The first UNet generates coarse segmentation maps, and the second UNet refines coarse predictions to segment the LA at a higher resolution accurately. Yang et al. [21] used an atlas-based method to identify the LA cavity first and then used a super-pixel-based approach to detect the scars in that region. Campello et al. [4] introduced a CyclicGan to first increase the number of annotated LGE MRI scans followed by a modified UNet [19] network to perform scar tissue segmentation.

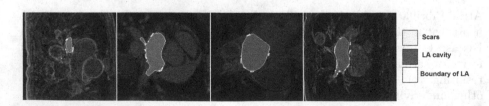

Fig. 1. Visualisation of LA cavity and scars from LAScarQS 2022 challenge dataset.

Challenges remain however, mostly because of the poor quality of annotated LGE MRI scans, the heterogeneity of LA shape and appearance, and the presence of small scars and thin tissue walls. Accordingly, the LAScarQS 2022 competition [14–16] seeks a solution to the aforementioned problems by focusing on the LA cavity and scars segmentation from LGE MRI. For illustration, Fig. 1 shows examples of LGE MRIs scan from the LAScarQS 2022 challenge dataset.

In this paper, we focus on segmenting the LGE MRI scans over multiple scales by concurrently sharing the weights and enabling the kernels to learn shared representations of features using MSWS-Net. In a second stage, we propose a Boundary2Patches method to detect the scars around the LA boundary and quantify the scars using patches and a modified UNet architecture.

2 Proposed Approach

Fig. 2 presents the proposed sequential segmentation framework, for both the LA cavity and scars segmentation. First, we segment the LA cavity using MSWS-Net and then use its output as an initialization step for scar quantification. In Fig. 2, the black arrows represent the workflow for LA cavity segmentation, the lime green arrows for scars segmentation (Boundary2Patches method), and the orange color is used only for visualisation, i.e. it is not part of training or inference. For both tasks, the training is performed separately; but the two steps are merged together during inference in an sequential manner. The following subsections will explain in detail each network and the post-processing steps adopted during training and testing.

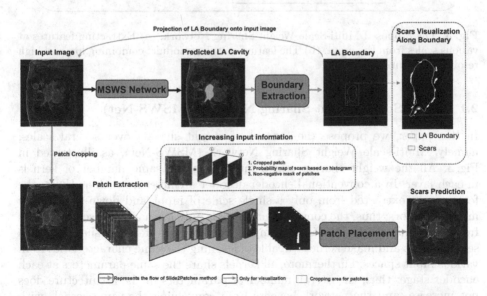

Fig. 2. A schematic of the proposed sequential approach for LA and atrial scars segmentation.

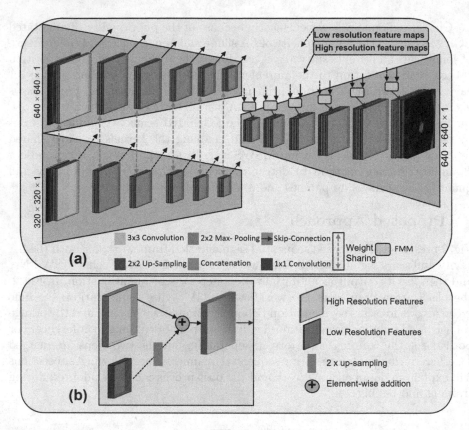

Fig. 3. The proposed Multi-Scale Weight Sharing Network. (a) Extracting features at various scales from the input. (b) The feature merging module; combining low and high resolution features.

2.1 Multi-Scale Weight Sharing Network (MSWS-Net)

In this paper, we propose the concept of weight sharing over several scales, namely, Multi-scale Weight Sharing Network (MSWS-Net), as illustrated in Fig. 3. All the weight sharing stages must have the same number of kernels in each layer. In a conventional encoder-decoder architecture such as UNet, the features are extracted from only a single scale of input and down-sampled by multiple factors; thus, the convolutional kernels only learn a single scale features from the input space. Instead, we employ the concept of kernel sharing across several scales and make kernels capable of learning the same characteristics from various input spaces. Furthermore, all kernels share the same parameters at each encoder stage; thus, the overall number of parameters in the architecture does not increase, and the network benefits from convolving the same kernels with varying dimensions of incoming feature maps. We experimented with different numbers of encoders $n \in [2, 4]$ and discovered that n = 2 performed best while $n > 2$ did not improve the results significantly, detailed experiments are mentioned in Table 1. We speculate that the LA cavity appears self-similar at these two scales, and increasing the number of encoders beyond 2 has no effect on the network's learning ability. Therefore, in our final implementation, we set n = 2. The optimal number of multi-scale levels depends upon the dataset's self-similarity across scale, and a performance boost may vary for different datasets.

The proposed multi-scale weight sharing (MSWS) architecture is depicted in Fig. 3. It takes two images as input with dimensions [H x W x C] and [H/2 x W/2 x C]; note that number of channels should be the same for both images. For this challenge, we resized all images to H = 640 and W = 640 using zero padding. Furthermore, each 2D scan was normalized to zero mean and unit variance. Two consecutive 3×3 convolutions are performed at each encoder stage, followed by ReLU activation and batch-normalization. The proposed weight-sharing strategy across multiple scales will help the network to learn the features of different scales. The shared weights are represented by an orange vertical dotted arrow. At the decoder side, the features of various scales are combined using a feature merging module (FMM) at each stage. The FMM merges the information across two-resolution representations. First, it upsamples the lower resolution features with a factor = 2, and then it preforms an element-wise addition with the corresponding incoming features from the other encoder. The resultant representation is semantically richer and spatially more precise; helping to segment various shapes of LA cavity efficiently. In Fig. 3, the black arrow, dotted black arrow and blue arrow represents features of higher-resolution, lower-resolution, and merged features, respectively.

2.2 Boundary Processing with the Boundary2Patches Method

Fig. 2 depicts a broad overview of the proposed boundary-based processing method, namely, Boundary2Patches for the scars segmentation. As previously indicated, the proportion of scars is relatively small compared to the entire image; therefore, we restricted the search area using the Boundary2Patches approach to concentrate more on the scars. Current literature implies that scars are most prevalent across the LA cavity's boundary; hence, we solely search for scars in the region adjacent to the LA wall. From the LA cavity segmentation, the boundary of the LA cavity is identified and 64×64 patches from the original image are extracted along the boundary, as illustrated in Fig. 2. The patch size of 64×64 is selected as it incorporates all the surrounding scars if we reconstruct the ground truth from these patches. For Boundary2Patches method, we trained another encoder-decoder network separately and ran it sequentially with MSWS-Net during inference. The architecture used for Boundary2Patches method is shown in Fig. 4. It has four stages (two consecutive 3×3 convolutions at each stage with ReLU activation and batch-normalization) at the respective encoder and decoder sides. For the encoder, features are down-sampled twice using strided convolution with stride = 2 to avoid the loss of information for small-size scars. On the decoder side, transposed convolutions are used to upsampled the incoming features, and the upsampled features are concatenated with corresponding

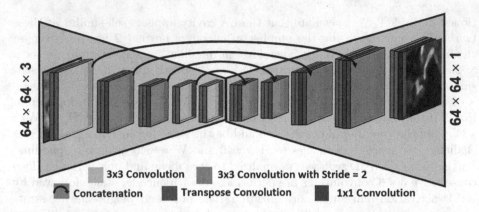

Fig. 4. The modified UNet architecture for scars segmentation.

features of the encoder for better gradient flow. Sigmoid was used as an activation function for the last output layer with 1×1 convolution to generate the segmentation map for scars.

In the final implementation, we further increased the input information by concatenating the patches with a probability map of scar based on histogram and non-negative values obtained after z-score normalization. We discovered that in LGE MRI, scars have greater intensities than the surrounding areas, thus we computed the histogram of higher intensities and used it in conjunction with extracted patches and a non-negative mask of scars, as illustrated in Fig. 2.

3   Dataset Description

The dataset was provided by the LAScarQS 2022 Challenge, which intends to develop automated/semi-automated methods for segmenting the LA Multi-Center LGE MRIs and quantifying scars. The dataset consists of 194 LGE MRIs. The MRI scans of LGE were produced at two distinct locations using scanners with varying resolutions. The included gold standard labels consist of the LA blood pool (atriumSegImgMO.nii.gz) as well as the LA scars (scarSegImgM.nii.gz). Furthermore, training and testing on the dataset can be conducted remotely from several local centers while the dataset remains concealed to preserve data privacy. During the training phase, the dataset was subdivided into 70% for training, 20% for validation, and 10% for inference to evaluate our proposed models and undertake ablation experiments.

4   Experimental Details

The proposed framework was implemented in PyTorch, and all the experiments were performed using a cluster of NVidia A100 GPUs [1]. For both approaches,

MSWS-Net and Boundary2Patches, the models were trained using Adam optimization [11], with β_1, $\beta_2 = [0.9, 0.99]$, and the learning rate was set to $= 0.0001$. During training, we set the maximum number of epochs to 100 and the batch size to 24. In addition, we employed a custom early stopping mechanism from terminating the training before the model overfits the data. In our customized early stopping method, we monitored the validation loss and Dice score and halted training if either was not improving for five consecutive epochs.

4.1 Loss Function

While analyzing the data, we found that the LA cavity and scars occupy a small fraction of the full image. Such imbalance in the data could not be handled by commonly used loss functions for segmentation, such as the Dice loss or binary cross entropy loss, as listed in Table 2. Initially, MSWS-Net was trained with a weighted Dice loss, but this led to a greater number of false negatives (FNs) than false positives (FPs). Consequently, we trained both networks with the Focal Tversky loss function [2] given by Eqs. 1 and 2,

$$TI_c = \frac{\sum_{i=1}^{N} \hat{y}_{ic} y_{ic} + \epsilon}{\sum_{i=1}^{N} \hat{y}_{ic} y_{ic} + \beta \sum_{i=1}^{N} (1 - \hat{y}_{i\bar{c}}) y_{ic} + \alpha \sum_{i=1}^{N} \hat{y}_{ic} (1 - y_{i\bar{c}}) + \epsilon} \quad (1)$$

$$FTL_c = \sum_c (1 - TI_c)^{1/\gamma} \quad (2)$$

where $\hat{y}_{ic}$ is the probability that the pixel is from the LA cavity and y_{ic} is the probability of background class. The hyperparameter α focuses on FPs, β focuses on FNs, and γ focuses on hard examples. These hyperparameters are tuned to get a balance between precision and recall in the case of large class imbalance. In our experiments, we trained MSWS-Net with α, β, $\gamma = [0.3, 0.7, 0.75]$ and the Boundary2Patches method with α, β, $\gamma = [0.4, 0.6, 0.75]$.

5 Results and Discussion

This section describes the results of our methods applied to the validation data for Tasks 1 and 2 of the LAScarQS 2022 challenge. In addition, we performed ablation studies to measure the effectiveness of the proposed methods. Finally, MSWS-Net is compared to two of its ablated variants, while Boundary2Patches was compared to two baseline schemes. The following list overviews four experiments conducted in this paper.

1. **Standard UNet Architecture:** The ability of proposed MSWS-Net to extract features at multiple-scales is compared to a standard UNet architecture with a single encoder and the same number of stages as MSWS-Net.

2. **MSWS-Net without weight sharing:** The weight sharing strategy is evaluated by training the MSWS-Net without sharing the weights of two encoders.

3. **Center-Cropping:** We trained the network depicted in Fig. 4 on centred cropped images for scar quantification and compared the results with the patch-based technique.

4. **Without using the increased input information:** We solely used the cropped patches in the Boundary2Patches method to evaluate the benefit of employing the additional information concatenated at the input of the network.

5. **Choice of Loss function:** We experimented with various loss functions and their combinations. Due to the small volume of the to-be-segmented region of interest, we modified the focal loss using Tversky loss to reduce the number of false negatives and achieve the optimal tradeoff between precision and recall. Table 2 summarizes the results of various loss functions.

6. **Number of Weight-Sharing Encoders for MSWS-Net:** For MSWS-Net, we increased the number of encoders from 1 to 4 while sharing the weights and having spatial dimensions in the range of H × W to $\frac{H}{2^n} \times \frac{W}{2^n}$, where 'n' is the number of encoders. We found that n = 2 is the optimal tradeoff between performance and network complexity for the task at hand. By increasing the 'n', the performance gain was statistically insignificant at the expense of slower processing and requiring more resources. Table 1 shows the results of ablation studies conducted to choose optimal number of Weight-Sharing Encoders for MSWS-Net.

Table 1. Ablation studies to choose optimal number of weight sharing encoders, Giga Floating Point Operations per Second (GFLOPs), Input Size, and Dice score.

# of Encoders	GFLOPs ↓	Input Size (MB) ↓	Dice Score ↑
1	**310.80**	**1.56**	0.828
2	339.31	1.95	0.918
3	346.44	2.05	0.920
4	348.22	2.10	**0.922**

Table 2. Comparison of different loss functions on validations set of task: 1. TPs: True Positives, FPs: False Positives, FNs: False Negatives, IoU: Intersection over Union.

Loss Function	Dice Score ↑	TPs ↑	FPs ↓	FNs ↓
Binary-Cross Entropy	0.895	1,821,410	112,551	305,740
1-IoU	0.906	1,857,001	106,154	270,149
Focal Tversky	**0.918**	**1,847,210**	**109,765**	**136,254**

5.1   LA Cavity Segmentation: Task 2

For this task, MSWS-Net is able to segment the LA cavity of different shapes accurately, achieving a Dice score of 0.846 on the validation set. Table 3 shows the results of the aforementioned ablation experiments and demonstrates the effectiveness of multiple scale encoders and weight-sharing schemes. Different evaluation metrics such as Dice score (DS), Hausdorff Distance (HD), average surface distance (ASD), and sensitivity were used to quantify the segmentation performance. The qualitative results are shown in Fig. 5, comparing the visual performance of MSWS-Net with its ablated versions. The third row indicates the results of MSWS-Net, whereas the first and second rows represent the results of standard UNet and MSWS-Net without the weight sharing approach.

For visualization purposes, we have projected the ground truth and predicted segmentation maps on the input images. In addition, we have assigned different colors to all qualitative results reported in this paper (Green represents false positives, Red represents false negatives, and Yellow represents true positives).

5.2   LA Cavity and Scars Segmentation: Task 1

Task 1 of the challenge aims to segment the LA cavity and the atrial scars. For scar quantification, we first segmented the LA cavity and then used the Boundary2Patches approach to find scars along the LA boundary, where they are predominantly present. The performance of the scar segmentation relies on the precise segmentation of the LA cavity. To improve the segmentation of the LA cavity, we first trained the MSWS-Net on training data from Task 2 and then fine-tuned it on Task 1. Ultimately, we obtained a Dice score of 0.938 for the LA cavity segmentation of Task 1 on the validation set. Figure 6 presents qualitative results for LA cavity segmentation from Task 1 of the challenge.

For scar quantification, we used the boundaries of predicted LA cavities, which are predicted via MSWS-Net, to crop the patches during the inference stage. The number of cropped patches during inference differed for each image, depending upon the area of the segmented LA cavity. Table 4 summarizes the performance of the proposed Boundary2Patches method for scar segmentation. For comparison purposes, we centred cropped the images (384 × 384) and tried to predict the scars, which resulted in lower performance, as listed in Table 4. We also highlighted the importance of using the increased input information at

Table 3. Validation dataset benchmarks quantitative results for Task 2 of LA cavity segmentation and comparison of MSWS-Net with its ablated versions.

Method	Dice Score ↑	HD (mm) ↓	ASD (mm) ↓
Standard UNet architecture	0.728	**96.5**	**3.22**
MSWS-Net without weight sharing	0.708	107.2	5.6
MSWS-Net	**0.846**	105.7	3.39

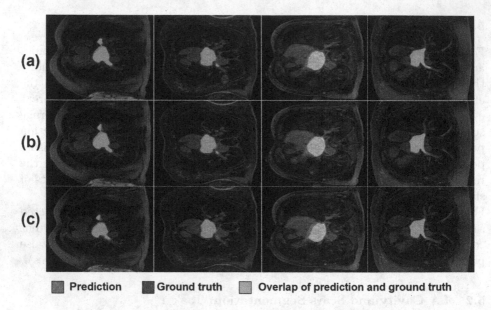

Prediction   Ground truth   Overlap of prediction and ground truth

Fig. 5. Qualitative results for Task 2 (LA cavity segmentation). Results of (a) proposed MSWS-Net (b) Standard UNet architecture (c) MSW-Net without weight sharing strategy.

the input of our network by comparing it to an ablated version of the Boundary2Patches method without the additional input derived from the histogram and non-negative mask. Some visual results of scar quantification are shown in Fig. 7.

We additionally applied the connected component analysis (CCA) [8] as a post-processing step on scar segmentation maps to eliminate small false positives from the final predictions, which resulted in a boost of 1.06% in the Dice score for scar quantification, as listed in Table 4. For the CCA implementation, we used the 4-connected component method and discarded components with less than 10 pixels or more than 450. These numbers were chosen empirically. The CCA algorithm also reduced the detection of true positives, but their dismissal ratio was

Table 4. Validation dataset benchmarks quantitative results for scars quantification and comparison of different ablation studies for the Boundary2Patches method.

Method	Dice Score ↑	Sensitivity ↑
Center-Cropping	0.407	0.412
Boundary2Patches (single channel input)	0.465	0.484
Boundary2Patches (three channel input)	0.547	0.559
Boundary2Patches (three channel input + post-processing with CCA)	**0.558**	**0.568**

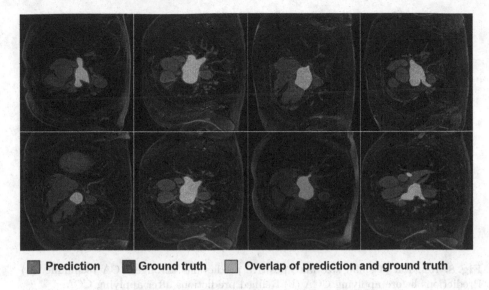

■ Prediction   ■ Ground truth   □ Overlap of prediction and ground truth

Fig. 6. Qualitative results for Task 1 of LA cavity segmentation.

far less than the removal of false positives, which resulted in improved performance. Figure 8 showcases the visual motivation of applying the CCA technique. It helped to remove the false positive outliers highlighted through the yellow dotted box.

Furthermore, the segmentation performance of the proposed MSWS-Net and Boundary2Patches method in the LAScarQS 2022 testing set is reported in Table 5. For task-1, the test set comprises 22 images, and for task-2, it has

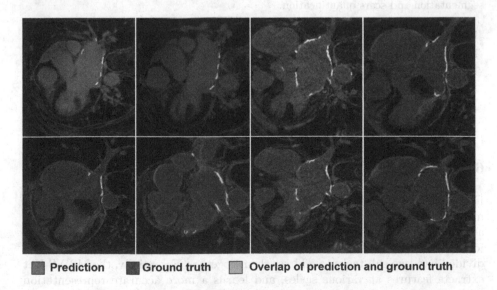

■ Prediction   ■ Ground truth   □ Overlap of prediction and ground truth

Fig. 7. Visual results for scar quantification of Task 1.

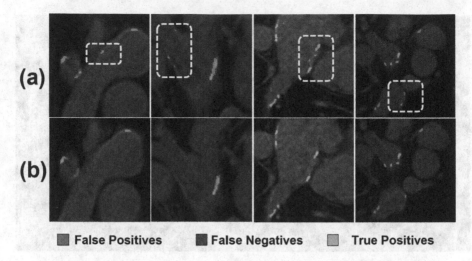

False Positives   **False Negatives**   **True Positives**

Fig. 8. Removal of small size false positive predictions through CCA technique. (a) Predictions before applying CCA (b) Refined predictions after applying CCA.

44. We observed that the overall performance on the test set is very similar to those of the validation benchmarks. For the test phase, the challenge required a docker file submission. The results are reported in terms of Dice score, HD, and ASD for LA cavity segmentation and for scars quantification; we evaluated the performance using Dice score and sensitivity metrics.

Table 5. LAScarQS 2022 testing dataset benchmarks quantitative results for LA cavity segmentation and scars quantification.

Task	Dice Score ↑	HD (mm) ↓	ASD (mm) ↓	Sensitivity ↑
Task-1 LA cavity segmentation	0.922	110.65	3.48	-
Task-2 LA cavity segmentation	0.792	67.45	2.89	-
Task-1 scars quantification	0.549	-	-	0.599

6   Conclusion

For the LAScarQS 2022 challenge, we propose a sequential approach to segment left atrium and atrial scars using a multi-scale weight-sharing network and boundary-based processing. As the challenge seeks to resolve two problems jointly, namely the LA cavity's segmentation and the quantification of scars, we divided into two sub-tasks to address them together. Essentially, the MSWS-Net extracts features at various scales, and learns a more accurate representation of features via multi-scaling and weight-sharing techniques. Additionally, the

Boundary2Patches method aids in focusing on and accurately segmenting small scars. Lastly, the proposed approach achieves an average Dice score of 0.938 and a Dice score of 0.558 for the segmentation of LA cavities and scars, respectively, in Task 1, as well as an average Dice score of 0.846 for the segmentation of LA cavities in Task 2.

Acknowledgements. This research work is funded by the mini-Centre for Doctoral Training (CDT) award through the Faculty of Science and Engineering, Queen Mary University of London, United Kingdom. The authors also thank project partners, including NVIDIA Corporation, Circle Cardiovascular Imaging, and Conavi Medical.

References

1. This research utilised queen mary's andrena HPC facility, supported by QMUL research-it. https://zenodo.org/record/438045 Accessed 20 May 2022
2. Abraham, N., Khan, N.M.: A novel focal Tversky loss function with improved attention u-net for lesion segmentation. In: 2019 IEEE 16th International Symposium on Biomedical Imaging (ISBI 2019), pp. 683–687. IEEE (2019)
3. Bian, C., et al.: Pyramid Network with Online Hard Example Mining for Accurate Left Atrium Segmentation. In: Pop, M., et al. (eds.) STACOM 2018. LNCS, vol. 11395, pp. 237–245. Springer, Cham (2019). https://doi.org/10.1007/978-3-030-12029-0_26
4. Campello, V.M., Martín-Isla, C., Izquierdo, C., Petersen, S.E., Ballester, M.A.G., Lekadir, K.: Combining Multi-Sequence and Synthetic Images for Improved Segmentation of Late Gadolinium Enhancement Cardiac MRI. In: Pop, M., et al. (eds.) STACOM 2019. LNCS, vol. 12009, pp. 290–299. Springer, Cham (2020). https://doi.org/10.1007/978-3-030-39074-7_31
5. Centers for Disease Control and Prevention CDC: centers for disease control and prevention CDC, Atrial Fibrillation (2017). https://www.cdc.gov/heartdisease/atrial_fibrillation.htm Accessed 12 July 2022
6. Chugh, S.S., et al.: Worldwide epidemiology of atrial fibrillation: a global burden of disease 2010 study. Circulation **129**(8), 837–847 (2014)
7. Detsky, J.S., Paul, G., Dick, A.J., Wright, G.A.: Reproducible classification of infarct heterogeneity using fuzzy clustering on multi contrast delayed enhancement magnetic resonance images. IEEE Trans. Med. Imaging **28**(10), 1606–1614 (2009)
8. Fu, Y., Chen, X., Gao, H.: A new connected component analysis algorithm based on max-tree. In: 2009 8TH IEEE International Conference on Dependable, Autonomic and Secure Computing, pp. 843–844 IEEE (2009)
9. Jia, S., et al.: Automatically Segmenting the Left Atrium from Cardiac Images Using Successive 3D U-Nets and a Contour Loss. In: Pop, M., et al. (eds.) STACOM 2018. LNCS, vol. 11395, pp. 221–229. Springer, Cham (2019). https://doi.org/10.1007/978-3-030-12029-0_24
10. Kim, R.J., et al.: Relationship of MRI delayed contrast enhancement to irreversible injury, infarct age, and contractile function. Circulation **100**(19), 1992–2002 (1999)
11. Kingma, D.P., Ba, J.: Adam: a method for stochastic optimization (2014) arXiv preprint arXiv:1412.6980
12. Kolipaka, A., Chatzimavroudis, G.P., White, R.D., O'Donnell, T.P., Setser, R.M.: Segmentation of non-viable myocardium in delayed enhancement magnetic resonance images. Int. J. Cardiovasc. Imaging **21**(2), 303–311 (2005)

13. Li, L., et al.: Atrial Scar Segmentation via Potential Learning in the Graph-Cut Framework. In: Pop, M., et al. (eds.) STACOM 2018. LNCS, vol. 11395, pp. 152–160. Springer, Cham (2019). https://doi.org/10.1007/978-3-030-12029-0_17

14. Li, L., Zimmer, V.A., Schnabel, J.A., Zhuang, X.: Atrial General: domain generalization for left atrial segmentation of multi-center LGE MRIs. In: de Bruijne, M., et al. (eds.) MICCAI 2021. LNCS, vol. 12906, pp. 557–566. Springer, Cham (2021). https://doi.org/10.1007/978-3-030-87231-1_54

15. Li, L., Zimmer, V.A., Schnabel, J.A., Zhuang, X.: Atrialjsqnet: a new framework for joint segmentation and quantification of left atrium and scars incorporating spatial and shape information. Med. Image Anal. **76**, 102303 (2022)

16. Li, L., Zimmer, V.A., Schnabel, J.A., Zhuang, X.: Medical image analysis on left atrial LGE MRI for atrial fibrillation studies: A review. Med. Image Anal., p. 102360 (2022)

17. Lu, Y., Yang, Y., Connelly, K.A., Wright, G.A., Radau, P.E.: Automated quantification of myocardial infarction using graph cuts on contrast delayed enhanced magnetic resonance images. Quant. Imaging Med. Surg. **2**(2), 81 (2012)

18. Njoku, A., et al.: Left atrial volume predicts atrial fibrillation recurrence after radiofrequency ablation: a meta-analysis. Ep Europace **20**(1), 33–42 (2018)

19. Ronneberger, O., Fischer, P., Brox, T.: U-Net: Convolutional Networks for Biomedical Image Segmentation. In: Navab, N., Hornegger, J., Wells, W.M., Frangi, A.F. (eds.) MICCAI 2015. LNCS, vol. 9351, pp. 234–241. Springer, Cham (2015). https://doi.org/10.1007/978-3-319-24574-4_28

20. Vesal, S., Ravikumar, N., Maier, A.: Dilated Convolutions in Neural Networks for Left Atrial Segmentation in 3D Gadolinium Enhanced-MRI. In: Pop, M., et al. (eds.) STACOM 2018. LNCS, vol. 11395, pp. 319–328. Springer, Cham (2019). https://doi.org/10.1007/978-3-030-12029-0_35

21. Yang, G., et al.: Fully automatic segmentation and objective assessment of atrial scars for long-standing persistent atrial fibrillation patients using late gadolinium-enhanced mri. Med. Phys. **45**(4), 1562–1576 (2018)

LA-HRNet: High-Resolution Network for Automatic Left Atrial Segmentation in Multi-center LEG MRI

Tongtong Xie[ID], Zhengeng Yang[ID], and Hongshan Yu[✉][ID]

College of Electrical and Information Engineering, Hunan University,
Changsha 410082, China
yuhongshancn@163.com

Abstract. Atrial fibrillation has become one of the biggest epidemics and public health challenges, and analysis by the late gadolinium-enhanced magnetic resonance imaging (LEG MRI)is of great clinical importance for its diagnosis and treatment. Deep learning-based methods have achieved great success in left atrial segmentation when the MRI data comes from a specific center. However, since images from multiple centers often show large differences, current left atrial segmentation methods designed for single centers often suffer from significant performance degradation when applied to multi-center images. In this paper, we developed a deep network named LA-HRNet for left atrial segmentation in multi-center LGE MRI based on VoxHRNet, a network used for whole-brain segmentation. We made three improvements over the VoxHRNet to make it suited for left atrial segmentation. First, We propose a feature fusion method capable of generating richer features. Second, we propose feature reuse to fuse the multi-scale features generated in the network with subsequent features. Third, we introduce an auxiliary loss in the network. The experimental results on LAScarQS 2022 dataset show that Our proposed improved model has better performance and realizes stronger generalization ability on the multi-center images.

Keywords: Left atrial segmentation · LGE MRI · Atrial Fibrillation

1 Introduction

Atrial fibrillation (AF) is the most common clinical arrhythmia. AF is caused by the impaired electrical activity within the atria which leads to myocardial fibers contracting rapidly in an irregular manner [1]. The incidence and prevalence of AF are increasing every year, especially in countries with medium socio-demographic indices. Now, AF has become one of the biggest cardiovascular epidemics and public health challenges [2].

In recent years, the late gadolinium-enhanced magnetic resonance imaging (LGE MRI) has been proven useful for accurately detect, quantify and characterize atrial fibrosis and predict patient outcomes after AF ablation [3]. LGE

X. Zhuang et al. (Eds.): LAScarQS 2022, LNCS 13586, pp. 83–92, 2023.
https://doi.org/10.1007/978-3-031-31778-1_8

MRI can be used to visualize and quantify left atrial (LA) scarring as well as its location, which provides important information on the pathophysiology and progression of AF. In other words, analysis of LGE MRI plays an essential role in the clinical diagnosis and individualized treatment of patients with AF [4]. However, manual segmentation of the atria or scars would be a very time-consuming and labor-intensive task. Thus, automated LGE MRI analysis system has received great attention in past decade, especially after the widespread use of deep learning techniques in medical image analysis.

The segmentation task of the LA faces great challenges due to the shape of the LA, poor image quality, and unclear boundaries. Li et al. [4] provided a review about current analysis methods for LA LGE MRI for AF studies. Among those reviewed methods, Li et al. [5]proposed a network for LA and scar segmentation and quantification that combined spatial and shape information. And they showed good generalization ability and achieved optimal segmentation performance. Also, it was pointed out in [4] that most of current LA segmentation algorithms are trained and evaluated on LGE MRI data from a specific center. However, due to the lack of a standard protocol for LGE MRI device, there is a lot of variation in the images from different medical centers, resulting in poor re-producibility of LGE MRI [4]. Li et al. [6] investigated domain generalization of LA segmentation based on multi-center LGE MRI. The generalization ability of four common semantic segmentation networks for segmenting LA in multi-center LGE MRI was experimentally evaluated. It was found that most models encounter a significant performance degradation when they are applied to unknown domains, i.e., different centers. And they evaluated the effectiveness of several domain generalization strategies, all of which were able to mitigate performance degradation. In other words, there are still lots room for improvement for the goal of improving the performance of LA segmentation on multi-center data. Therefore, LAScarQS 2022 [7] organized a quantification and segmentation challenge on multi-center LGE MRI of the LA and scars. This will help to validate the robustness and generality of the algorithm on a multi-center dataset and to promote the application of the algorithm in practice.

In this paper, we develop a LA segmentation method for multi-center LGE MRI, which we call LA-HRNet. We choose the same backbone as the one used in VoxHRNet [8], which is designed for whole-brain segmentation. We redesign the feature fusion layer and propose feature reuse to enrich the high-resolution features with much more semantic information. Finally, we introduce auxiliary loss to accelerate the convergence of the network. The overall flow of our method is shown in Fig. 1: (1) In the first stage, the aim of this stage is to achieve target localization. We resample the original image and achieve a rough segmentation of the LA, and crop the target area in the original image to reduce memory consumption; (2) In the second stage, a fine-grained segmentation network is trained based on the cropped target region obtained in our first stage, after which the predictions are restored to the original input size. Both stages of the segmentation network were performed using our LA-HRNet design and we trained and evaluated the segmentation accuracy of our network using the dataset provided by the LAScarQS 2022 challenge [7]. Finally, we perform ablation experiments and compare them with VoxHRNet.

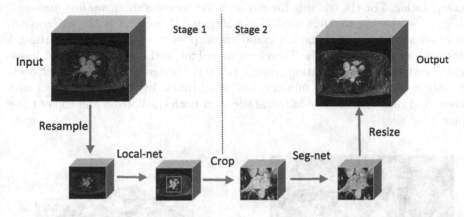

Fig. 1. Two-Stage LA Segmentation Network Process.

2   Methods

2.1   Data Pre-processing

Data Acquisition. The data we used were all from the LAScarQS 2022 challenge for quantification and segmentation of the LA and scar. We participate in task 2 named "Left Atrial Segmentation from Multi-Center LGE MRIs". The dataset for task 2 contains 130 and 20 LGE MRIs for training and validation, respectively. These MRI datas are sampled from patients with AF in a real clinical setting in three centers. The three centers include the University of Utah, Beth Israel Deaconess Medical Center and King's College London, where they may choose different equipment and imaging parameters. The original voxel spacing of the training data provided was $0.625 \times 0.625 \times 2.5 \ mm^3$ with dimensions of $576 \times 576 \times 44/640 \times 640 \times 44$, while the image voxel spacing in the validation dataset was $0.3472 \times 0.3472 \times 2 \ mm^3/0.625 \times 0.625 \times 1.3 \ mm^3$, etc. The training data and the validation data are from different centers and the images are also very different due to different acquisition methods. This is a big challenge for the segmentation task, so we pre-processed the data carefully.

Resampling and Crop. Firstly, to avoid adverse effects on prediction accuracy due to different sampling devices and sampling protocols, we adapted the training data to the same voxel spacing and size. We first resample the voxel spacing of the images to $1.875 \times 1.875 \times 3.75 \ mm^3$ and then use them to train the rough segmentation network. The interpolation method used for image resampling is B spline interpolation and the labels were interpolated using nearest-neighbor interpolation. For the training images used for segmentation, we first resample their voxel spacing to $0.625 \times 0.625 \times 1.25 \ mm^3$. Note that a 256×256 patch cropped at the center of the LA could encompass the entire region of the LA through our statistical study. Therefore, we calculate the center of the LA based on the results of the localization and then crop the image to a size of $256 \times 256 \times h$. As shown in Fig. 2, h is the number of slices obtained by choosing all slices with labels and then choosing 5 additional slices on both the bottom and top of these annotated slices.

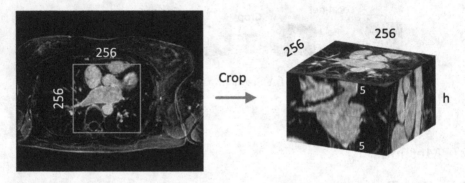

Fig. 2. According to the location information of the LA provided by the rough segmentation network, the image for accurate segmentation is cropped to a size of $256 \times 256 \times h$.

Normalization and Data Augmentation. We observed significant differences in the intensity of the data from different centers. In order to adapt the model to the multi-center data, we use a random affine transformation and add Gaussian noise to the data to simulate the differences caused by different sampling methods. Finally, the data is pre-processed with contrast limited adaptive histogram equalization (CLAHE) to enhance the contrast of the images, and then the image is further processed by z-score normalization.

2.2 Network Architectures

We choose VoxHRnet [8] as our backbone. The VoxHRNet is developed from the well-known HRNet [9]. To allow the network to learn rich spatial representations and produce accurate semantic segmentation results on whole brain, Li et al. designed VoxHRNet based on HRNetV2 [10]. The first version of HRNet was designed for human posture estimation task. Since the high-resolution spatial information plays an important role in human posture estimation, the HRNet maintains a high-resolution representation at all stages of the network and performs repetitive multi-scale feature fusion. Subsequently, HRNetV2 makes predictions by aggregating features from all resolutions and applies it to semantic segmentation and object detection tasks. VoxHRNet retains the benefits of HRNetV2 with relevant modifications to suit the whole brain segmentation problem. First, VoxHRNet adds a stem block to reduce the size of the input image to $H/2 \times W/2 \times D/2$, which reduces the memory requirement of the GPU. In addition, the VoxHRnet adds a classification subnet at the end of feature extraction. The classification sub-network first upsamples the features from different branches and uses the result of their stitching as input, and then outputs a prediction.

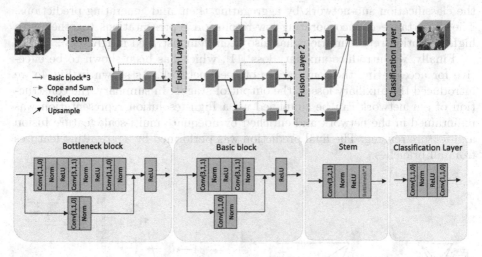

Fig. 3. Our network model and the blocks in it. Conv(a, b, c) indicates that the convolutional layer has a kernel size of $a \times a \times a$, a stride of b and a padding size of c.

The backbone of VoxHRNet consists of three stages and we have kept only two of them, which formed our two-stage backbone shown in Fig. 3. The first stage of our network contains two branches with input dimensions equal to $H/2 \times W/2 \times D/2 \times 16$ and $H/4 \times W/4 \times D/4 \times 32$ respectively, where H, W, D are the dimensions of the input images, and the last dimension is the feature channel. The second stage consists of three branches, the first two branches keep the same input dimensions as one used in the first stage, and the third branch accepts input with dimensions $H/8 \times W/8 \times D/8 \times 64$.

To produce a rich high-resolution representation, we also used multi-scale feature fusion at the end of each stage. As shown in Fig. 4a, the original multi-scale feature is obtained by accumulating feature generated from all branches.

The fusion of various scales of feature is achieved by interpolation or strided convolution. Inspired by Gauss-Seidel method, we redesigned the feature fusion module. The Gauss-Seidel method is an iterative method in numerical linear algebra and its basic idea is to try to use the latest obtained parameters to participate in the iterative computation. We also use the latest obtained features for subsequent feature fusion whenever possible. In the proposed fusion layer (Fig. 4b), we first obtain feature of the low-resolution branch. Then, the feature is utilized to produce high-resolution latent. The red arrow in the figure is our improved new feature transfer path. This modification will encode much more high-level semantic information into high-resolution features. Inspired by the feature-reusing mechanism used in Unet, we fused the input and output features for each stage, which aims to make full use of the features generated by the network. The red dotted line in Fig. 3 shows the location and transfer path of feature-reusing. After the backbone network, the multi-scale features are fed into the classification sub-network by aggregating them and generating predictions. The importance of incorporating low-resolution representations together with high-resolution representations has also been demonstrated in HRNetV2.

Finally, we introduce auxiliary loss [11], which has been shown to be effective for accelerating the convergence of deep network. As shown in Fig. 4c we introduced the auxiliary loss at the output of stage1. In summary, the construction of our network can be simplified as: a high-resolution representation was maintained in the network and enriched by adequate multi-scale feature fusion and feature reusing. The final prediction was performed by aggregating features from all branches.

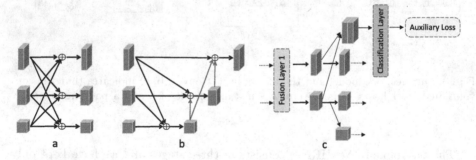

Fig. 4. The location where our proposed feature fusion layer and auxiliary loss are added. (a) The original feature fusion layer. (b) Our proposed improved feature fusion layer. (c) Auxiliary loss structure and location.

3   Results and Discussion

We trained our model on an NVIDIA TESLA T4 with an initial learning rate set to 0.001. The total training iterations was set to 200 epochs and the parameter was optimized with RAdam algorithm [12]. For the loss functions, we chose the Dice loss and CE loss, which are widely used in medical segmentation task. Thus, our final loss can be formally written by

$$l_{Comb} = l_{Dice} : \left(1 - \frac{1}{B}\sum_{i \in B}\frac{2^* \sum_n y_i y_i'}{\sum_n (y_i + y_i')}\right) + l_{CE} : \left(-\frac{1}{B}\sum_{i \in B} y_i \log P y_i'\right) \quad (1)$$

where B represents the batch size, y_i' represents the prediction result, and y_i represents the true label.

The weight of the auxiliary loss and the weight of the main loss are both set to 1. Finally, we divide the training set and the validation set by a ratio of 4:1. We use the Dice Similarity Coefficient (DC) to evaluate the performance of model during training.

Our rough segmentation network achieved a DC of 0.9552/0.8989 on the training/validation set. Figure 5 shows two of the segmentation results of our rough segmentation network on the validation dataset. It can be seen that the network segment the LA well and provide the precise location of the LA. This is helpful for subsequent cropping and precise segmentation.

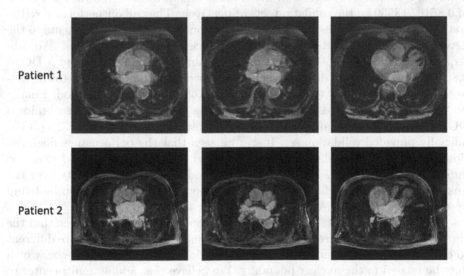

Fig. 5. LA segmentation results of the rough segmentation network. A total of two validation patient images were selected and three random slices are shown in each row. The yellow part represents the segmented result. (Color figure online)

Table 1. The performance of our model (LA-HRNet) and VoxHRNet* with the same number of stages on each dataset. The evaluation index used is the DC and Hausdorff distance (HD). HD is the maximum Euclidean distance among all the minimum Euclidean distances between two finite points sets and smaller HD value means smaller surface distance. F means using the new feature fusion layer and R means using feature-reusing.

Methods	Train/validation Data	Validation Data (DC / HD)
VoxHRNet*	0.9535 / 0.9176	0.8385 / 32.998
VoxHRNet* + F	0.9539 / 0.9178	0.8610 / 30.953
VoxHRNet* + R	0.9552 / 0.9170	0.8550 / 33.945
VoxHRNet* + F + R	0.9545 / 0.9172	0.8646 / 25.675
LA-HRNet	**0.9536 / 0.9202**	**0.8719 / 22.394**

The segmentation results of the LA based on the output of rough segmentation network are shown in Table 1. The original VoxHRNet achieved 0.9176 DC on the validation set used for training and a DC of 0.8385 on the officially provided validation set that comes from centers different from those used in training. It can be seen that the DC value was reduced by 0.1150 when the trained model was applied to unseen validation data, suggesting that image from multi-center poses a greater challenge to the network. When we applied the proposed new feature fusion layer and feature-reusing method to the network, respectively, we obtained DC of 0.9178/0.9170 on the trained validation set. And they get a DC of 0.8610/0.8550 on the validation set, respectively. They all outperform VoxHR-Net*, which demonstrates the effectiveness of our proposed improvements to the network for the multicenter-based LGE MRI task of LA segmentation. We subsequently obtained a DC of 0.9172 on the training validation set and a DC of 0.8646 on the validation dataset when we applied both improvements to the network. This again proves the advanced nature of our proposed method. Finally we introduce auxiliary loss, which leads to the model LA-HRNet. It obtains a DC of 0.9202 on the validation set used for training and a DC of 0.8719 on the officially provided validation set. It can be seen that the performance degradation on the unseen validation set was reduced by 3.33% point. And this also indicates that the proposed network has a good generalization ability over the unknown domain. The effectiveness of our proposed methods can also be found by comparing HD and LA-HRNet achieves the lowest HD of 22.394.

The qualitative results of our method was shown in Fig. 6. It can seen that the three images may come from different centers since the style of them are different to each other. We can find that the segmentation of the LA wall is poor, which may be related to the unclear boundary. We believe that adding multi-center to the training data or simulating the generation of data from unknown domains through data augmentation, generative adversarial strategies, etc. will further improve the domain generalization capability of the model.

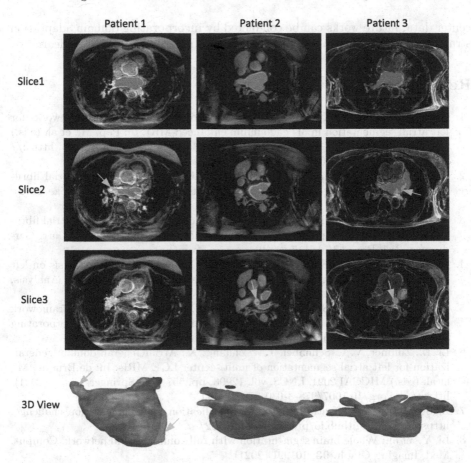

Fig. 6. LA segmentation results. We show segmentation results for three patients and randomly select three slices. The last row is the 3D reconstructed image of the segmentation result. Yellow is the label and red is the model prediction (Color figure online)

4 Conclusion

In this paper, we present a two-stage framework for automatic segmentation of the LA in LGE-MRI, which can be used to aid the diagnosis, treatment of patients with atrial fibrillation. First, we propose a data pre-processing and data enhancement solution to minimize the input variations of data come from multi-center. In light of the excellent performance of HRNet achieved on semantic segmentation task, we adapted it to LA segmentation by incorporating a novel multi-scale feature fusion strategy and feature reusing. In addition, we introduce an auxiliary loss to accelerate the convergence of the network. Experiments show that our method can improve the domain generalization ability of the baseline, i.e., the VoxHRNet. To further improve the segmentation performance on multi-center data, future works can be conducted by incorporating domain adaptation strategies such as adversarial training based domain invariant feature learning.

References

1. Vesal, S., Ravikumar, N., Maier, A.: Dilated convolutions in neural networks for left atrial segmentation in 3D gadolinium enhanced-MRI. In: Pop, M., et al. (eds.) STACOM 2018. LNCS, vol. 11395, pp. 319–328. Springer, Cham (2019). https://doi.org/10.1007/978-3-030-12029-0_35
2. Lippi, G., Sanchis-Gomar, F., Cervellin, G.: Global epidemiology of atrial fibrillation: an increasing epidemic and public health challenge. Int. J. Stroke **16**(2), 217–221 (2021)
3. Benito, E.M., Alarcon, F., Mont, L.: LGE-MRI characterization of left atrial fibrosis: a tool to establish prognosis and guide atrial fibrillation ablation. Curr. Cardiovasc. Risk Rep. **13**(5), 1–7 (2019)
4. Li, L., Zimmer, V.A., Schnabel, J.A., Zhuang, X.: Medical image analysis on left atrial LGE MRI for atrial fibrillation studies: a review. Medical Image Analysis, p. 102360 (2022)
5. Li, L., Zimmer, V.A., Schnabel, J.A., Zhuang, X.: Atrialjsqnet: a new framework for joint segmentation and quantification of left atrium and scars incorporating spatial and shape information. Med. Image Anal. **76**, 102303 (2022)
6. Li, L., Zimmer, V.A., Schnabel, J.A., Zhuang, X.: AtrialGeneral: domain generalization for left atrial segmentation of multi-center LGE MRIs. In: de Bruijne, M., et al. (eds.) MICCAI 2021. LNCS, vol. 12906, pp. 557–566. Springer, Cham (2021). https://doi.org/10.1007/978-3-030-87231-1_54
7. LAScarQS 2022: Left atrial and scar quantification and segmentation challenge. https://zmiclab.github.io/projects/lascarqs22/
8. Li, Y., et al.: Whole brain segmentation with full volume neural network. Comput. Med. Imaging Graph. **93**, 101991 (2021)
9. Sun, K., Xiao, B., Liu, D., Wang, J.: Deep high-resolution representation learning for human pose estimation. In: Proceedings of the IEEE/CVF Conference on Computer Vision and Pattern Recognition, pp. 5693–5703 (2019)
10. Sun, K., et al..: High-resolution representations for labeling pixels and regions. arXiv preprint arXiv:1904.04514 (2019)
11. Lee, C.Y., Xie, S., Gallagher, P., Zhang, Z., Tu, Z.: Deeply-supervised nets. In: Artificial intelligence and statistics, pp. 562–570. PMLR (2015)
12. Liu, L., et al.: On the variance of the adaptive learning rate and beyond. arXiv preprint arXiv:1908.03265 (2019)

Edge-Enhanced Feature Guided Joint Segmentation of Left Atrial and Scars in LGE MRI Images

Siping Zhou⬢, Kai-Ni Wang⬢, and Guang-Quan Zhou(✉)⬢

School of Biological Science and Medical Engineering, Southeast University,
Nanjing, China
guangquan.zhou@seu.edu.cn

Abstract. Automatic segmentation of the left atrial (LA) cavity and atrial scars in late gadolinium enhancement magnetic resonance imaging has significant clinical relevance to diagnosing atrial fibrillation (AF). Nevertheless, automatic segmentation remains challenging because of the poor image quality, the shape variability of LA, and the small size of scars. Therefore, this study proposes a multi-task learning model in a coarse-to-fine framework, among which the fine model simultaneously segmenting the LA cavity and scars. Specially, we develop an edge-enhanced feature-guided module (EFGM) to exploit the spatial relationship between LA and scars using a 3D central difference convolution, exploring the feature dependence from multi-task learning. Also, a dilated inception module (DIM) is plugged in to learn multi-scale representation, further improving the joint segmentation considering the shape difference between the LA cavity and scar. We evaluate our model on the LAScarQS 2022 validation set. The average Dice scores of the LA cavity and scar are 0.875 and 0.631. Also, the Average Surface Distance (ASD) and Hausdorff Distance (HD) of the LA cavity are 2.233 mm and 24.731 mm, respectively. The accuracy, specificity, sensitivity, and generalized Dice score of LA scar are 0.999, 0.999, 0.603, and 0.916, respectively.

Keywords: Deep learning · Cardiac Segmentation · Joint optimization · Difference convolution

1 Introduction

Atrial fibrillation (AF) is the most common cardiac arrhythmia observed in clinical practice, occurring in up to 2% of the population and rising fast with advancing age [10]. Recently, late gadolinium enhancement magnetic resonance imaging (LGE MRI) has been considered as a promising and reliable technique to visualize and quantify left atrial scars [11]. The segmentation or quantification of LA and scars provides important information for the clinical diagnosis and the treatment of AF patients. Since manual delineations of LA and scars are time-consuming and subjective, it is crucial to develop techniques for automatic segmentation of the LA cavity and scar for LGE MRI.

© The Author(s), under exclusive license to Springer Nature Switzerland AG 2023
X. Zhuang et al. (Eds.): LAScarQS 2022, LNCS 13586, pp. 93–105, 2023.
https://doi.org/10.1007/978-3-031-31778-1_9

However, the poor image quality in LGE MRI, various shapes of LA, the surrounding enhanced noise, and the complex patterns of scars make it challenging to automatically and accurately segment LA and scars. Li et al. reviewed algorithms proposed to perform the LA cavity and scar segmentation or quantification from medical images in [2]. Among them, deep learning-based methods are dominant in these two tasks and they achieved promising results [1,15,16,19–22]. Nevertheless, most of the methods mentioned in [2] normally solved the two tasks independently and ignored the intrinsic spatial relationship between LA and scars which are located on the LA wall, as Fig. 1 shows. The performance of segmenting the LA cavity and scar may be bottlenecked by the failure in exploiting the correlation between these two tasks. Multi-task learning has been shown to outperform methods considering related tasks separately by leveraging the relationship between different tasks. Recently, Li et al. [1] developed a novel framework where LA segmentation, scar projection onto the LA surface, and scar quantification are performed simultaneously in an end-to-end style. The relationship between LA segmentation and scar quantification was explicitly explored and has shown significant performance improvements for both tasks in their work.

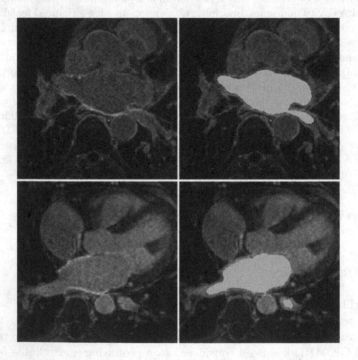

Fig. 1. Examples of axial views from two cases in the LAScarQS2022 dataset. The LA cavity and scar are highlighted in blue and red, respectively. One can see that scars are located on the LA wall. (Color figure online)

This paper, inspired by [1], proposes a coarse-to-fine framework to achieve joint segmentation of LA and scars. In the coarse stage, a vanilla 3D U-Net [14] is trained to coarsely segment LA and crop a region of interest (ROI) that contains the whole LA. In the fine stage, a modified dual-task learning 3D U-Net consisting of two decoders for LA and scars segmentation respectively, is proposed to segment LA and scars simultaneously. We also introduce an edge-enhanced feature-guided module (EFGM) at the skip connection between the shared encoder and the decoder layers for scar segmentation. It includes a difference convolution submodule based on 3D central difference convolution (CDC) [7], followed by a spatial attention submodule. We argue that it can help pass the edge-enhanced features to guide the localization and segmentation of scars as they are located at the LA wall while utilizing the spatial relationship between LA and scars. In addition, a dilated inception module (DIM) to extract multi-scale features is plugged in at the bottleneck of the modified 3D U-Net.

2 Methods

Figure 2 shows the pipeline of our coarse-to-fine joint segmentation framework. In our work, we develop a two-stage strategy to perform coarse-to-fine joint segmentation of the LA cavity and scar. In the coarse stage, a vanilla 3D U-Net is first trained to segment the ROI which contains the whole LA from the entire 3D volume of each MRI. After the ROIs are detected, they are all cropped out with a fixed size from the processed MRIs and then fed into the proposed modified multi-task learning 3D U-Net to obtain segmentation results of LA cavity and scars simultaneously in the fine stage.

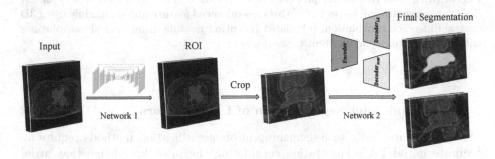

Fig. 2. The overall pipeline of our coarse-to-fine joint segmentation of left atrial and scars framework. The network 1 is a vanilla 3D U-Net to segment the ROI coarsely. The network 2 is a modified 3D U-Net consisting of two decoders for LA and scar segmentation respectively to get more accurate segmentation results.

2.1   Coarse Segmentation of ROIs

As shown in Fig. 1, the regions of the LA cavity and scar are only part of the
whole volume, especially for a scar of such a small size. Therefore, we first employ
a coarse segmentation stage to segment the ROI containing the LA cavity and
scar,aiming at alleviating the class imbalance problem and discarding redundant
or irrelevant surrounding voxels. We choose the vanilla 3D U-Net as our coarse
segmentation network for its effectiveness in various medical image segmentation
tasks without any complex design.

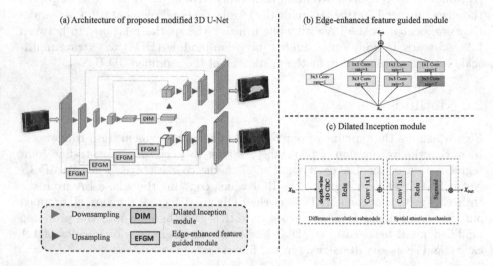

Fig. 3. (a)An overview of our proposed modified 3D U-Net with two decoders for LA
and scar segmentation, respectively. (b)Edge-enhanced feature-guided module using 3D
central difference convolution. (c)Dilated Inception module using dilated convolutions
with different rates and shortcut connections.

2.2   Fine and Joint Segmentation of LA and Scars

Most of the automatic scar segmentation or quantification methods require an
accurate initial LA segmentation considering the prior knowledge that atrial
scars are located on the LA wall. Additionally, previous methods usually
solved the two tasks independently and ignored the intrinsic spatial relationship between LA and scars [2]. Therefore, we propose a modified 3D U-Net
consisting of two decoders for LA and scar segmentation and train it in a multi-
task learning manner in the fine stage. Figure 3 (a) provides an overview of
the proposed dual-task learning network architecture. First, an edge-enhanced
feature guided module (EFGM) is introduced at the skip connection between
the shared encoder and decoder layers for scar segmentation. Different from the
original skip connection, the EFGM, which can serve as an edge detector, helps

preserve differential or edge-related information via extracting edge-enhanced features and passing them to the corresponding layers at the scar segmentation decoder. In addition, a dilated inception module (DIM) is introduced at the end of the original encoder. With the equipment of DIM, the modified 3D U-Net can capture deep multi-scale semantic features, which is beneficial to the joint segmentation of LA cavities and scars as they are totally different in size. The details of the EFGM and the DIM are described below.

Edge-enhanced Feature Guided Module. Difference Convolution, which explicitly calculates pixel differences during convolution to aggregate local gradient information, has been gradually used in computer vision tasks such as edge detection [6], face recognition [5], gesture recognition [7], and so on in recent years. By contrast, vanilla convolution aggregates intensity-level information [6]. As a result, although modern CNNs based on vanilla convolution are powerful enough to learn rich and hierarchical image representations, it is still hard for them to focus on edge-related features due to the lack of explicit encoding for gradient information [5]. The formulations of vanilla convolution and difference convolution can be written as (take 2D convolution as an example):

$$y = \sum_{i=1}^{k \times k} w_i \cdot x_i \quad (vanilla\ convolution) \tag{1}$$

$$y = \sum_{x_i, x_j \in S} w_i \cdot (x_i - x_j) \quad (difference\ convolution) \tag{2}$$

where, x_i and x_j are the input pixels, w_i is the weight in the $k \times k$ convolution kernel. S is the local receptive filed over the feature map.

As mentioned before, scars are located on the LA wall, so we intuitively argue that the edge information of the LA cavity is important to the localization and further segmentation of scars. In the vanilla U-Net [13], long skip connections were introduced to pass features from the encoder path to the decoder path to recover spatial information lost during downsampling. However, original low-level features which are simply passed through the skip connections to fuse with high-level features may contain substantial redundant location or spatial information. Motivated by these assumptions, we propose the EFGM equipping difference convolution at the skip connection between the encoder and the decoder for scar segmentation in the modified 3D U-Net only to pass the edge-enhanced features containing rich edge-related information. With the implementation of the EFGM, our model can learn to suppress irrelevant regions and highlight salient regions (edge of LA cavity) useful for more precise localization and segmentation of scars due to the ability of difference convolution to extract local differential information from feature maps. Moreover, the edge-enhanced features can also be regarded as localization guidance for decoding high-level semantic features in the decoder path in scar segmentation, which benefits the segmentation of scars located on the LA wall.

Figure 3 (b) illustrates an edge-enhanced feature-guided module. Each module mainly includes a difference convolution submodule where we utilize a 3D central difference convolution (CDC) [7], which is formulated as follows::

$$y = \sum_{i \in C} w_i \cdot (x_i - x_0) \tag{3}$$

3D convolution with kernel size 3×3×3 and dilation 1 is used for demonstration. The local receptive field cube for the 3D convolution is $C = (-1, -1, -1), (-1, -1, 0), ..., (0, 1, 1), (1, 1, 1)$.

The same as [6], we use the separable depth-wise convolutional structure with a shortcut for fast inference and easy training. The residual path in this module includes a depth-wise convolutional layer, a ReLU layer, and a point-wise convolutional layer sequentially. To further highlight the edge-related features and filter background noise, we apply the spatial attention mechanism at the end of the difference convolution submodule.

Dilated Inception Module. Motivated by the Inception-ResNet-V2 module [8] and Atrous Spatial Pyramid Pooling (ASPP) [9], we propose the DIM to encode deep multi-scale features for both LA and scar segmentation. As shown in Fig. 3 (c), the DIM has four parallel paths with dilated convolutions with different dilation rates followed by one 1×1 convolution. At last, we directly add the original features with the other four multi-scale features to make a shortcut mechanism. Different dilation rates can increase the receptive field sizes of parallel convolution paths by adding zeros between kernel elements without incrementing parameters. As a result, the proposed DIM can capture features of objects of various sizes, such as LA cavities and scars, due to the combination of the dilation convolutions with different dilation rates.

2.3   Loss Function

For the coarse stage only regarding the segmentation of the LA cavity, our loss function is Dice Loss.

For the fine and joint segmentation stage, our loss function is the sum of the loss function of segmenting the LA cavity and the loss function of segmenting scar, as shown in Eq. 4:

$$Loss_{total} = Loss_{LA} + Loss_{scar} \tag{4}$$

The loss function used in LA segmentation is the sum of the Dice Loss and the Cross-Entropy Loss, as shown in Eq. 5:

$$Loss_{LA} = Loss_{ce} + Loss_{dice} \tag{5}$$

For scar segmentation, as the scar only takes up a small fraction of the whole volume, which can cause a severe class-imbalance problem, the loss function is the sum of the Dice Loss and the Weighted Cross Entropy Loss, as shown in Eq. 6:

$$Loss_{scar} = Loss_{wce} + Loss_{dice} \tag{6}$$

3 Experiments

3.1 Dataset and Data Preprocessing

MICCAI 2022-LAScarQS2022 (Left Atrial and Scar Quantification & Segmentation Challenge) [1–3] provides 194 LGE MRIs acquired in real clinical environment from patients suffering atrial fibrillation (AF) and is composed of two tasks: 1. LA Scar Quantification 2. Left Atrial Segmentation from Multi-Center LGE MRIs. In this study, we focus on task 1.

The training dataset provided for task 1 of the LAScarQS 2022 challenge [1–3] consists of 60 LGE-MRIs with segmentation annotations of LA cavities and scars. In our experiments, the images and masks were first resampled to the isotropic resolution of $1 \times 1 \times 1mm^3$. And then, all the volumes were cropped and zero-pad to the uniform size of $576 \times 576 \times 96$. Then we used a 3D version of contrast limited adaptive histogram localization (CLAHE) [4] to enhance the contrast of LGE-MRIs, and finally applied sample-wise normalization.

3.2 Implementation Details

Our experiments were run on NVIDIA GeForce RTX 3090 GPU with 24 GB RAM. We firstly down-sampled the input for the coarse segmentation from $576 \times 576 \times 96$ to $144 \times 144 \times 48$ due to memory restriction. The first network was trained for 100 epochs using the Adam optimizer with a fixed learning rate of 0.001. The batch size is 4. We randomly chose 48 out of the 60 MRIs as training data; the rest 12 are validation data. After the training procedure was completed, the model with the best dice scores on validation data was saved for ROI detection. For the fine and joint segmentation, we first computed the barycenter of the ground truth and cropped a region of size $288 \times 192 \times 96$ centered with the barycenter from the original data. Then the cropped ROIs were fed into the second network. The second network was trained for 100 epochs using the Adam optimizer with an initial learning rate of 0.001. The learning rate was reduced by 0.1 every 1000 iterations and the batch size is 2. We randomly split the data into training (48 subjects) and testing (12 subjects) subsets for the fine stage.

To reduce the risk of over-fitting and further improve the generalization ability of our framework, we also apply data augmentation including random flipping and rotation in both networks training.

At the inference stage, each MRI volume from the testing subset was firstly down-sampled to $144 \times 144 \times 48$ and fed into the first network. The network would output the predicted binary mask used to locate the ROI. We computed the barycenter of the predicted mask, cropped a region of size $288 \times 192 \times 96$ centered with this barycenter, and then fed it into the second network. The second network output the predicted masks of the LA cavity and scar simultaneously inside the target region and mapped them back to the original size volume, which finished the inference. The end-to-end segmentation process takes approximately 9 s for each case.

4 Results and Discussions

4.1 Ablation Experiments

We run a number of ablation experiments to evaluate the effectiveness of multi-task learning and the two proposed modules in our modified 3D U-Net. All the experiments were run in the coarse-to-fine framework mentioned above, sharing the same coarse stage and we only performed different models in the fine stage to conduct ablation experiments. Here, U-Net$_{LA}$ denotes the vanilla 3D U-Net architecture for LA segmentation individually. U-Net$_{scar}$ denotes the vanilla 3D U-Net architecture for scar segmentation individually. U-Net$_{LA\ and\ scar}$ denotes the multi-task learning 3D U-Net consists of a shared encoder and two decoders for joint segmentation of LA and scars, which is also our baseline model. Besides, we successively tested the performance of the baseline model incorporating the DIM, the baseline model incorporating the EFGM, and the baseline model incorporating both the EFGM and the DIM. All these experiments were conducted using the same aforementioned training configurations and loss functions.

All the models were evaluated through the validation platform provided by the LAScarQS2022 organizer. As shown in Table 1, the segmentation performance of LA was evaluated by the Dice score, average surface distance (ASD) and Hausdorff distance (HD). The scar's quantification performance was evaluated via first projecting the segmentation result onto the manually segmented LA surface. Then, the Accuracy, Specificity and Sensitivity measurement of the two areas in the projected surface, Dice score ($Dice$) and generalized Dice score ($Dice_g$) were used as indicators of the accuracy of scar quantification [1]. $Dice_g$ is a weighted Dice score by evaluating the segmentation of all labels [17,18], which is formulated as follow [1]:

$$Dice_g = \frac{2\sum_{k=0}^{N_k-1}|S_k^{auto}\cap S_k^{manual}|}{\sum_{k=0}^{N_k-1}(|S_k^{auto}+S_k^{manual}|)} \tag{7}$$

where S_k^{auto} auto and S_k^{manual} indicate the segmentation results of label k from the automatic method and manual delineation, respectively, and N_k is the number of labels.

Table 1. Summary of the quantitative evaluation results of LA segmentation and scar quantification on the LAScarQS 2022 validation set in ablation experiments. EFGM denotes the proposed edge-enhanced feature-guided module discussed in Sect. 2.2, and DIM denotes the proposed dilation inception module discussed in Sect. 2.2.

Method	LA			Scar				
	Dice	ASD(mm)	HD (mm)	Accuracy	Specificity	Sensitivity	Dice	$Dice_g$
U-Net$_{LA}$	0.860	2.625	30.028	N\ A	N\ A	N\ A	N\ A	N\ A
U-Net$_{scar}$	N\ A	N\ A	N\ A	0.999	0.999	0.534	0.580	0.909
Base(U-Net$_{LA\ and\ scar}$)	0.869	2.318	27.050	0.999	0.999	0.549	0.596	0.913
Base+EFGM	0.867	2.489	26.170	0.999	0.999	0.588	0.621	0.914
Base+DIM	0.871	2.355	25.636	0.999	0.999	**0.605**	0.617	0.914
Base+EFGM+DIM	**0.875**	**2.233**	**24.731**	0.999	0.999	0.603	**0.631**	**0.916**

Table 1 presents the quantitative results for LA segmentation and scar quantification. It demonstrates that our baseline model outperforms U-Net$_{LA}$ and U-Net$_{scar}$ which consider these two related tasks separately, verifying the superiority of multi-task learning. The relationship between LA segmentation and scar segmentation is exploited implicitly through multi-task learning. Figure 4 and Fig. 5 illustrate the segmentation results of the LA cavity and scar, respectively, from the mentioned ablation experiments. One can see that the boundary of segmentation results of U-Net$_{LA}$ is far from the boundary of the ground-truth and U-Net$_{scar}$ tends to make mistakes on non-LA wall regions and under-segment scars, while the baseline model results are closer to the ground truth.

Meanwhile, Table 1 illustrates the effectiveness of each proposed module, suggesting the advantage of the EFGM and the DIM. Compared to the baseline model, incorporating the DIM reduces about 2 mm in HD in segmenting LA and improves the Dice in segmenting scar by around 2%. This observation implies the need for learning deep multi-scale features when coping with segmenting targets of different sizes since scars are quite small compared with the LA cavity. Note that incorporating the EFGM into the baseline model improves the Dice in segmenting scar by around 2.5% compared to the baseline model and outperforms the baseline model only equipped with the DIM. As shown in Fig. 5, introducing the EFGM can alleviate the problem of under-segmenting scars observed in other models. Furthermore, it indicates that the edge-related information can effectively guide the segmentation of scars while encoding the prior spatial knowledge that scars are located at the LA wall into the framework, thus utilizing the spatial relationship between LA and scars more explicitly. However, the performance of the model which only incorporates the EFGM even degrades a little in Dice and ASD of segmenting LA compared to the baseline model. We argue that this is because the EFGM is mainly designed for the scar segmentation task, which is much more challenging than LA segmentation, so it may not improve the segmentation performance of LA.

The highest performance gain (about 1.5% in Dice of LA segmentation and 5% in Dice of scar segmentation compared to U-Net$_{LA}$ and U-Net$_{scar}$) is observed when incorporating both the DIM and the EFGM. Moreover, the model equipped with both two modules achieves the best segmentation performance in almost all metrics in both tasks. Figure 4 also demonstrates that the boundary of LA segmentation results is the most consistent with the ground truth among all the experiments, while Fig. 5 illustrates that our final model can detect and segment scars more precisely than any other model in our ablation experiments. It shows that the combination of two modules can further improve the performance of the framework. Note that the model incorporating both the DIM and the EFGM outperforms the model only incorporating the DIM in LA cavity segmentation, but the introduction of the EFGM cannot improve the segmentation of the LA cavity as mentioned above. This finding is probably attributed to the explanation that relatively good performance in the scar segmentation task can boost the LA segmentation task during the simultaneous optimization process in multi-task learning.

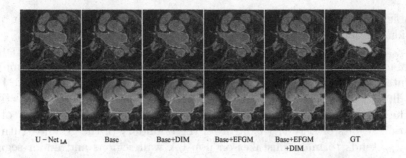

Fig. 4. Visualization of the LA cavity segmentation results on the LAScarQS 2022 validation set by using different training combinations.

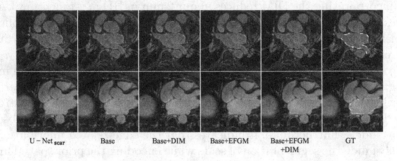

Fig. 5. Visualization of the scar segmentation results on the LAScarQS 2022 validation set by using different training combinations.

4.2   Comparison Experiments

We implemented U-Net with different loss functions to conduct comparison experiments for both LA segmentation and scar segmentation. We used the same hyper-parameters in these experiments for consistency.

Table 2 tabulates the quantitative comparison results for LA segmentation and scar quantification. For LA segmentation, our method achieves 0.875 in Dice, demonstrating its advantage in segmenting the LA cavity more accurately. Meanwhile, the proposed coarse-to-fine joint segmentation framework obtains the smallest HD and ASD, which means it can identify the correct boundaries of LA cavities despite their various shape. Figure 6 also proves that our proposed model can achieve better segmentation compared to other methods.

Note that our method shows significant improvement in scar quantification results. As demonstrated in Fig. 7, the vanilla U-Net models tend to under-segment scars while our method alleviates this problem. With the help of the DIM and the EFGM, edge-enhanced low-level and multi-scale features are fused while more contextual semantic information and more precise spatial information are integrated, facilitating the segmentation of scars which are hard to recognize and locate due to their small size, complex patterns, and surrounding noise.

Overall, our method outperformed superiorly to other methods, implying its effectiveness. This could result from the two major contributions in our framework. First, the multi-task learning model can effectively exploit the relationship between LA and scars. Moreover, the EFGM and the DIM are introduced to further boost the multi-task learning process through providing spatial guidance for segmenting scars and learning multi-scale representation. Second, the two-stage coarse-to-fine framework can suppress the background pixels that dominate foreground pixels in the scar segmentation, thus significantly mitigate the class imbalance problem.

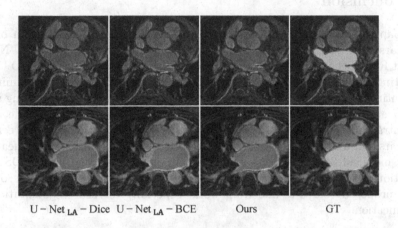

$\text{U}-\text{Net}_{\text{LA}}-\text{Dice}$ $\text{U}-\text{Net}_{\text{LA}}-\text{BCE}$ Ours   GT

Fig. 6. Visualization of the LA cavity segmentation results on the LAScarQS 2022 validation set compared with other classic methods.

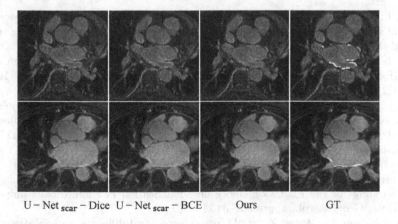

$\text{U}-\text{Net}_{\text{scar}}-\text{Dice}$ $\text{U}-\text{Net}_{\text{scar}}-\text{BCE}$ Ours   GT

Fig. 7. Visualization of the scar segmentation results on the LAScarQS 2022 validation set compared with other classic methods.

Table 2. Summary of the quantitative evaluation results of LA segmentation and scar quantification on the LAScarQS 2022 validation set in comparison experiments.

Method	LA			Scar				
	Dice	ASD(mm)	HD (mm)	Accuracy	Specificity	Sensitivity	Dice	$Dice_g$
U-Net$_{LA/scar}$-BCE	0.849	2.980	41.934	0.681	0.999	0.362	0.466	0.890
U-Net$_{LA/scar}$-Dice	0.845	3.227	43.622	0.670	0.999	0.340	0.427	0.883
Ours	**0.875**	**2.233**	**24.731**	**0.999**	**0.999**	**0.603**	**0.631**	**0.916**

5 Conclusion

This paper proposes a coarse-to-fine framework for joint segmentation of LA and scars from LGE MRI. The coarse segment network is a vanilla 3D U-Net to extract ROI of the volume, and the fine segment network is a modified 3D U-Net consisting of two decoders for LA and scar segmentation, respectively, aiming at segmenting the LA cavity and scar simultaneously in a multi-task learning manner. In addition, we introduce an edge-enhanced feature-guided module using 3D central difference convolution to exploit the spatial relationship between LA and scars and a dilated inception module to learn multi-scale semantic features in our modified 3D U-Net. We evaluated our method on the LAScarQS 2022 validation dataset, and the convincing results suggest the effectiveness of the newly proposed coarse-to-fine framework, especially for scar segmentation or quantification.

References

1. Li, L., Zimmer, V.A., Schnabel, J.A., et al.: AtrialJSQnet: a new framework for joint segmentation and quantification of left atrium and scars incorporating spatial and shape information. Med. Image Anal. **76**, 102303 (2022)
2. Li, L., Zimmer, V.A., Schnabel, J.A., et al.: Medical image analysis on left atrial LGE MRI for atrial fibrillation studies: a review. Medical Image Analysis, 102360 (2022)
3. Li, L., Zimmer, V.A., Schnabel, J.A., Zhuang, X.: AtrialGeneral: domain generalization for left atrial segmentation of multi-center LGE MRIs. In: de Bruijne, M., et al. (eds.) MICCAI 2021. LNCS, vol. 12906, pp. 557–566. Springer, Cham (2021). https://doi.org/10.1007/978-3-030-87231-1_54
4. Pizer, S.M., Johnston, R.E., Ericksen, J.P., Yankaskas, B.C., Muller, K.E.: Contrast-limited adaptive histogram equalization: speed and effectiveness. In: Proceedings of the First Conference on Visualization in Biomedical Computing, Atlanta, Georgia, vol., 1, pp. 337–345 (1990)
5. Yu, Z., Zhao, C., Wang, Z., et al.: Searching central difference convolutional networks for face anti-spoofing. In: Proceedings of the IEEE/CVF Conference on Computer Vision and Pattern Recognition, pp. 5295–5305 (2020)
6. Su, Z., Liu, W., Yu, Z., et al.: Pixel difference networks for efficient edge detection. In: Proceedings of the IEEE/CVF International Conference on Computer Vision, 5117–5127 (2021)

7. Yu, Z., Zhou, B., Wan, J., et al.: Searching multi-rate and multi-modal temporal enhanced networks for gesture recognition. IEEE Trans. Image Process. **30**, 5626–5640 (2021)
8. Szegedy, C., Ioffe, S., Vanhoucke, V., et al.: Inception-v4, inception-resnet and the impact of residual connections on learning. In: Thirty-first AAAI Conference on Artificial Intelligence (2017)
9. Chen, L.C., Papandreou, G., Kokkinos, I., et al.: DeepLab: semantic image segmentation with deep convolutional nets, atrous convolution, and fully connected CRFs. IEEE Trans. Pattern Anal. Mach. Intell. **40**(4), 834–848 (2017)
10. Chugh, S.S., Havmoeller, R., Narayanan, K., et al.: Worldwide epidemiology of atrial fibrillation: a global burden of disease 2010 study. Circulation **129**(8), 837–847 (2014)
11. Vergara, G.R., Marrouche, N.F.: Tailored management of atrial fibrillation using a LGE-MRI based model: from the clinic to the electrophysiology laboratory. J. Cardiovasc. Electrophysiol. **22**(4), 481–487 (2011)
12. Xiong, Z., Xia, Q., Hu, Z., et al.: A global benchmark of algorithms for segmenting the left atrium from late gadolinium-enhanced cardiac magnetic resonance imaging[J]. Med. Image Anal. **67**, 101832 (2021)
13. Ronneberger, O., Fischer, P., Brox, T.: U-Net: convolutional networks for biomedical image segmentation. In: Navab, N., Hornegger, J., Wells, W.M., Frangi, A.F. (eds.) MICCAI 2015. LNCS, vol. 9351, pp. 234–241. Springer, Cham (2015). https://doi.org/10.1007/978-3-319-24574-4_28
14. Çiçek, Ö., Abdulkadir, A., Lienkamp, S.S., Brox, T., Ronneberger, O.: 3D U-Net: learning dense volumetric segmentation from sparse annotation. In: Ourselin, S., Joskowicz, L., Sabuncu, M.R., Unal, G., Wells, W. (eds.) MICCAI 2016. LNCS, vol. 9901, pp. 424–432. Springer, Cham (2016). https://doi.org/10.1007/978-3-319-46723-8_49
15. Zhao, Z., Puybareau, E., Boutry, N., et al.: Do not treat boundaries and regions differently: an example on heart left atrial segmentation. In: 2020 25th International Conference on Pattern Recognition (ICPR), pp. 7447–7453. IEEE (2021)
16. Li, L., Wu, F., Yang, G., et al.: Atrial scar quantification via multi-scale CNN in the graph-cuts framework. Med. Image Anal. **60**, 101595 (2020)
17. Crum, W.R., Camara, O., Hill, D.L.G.: Generalized overlap measures for evaluation and validation in medical image analysis. IEEE Trans. Med. Imaging **25**(11), 1451–1461 (2006)
18. Zhuang, X.: Challenges and methodologies of fully automatic whole heart segmentation: a review. J. Healthc. Eng. **4**(3), 371–407 (2013)
19. Borra, D., Andalò, A., Paci, M., et al.: A fully automated left atrium segmentation approach from late gadolinium enhanced magnetic resonance imaging based on a convolutional neural network. Quant. Imaging Med. Surgery **10**(10), 1894 (2020)
20. Du, X., Yin, S., Tang, R., et al.: Segmentation and visualization of left atrium through a unified deep learning framework. Int. J. Comput. Assist. Radiol. Surg. **15**(4), 589–600 (2020)
21. Chen, J., et al.: Multiview two-task recursive attention model for left atrium and atrial scars segmentation. In: Frangi, A.F., Schnabel, J.A., Davatzikos, C., Alberola-López, C., Fichtinger, G. (eds.) MICCAI 2018. LNCS, vol. 11071, pp. 455–463. Springer, Cham (2018). https://doi.org/10.1007/978-3-030-00934-2_51
22. Yang, G., Chen, J., Gao, Z., et al.: Simultaneous left atrium anatomy and scar segmentations via deep learning in multiview information with attention. Future Gener. Comput. Syst. **107**, 215–228 (2020)

TESSLA: Two-Stage Ensemble Scar Segmentation for the Left Atrium

Shaheim Ogbomo-Harmitt[(⊠)] ⓘ, Jakub Grzelak, Ahmed Qureshi ⓘ,
Andrew P. King ⓘ, and Oleg Aslanidi ⓘ

School of Biomedical Engineering and Imaging Sciences, King's College London, London, UK
shaheim.ogbomo-harmitt@kcl.ac.uk

Abstract. Atrial fibrillation (AF) is the most common cardiac arrhythmia world-wide; however, the current success rates for catheter ablation (CA) therapy, the first-line treatment for AF, are suboptimal. Therefore, extensive research has focused on the relationship between scar tissue in the left atrium (LA) and AF, and its application for patient stratification and more effective CA therapy strategies. However, quantifying and segmenting LA scar tissue requires significant data pre-processing from well-trained clinicians. Hence, deep learning (DL) has been proposed to automatically segment the LA fibrotic scar from late gadolinium-enhanced cardiac magnetic resonance (LGE-CMR) images. Segmenting LA scar with DL is challenging as fibrosis from LGE-CMR images has a relatively small volume and regions surrounding the scar are also enhanced. Therefore, we propose a two-stage ensemble DL model (TESSLA: two-stage ensemble scar segmentation for the LA) that segments the blood pool of the LA, estimates the LA wall, applies an image intensity ratio with Z-score normalisation and combines a scar segmentation from two independent networks. TESSLA outperformed its constituent models and achieved state-of-art accuracy on the LAScar 2022 challenge evaluation platform for LA scar segmentation with a Dice score of 0.63 ± 0.14 and a Dice score of 0.58 ± 0.11 for the final test phase. Our workflow provides a fully automatic estimation of LA fibrosis from clinical LGE CMR scans.

Keywords: Left Atrial Scar · Deep Learning · Segmentation · Atrial Fibrillation

1 Introduction

Atrial fibrillation (AF) is the most common type of cardiac arrhythmia, affecting more than 46 million people worldwide. It is characterised by rapid and irregular electrical activations of the atrial chambers, resulting in reduced cardiac output [1, 2]. AF is not directly lethal, but it is associated with an increased risk of stroke and heart failure if sustained for long periods (known as persistent AF). In a study investigating the risk factors of cardiovascular diseases with approximately 5000 participants, AF was found to increase the risk of stroke by 1.5% for ages 50–59 years old and 23.5% for ages 80–89 years old [3]. The first-line treatment for AF is catheter ablation (CA) therapy. CA involves using a catheter to ablate (isolate or destroy) arrhythmogenic atrial tissue that

© The Author(s), under exclusive license to Springer Nature Switzerland AG 2023
X. Zhuang et al. (Eds.): LAScarQS 2022, LNCS 13586, pp. 106–114, 2023.
https://doi.org/10.1007/978-3-031-31778-1_10

harbours AF triggers, thus restoring sinus rhythm and potentially the heart's biomechanical function [4]. However, when treating persistent AF, CA therapy has a suboptimal AF reoccurrence rate of up to ~ 70% post-intervention [5, 6].

Extensive research has focused on the relationship between scar tissue in the left atrium (LA) and AF, and its application for patient stratification and more effective CA therapy strategies, including the DECAAF I and II clinical trial that rely on preprocessed late gadolinium enhanced (LGE) cardiac magnetic resonance (CMR) images [7, 8]. The preprocessing of LGE-CMR images involves manual segmentation of the left atrium (LA) and scar tissue by a well-trained clinician. This creates a bottleneck for routine clinical usage of LA scar quantification and segmentation as it is time-consuming and requires specialists to perform it.

The standard approach for LA scar segmentation employs thresholding techniques, which involves evaluating a threshold value based on a fixed number of standard deviations above the average intensity value of the LA wall or blood pool. However, the selection of threshold values is subjective, and the values can be affected by several factors such as scanner variability, acquisition timing after gadolinium administration and whether the LGE-CMR image is pre-or post-ablation [9]. Therefore, to automatically segment LA and scar tissue from LGE-CMR images, deep learning (DL) has been proposed as an efficient and accurate solution. DL was first applied to LA scar segmentation by Yang et al., who used super-pixel over-segmentation for feature extraction and stacked sparse auto-encoders [10]. Meanwhile, other studies adopted a DL model for simultaneous segmentation of the LA wall and LA scar [9]. However, the primary/key issues when segmenting LA scars from LGE-CMR images are its relatively small volume and enhanced regions of intensity surrounding it – creating noise during segmentation. Li et al. addressed this issue by utilising the spatial relationship of the LA and its scar to jointly segment both using an attention mask on the predicted scar probability map for shape attention [11]. Following on from utilising the spatial relationship of the LA and its scar, we propose an ensemble two-stage DL network (TESSLA: two-stage ensemble scar segmentation for the LA). In addition, to overcome the limitation of generalisability of the model developed by Li et al., we propose using an intensity ratio (IIR) normalisation, applied by traditional methods to reduce inter-patient and scanner effects [12, 13]. To summarise, the contributions of this work are:

- First method to feature a two-stage DL model to segment blood pool, estimate LA wall and predict scar segmentation from LA wall and original LGE-CMR images.
- First DL model to implement IIR normalisation for LA scar segmentation.

2 Methods

2.1 Dataset

The dataset was provided by the Left Atrial and Scar Quantification & Segmentation Challenge 2022, which includes 60 LGE-CMR images from patients post- and pre-ablation with corresponding LA blood pool and scar segmentation masks. The images were collected across three centres (University of Utah, Beth Israel Deaconess Medical Center and King's College London). The spatial resolution of the LGE-CMR images was either $1.25 \times 1.25 \times 2.5$ mm^3 (University of Utah), $1.4 \times 1.4 \times 1.4$ mm^3 (Beth Israel Deaconess Medical Center) or $1.3 \times 1.3 \times 4.0$ mm^3 (King's College London) [9, 11, 14].

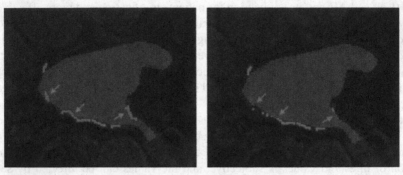

Fig. 1. Ground truth segmentation. Left: scar segmentation (green) and LA blood pool (red) ground truth masks. Right: Same masks with scar projected onto closest point on endocardial wall. Scar in blood pool and subsequent projections are highlighted with arrows (blue).

Due to 20–35% of the voxels of the scar segmentation masks being within the blood pool segmentation masks, prior to being used in model training, scar voxels within the blood pool were projected to the LA surface along the normal direction of the closest LA endocardial wall voxel (see Fig. 1).

2.2 Proposed Model and Implementation

The proposed model consists of three 3D nn-UNets [15], which form two distinct paths to predict scar. In the first path (A in Fig. 2) a nn-UNet predicts the segmentation mask of the LA blood pool from the LGE-CMR image, and a second nn-UNet predicts the LA scar from the LGE-CMR image and IIR normalised LA wall (derived from the blood pool prediction and LGE-CMR image). In the second path (B in Fig. 2) a nn-UNet predicts LA scar directly from the LGE-CMR image (see Fig. 2).

The final LA scar mask is formed by the union of the predictions from the two paths (post-softmax probability thresholding and nn-UNet postprocessing), to provide a final ensemble prediction of LA scar (Fig. 3). nn-UNet was chosen for the segmentation as it automatically configures the optimal U-Net architecture, hyperparameters and image preprocessing and postprocessing steps and has demonstrated state-of-the-art performance in a range of segmentation challenges [15]. Data augmentation was performed during training and included techniques such as rotations, scaling, Gaussian noise, blur, brightness, contrast, low-resolution simulation, gamma correction and mirroring [15].

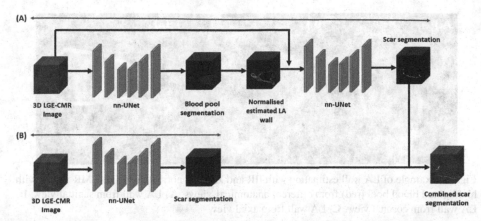

Fig. 2. Diagram of the proposed TESSLA model, outlining each stage of the model: blood pool segmentation, LA wall estimation and normalisation, LA scar segmentation from both nn-UNets and combined scar segmentation.**A**) Represents first path of TESSLA which predicts LA scar from normalised LA wall and LGE-CMR image. **B**) Represents second path of TESSLA which predicts LA scar from LGE-CMR image.

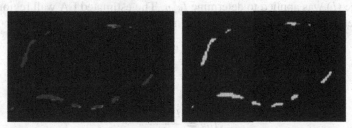

Fig. 3. Example of how the two different scar predictions (colours red and blue representing each scar prediction) (left image) are combined for the final prediction (right image).

2.3 LA Wall Estimation and Normalisation

The LA wall was estimated by obtaining the predicted blood pool segmentation mask to evaluate the boundary of the blood pool/LA endocardial wall and then dilating the wall boundary outwards (in 3D) by 3 voxels (each LGE-CMR image had a resolution of ~ 1 mm). A 3 voxel dilation amount was chosen based on the CT and MRI studies that found LA wall mean thickness was between 2 and 3 mm (Fig. 4) [16, 17].

The outward dilation was achieved by first dilating and eroding the blood pool boundary. Then, as shown in Eq. 1 below, the LA wall segmentation mask (M_{wall}) was found by the matrix subtracting the blood pool segmentation mask (B) and the eroded boundary (B_E) from the dilated boundary (B_D). The subtraction of B_D ensured that no dilation was within the LA blood pool. Lastly, if a voxel's LGE-CMR image intensity was less than 1, it was set to 0. The voxel intensity was then normalised and thresholded, such that a voxel intensity of 1 corresponded to LA wall voxels and 0 corresponded to background voxels. This process took ~ 5s to run for a single subject on a 12th Gen

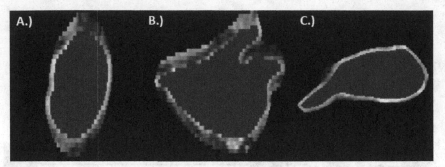

Fig. 4. Example of LA wall estimation with IIR and Z-score normalised LGE-CMR values with highlighted blood bool (red) from different anatomical views. **A)** LA wall from sagittal view. **B)** LA wall from coronal view. **C)** LA wall from axial view

Intel(R) Core (TM) i7-12700KF 3.61 GHz.

$$M_{wall} = B_D - B_E - B \tag{1}$$

An element-wise product, $\odot$, of the LA wall segmentation mask (M_{wall}) and LGE-CMR image (I) was applied to determine I_{wall}. The estimated LA wall region (LA_{wall}) was then defined to be all voxels where the intensities of image I_{wall} were above zero.

$$I_{wall} = I \odot M_{wall} \tag{2}$$

$$LA_{wall} = \{X \mid X \in I_{wall}, X > 0\} \tag{3}$$

$$I_{IIR} = \frac{LA_{wall}}{\tilde{X}_B} \tag{4}$$

IIR normalisation was then performed by dividing the LA_{wall} by, $\tilde{X}_B$, the mean blood pool voxel intensity (Eq. 4) [13]. Note that only the voxel intensities of the estimated LA wall from I are divided by $\tilde{X}_B$ as they are the only non-zero intensity voxels. The motivation for LA wall IIR normalisation was to provide the second nn-UNet with a set of features which are partially homogenised across multiple inter-individual factors (interscan variability in intensities, contrast dose, the delay time of image acquisition after contrast injection, body mass index, hematocrit, and renal function) to assist in model generalisability [18].

$$I^* = \frac{I_{IIR} - \mu}{\sigma} \tag{5}$$

Using the rule-based preprocessing of the nn-UNet pipeline, all IIR LA wall (I_{IIR}) voxels were Z-score normalised to get I^* (Eq. 5, where the mean voxel intensity of I_{IIR} is μ and the standard deviation is σ) as better convergence can be achieved during backpropagation if the average of each input variable over the training set is close to zero. The latter quality has led Z-score normalisation to becoming a de-facto practice in computer vision [19].

3 Results

3.1 Model Implementation and Training

Each nn-UNet model was trained independently for their respective task (blood pool or LA scar segmentation). The proposed framework was trained using 48 LGE-CMR images and a further 12 such images were used as a validation set. Each nn-UNet was trained for 1000 epochs using a combined cross-entropy and Dice loss function, Stochastic gradient descent was used with Nesterov momentum ($\mu = 0.99$) with an initial learning rate of 0.01 on an NVIDIA RTX 48GB A6000 GPU; each nn-UNet took ~ 24 h to train [20–22].

3.2 Validation and Test Set Results

As reflected in Tables 1 and 2, TESSLA outperformed both of its constituent models, justifying the use of an ensemble prediction. Figure 5 further supports this justification, as it illustrates how the two different nn-UNets predict LA scars that are overlapping but also different which is reflected in the increase of Dice score and sensitivity. Therefore, combining the two scar segmentations can predict better LA scar coverage.

On the LAScar 2022 test phase (hold out test set of 24 LGE-CMR images), TESSLA had a LA scar Dice score of 0.581 ± 0.112 and sensitivity of 0.529 ± 0.145.

Table 1. Validation set results for proposed model and constituent models.

Model	Scar		Blood
	Dice Score	Sensitivity	Dice Score
TESSLA	**0.529 ± 0.070**	**0.531 ± 0.133**	0.927 ± 0.020
nn-UNet (LGE-CMR)	0.506 ± 0.090	0.454 ± 0.134	N/A
nn-UNet (LGE-CMR + LA wall)	0.510 ± 0.080	0.474 ± 0.125	0.927 ± 0.020

Table 2. LAScarQ 2022 evaluation platform results from the hold-out test set (10 3D LGE-CMR) images from the challenge evaluation platform for the proposed model and constituentmodels.

Model	Scar		Blood Pool
	Dice Score	Sensitivity	Dice Score
TESSLA	**0.634 ± 0.142**	**0.578 ± 0.162**	0.890 ± 0.075
nn-UNet (LGE-CMR)	0.608 ± 0.149	0.524 ± 0.165	N/A
nn-UNet (LGE-CMR + LA wall)	0.593 ± 0.152	0.497 ± 0.152	0.890 ± 0.075

nn-UNet (LGE-CMR)   nn-UNet (LGE-CMR + LA wall)   TESSLA

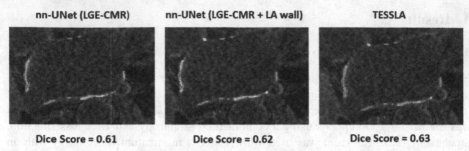

Dice Score = 0.61   Dice Score = 0.62   Dice Score = 0.63

Fig. 5. Comparison of model prediction from a validation set subject with corresponding scar segmentation Dice score, where predicted scar is in red and ground truth is in green.

LGE-CMR image quality plays a vital role in accurate TESSLA LA scar prediction, as shown in Fig. 6 and 7, as images with non-prevalent fibrotic gadolinium binding or motion artefacts had worse Dice scores. Furthermore, this explains the increase in LA scar Dice score in the LAScar 2022 evaluation platform results compared to the validation set results in training, as the evaluation platform set of LGE-CMR images only had one image with poor quality while the validation set had three. Meanwhile, this also explains the decrease of scar Dice score on the test phase dataset compared to the evaluation platform results.

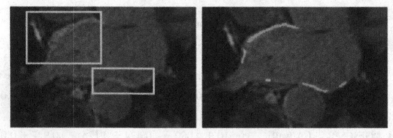

Dice score = 0.60

Fig. 6. Example of good quality LGE-CMR image with highlighted regions (gold boxes) of good gadolinium binding to fibrotic tissue (image on left) and corresponding Dice score. Predicted (red) and ground truth (green) scar highlighted on the image on the right.

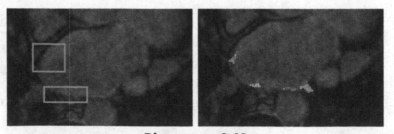

Dice score = 0.40

Fig. 7. Example of poor quality LGE-CMR image with highlighted regions of poor (gold boxes) gadolinium binding to fibrotic tissue (image on left) and corresponding Dice score. Predicted (red) and ground truth (green) scar highlighted on the image on the right.

4   Discussion and Conclusion

This study introduces a novel DL model, TESSLA, a two-stage ensemble model for LA scar segmentation. TESSLA achieved accuracy comparable to the state-of-the-art on the LAScar 2022 evaluation platform test set by utilising LA wall IIR-Z-score normal-isation and nn-UNets. To effectively compare these results to the gold standard, a study of inter-observer variability in manual segmentation would be required. Moreover, the model results show that poor image quality significantly impacts its performance. Hence, future work should focus on implementing a method to reduce its effects for better robustness. The study also demonstrated that integrating an IIR-Z-score normal-isation to the LA wall into an ensemble model can predict better LA scar coverage. Therefore, our proposed DL model provides better model generalisability for LA scar segmentation than a single model with LGE-CMR input.

The novel automatic tool for LA scar tissue quantification developed in this study can be applied in the clinic. Previous studies have suggested that DL LA scar segmentation tend to have higher Dice score accuracies than conventional thresholding-based methods [9]. Hence, DL models like TESSLA can be superior to the current gold standard of IIR thresholding, both in accuracy and speed of the LA scar assessment. This could lead to better patient stratification and AF treatment planning. Furthermore, this will also aid the clinical implementation of emerging technologies for AF management, such as digital twins, patient-specific models and AI therapy predictors [23–26].

Acknowledgements. This work was supported by funding from the Medical Research Council [MR/N013700/1], the British Heart Foundation [PG/15/8/31130], and the Wellcome/EPSRC Centre for Medical Engineering [WT 203148/Z/16/Z].

References

1. Hart, R.G., Halperin, J.L.: Atrial fibrillation and stroke: concepts and controversies. Stroke **32**, 803–808 (2001)
2. Chugh, S.S., et al.: Worldwide epidemiology of atrial fibrillation: a Global Burden of Disease 2010 Study. Circulation **129**, 837–847 (2014)
3. Wolf, P.A., Abbott, R.D., Kannel, W.B.: Atrial fibrillation as an independent risk factor for stroke: the Framingham Study. Stroke **22**, 983–988 (1991)
4. Amin, A., Houmsse, A., Ishola, A., Tyler, J., Houmsse, M.: The current approach of atrial fibrillation management. Avicenna J. Med. **6**, 8–16 (2016)
5. Brundel, B.J.J.M., Ai, X., Hills, M.T., Kuipers, M.F., Lip, G.Y.H., de Groot, N.M.S.: Atrial fibrillation. Nat Rev Dis Primers. **8**, 21 (2022). https://doi.org/10.1038/s41572-022-00347-9
6. Karamichalakis, N., et al.: Managing atrial fibrillation in the very elderly patient: challenges and solutions. Vasc. Health Risk Manag. **11**, 555–562 (2015)
7. Marrouche, N.F., et al.: Association of atrial tissue fibrosis identified by delayed enhancement MRI and atrial fibrillation catheter ablation: the DECAAF study. JAMA **311**, 498–506 (2014)
8. Marrouche, N.F., et al.: DECAAF II Investigators: Efficacy of LGE-MRI-guided fibrosis ablation versus conventional catheter ablation of atrial fibrillation: The DECAAF II trial: Study design. J. Cardiovasc. Electrophysiol. **32**, 916–924 (2021)
9. Li, L., Zimmer, V.A., Schnabel, J.A., Zhuang, X.: Medical image analysis on left atrial LGE MRI for atrial fibrillation studies: A review. Med. Image Anal. **77**, 102360 (2022)

10. Yang, G., et al.: A fully automatic deep learning method for atrial scarring segmentation from late gadolinium-enhanced MRI images. In: 2017 IEEE 14th International Symposium on Biomedical Imaging (ISBI 2017), pp. 844–848 (2017)

11. Li, L., Zimmer, V.A., Schnabel, J.A., Zhuang, X.: AtrialJSQnet: A New framework for joint segmentation and quantification of left atrium and scars incorporating spatial and shape information. Med. Image Anal. **76**, 102303 (2022)

12. Roy, A., Varela, M., Aslanidi, O.: Image-Based Computational Evaluation of the Effects of Atrial Wall Thickness and Fibrosis on Re-entrant Drivers for Atrial Fibrillation. Front. Physiol. **9**, 1352 (2018)

13. Roy, A., et al.: Identifying locations of re-entrant drivers from patient-specific distribution of fibrosis in the left atrium. PLoS Comput. Biol. **16**, e1008086 (2020)

14. Li, L., Zimmer, V.A., Schnabel, J.A., Zhuang, X.: AtrialGeneral: Domain Generalization for Left Atrial Segmentation of Multi-center LGE MRIs. In: de Bruijne, M., et al. (eds.) MICCAI 2021. LNCS, vol. 12906, pp. 557–566. Springer, Cham (2021). https://doi.org/10.1007/978-3-030-87231-1_54

15. Isensee, F., Jaeger, P.F., Kohl, S.A.A., Petersen, J., Maier-Hein, K.H.: nnU-Net: a self-configuring method for deep learning-based biomedical image segmentation. Nat. Methods. **18**, 203–211 (2021)

16. Beinart, R., et al.: Left atrial wall thickness variability measured by CT scans in patients undergoing pulmonary vein isolation. J. Cardiovasc. Electrophysiol. **22**, 1232–1236 (2011)

17. Varela, M., et al.: Novel MRI Technique Enables Non-Invasive Measurement of Atrial Wall Thickness. IEEE Trans. Med. Imaging. **36**, 1607–1614 (2017)

18. Benito, E.M., et al.: Left atrial fibrosis quantification by late gadolinium-enhanced magnetic resonance: a new method to standardize the thresholds for reproducibility. Europace **19**, 1272–1279 (2017)

19. LeCun, Y., Bottou, L., Orr, G.B., Müller, K.-R.: Efficient BackProp. In: Orr, G.B., Müller, K.-R. (eds.) Neural Networks: Tricks of the Trade. LNCS, vol. 1524, pp. 9–50. Springer, Heidelberg (1998). https://doi.org/10.1007/3-540-49430-8_2

20. Sudre, C.H., Li, W., Vercauteren, T., Ourselin, S., Jorge Cardoso, M.: Generalised Dice Overlap as a Deep Learning Loss Function for Highly Unbalanced Segmentations. In: Cardoso, M.J., et al. (eds.) DLMIA/ML-CDS -2017. LNCS, vol. 10553, pp. 240–248. Springer, Cham (2017). https://doi.org/10.1007/978-3-319-67558-9_28

21. Sabuncu, Z.: Generalized cross entropy loss for training deep neural networks with noisy labels. Adv. Neural Inf. Process. Syst., **31** (2018)

22. Paszke, A., et al: PyTorch: An imperative style, high-performance deep learning library. In: Wallach, H., Larochelle, H., Beygelzimer, A., d\textquotesingle Alché-Buc, F., Fox, E., and Garnett, R. (eds.) Adv. Neural Inf. Process. Syst. Curran Associates, Inc. **32**, pp. 8026–8037 (2019)

23. Corral-Acero, J., et al.: Others: The Digital Twin to enable the vision of precision cardiology. Eur. Heart J. **41**, 4556–4564 (2020)

24. Muffoletto, M., et al.: Toward Patient-Specific Prediction of Ablation Strategies for Atrial Fibrillation Using Deep Learning. Front. Physiol. **12**, 674106 (2021). https://doi.org/10.3389/fphys.2021.674106

25. Roney, C.H., et al.: Predicting atrial fibrillation recurrence by combining population data and virtual cohorts of patient-specific Left atrial models. Circ. Arrhythm. Electrophysiol. **15**, e010253 (2022)

26. Muizniece, L., et al.: Reinforcement Learning to Improve Image-Guidance of Ablation Therapy for Atrial Fibrillation. Front. Physiol. **12**, 733139 (2021). https://doi.org/10.3389/fphys.2021.733139

Deep U-Net Architecture with Curriculum Learning for Left Atrial Segmentation

Lei Jiang[1,2], Yan Li[1,2], Yifan Wang[1,2], Hengfei Cui[1,2(✉)], Yong Xia[1,2], and Yanning Zhang[1]

[1] National Engineering Laboratory for Integrated Aero -Space -Ground -Ocean Big Data Application Technology, School of Computer Science, Northwestern Polytechnical University, Xi'an 710072, China
hfcui@nwpu.edu.cn

[2] Centre for Multidisciplinary Convergence Computing (CMCC), School of Computer Science, Northwestern Polytechnical University, Xi'an 710072, China

Abstract. Segmentation of the late-stage gadolinium-enhanced magnetic resonance imaging (LGE-MRI) is a critical step in the ablation therapy for atrial fibrillation (AF). In this work, we propose an end-to-end deep learning-based segmentation method for delineating 3D left atrial (LA) structures in multiple domains. The proposed method uses the 6 layers deep U-Net architecture as the segmentation backbone. Curriculum learning is integrated into the deep U-Net architecture, helping the network learn step by step from easy to difficult scene. We have tested normal and strong version of data augmentation methods, to verify the effect of reducing domain shifts. Other techniques like Fourier-based data augmentation and Swin Transformer Block have also been explored to further improve the segmentation performance. The experimental results demonstrate that the strong version of data augmentation method can reduce the domain shifts and achieve more accurate result, with mean Dice score of 0.881 on the validation set of LAScarQS 2022 challenge. The evaluation results demonstrate our method's effectiveness on left atrial segmentation in multi-sequence cardiac magnetic resonance (CMR) data.

Keywords: Late-stage gadolinium-enhanced MRI · Left atrial segmentation · Deep U-Net · Curriculum learning

1 Introduction

Atrial fibrillation (AF) is one of the most common arrhythmia, affecting around 1% of the population all around the world. Delineating diseased 3D left atrial (LA) structures is of great importance for ablation treatment of AF and the quantification of atrial fibrosis. However, due to the nature of unclear boundaries, heterogeneous intensity distribution, and complex enhancement patterns [1–4] in the late gadolinium-enhanced magnetic resonance imaging, it is still challenging to apply fully automatic deep learning based segmentation method on this task. Moreover, the performance of the network often drops when it is applied to another domain.

© The Author(s), under exclusive license to Springer Nature Switzerland AG 2023
X. Zhuang et al. (Eds.): LAScarQS 2022, LNCS 13586, pp. 115–123, 2023.
https://doi.org/10.1007/978-3-031-31778-1_11

In recent years, many methods have been proposed for the segmentation of 3D LA and other structures. Some methods [5–7] adopted a two-stage framework, which first locating region of interest (ROI), and then using another network for fine segmentation. Nevertheless, such method is troublesome and time-consuming. As for the problem of domain shifts in cardiac image segmentation, Parreño et al. [8] trained a classifier to distinguish images from different domains, and then used error propagation to modify original images. Scannell et al. [9] utilized both segmentation loss and classification loss to improve robustness of the model. Liu et al. [10] used meta learning for domain generalization on cardiac images. However, the above mentioned methods needed class information for different domains, which was not available and could not be acquired in the data provided by LAScarQS 2022 challenge.

Unlike the large domain gaps between the balanced-steady free precession (bSSFP) and LGE images, we assumed that domain shifts of images from different centers can be reduced by properly choosing the data augmentation (DA) methods. In this work, we propose an end-to-end deep learning-based method for segmenting 3D left atrial (LA) structures in multiple domains. Our contributions are summarized as follows:

- We propose a simple end-to-end supervised method for solving the problem of left atrial segmentation in LAScarQS 2022 (Left Atrial and Scar Quantification & Segmentation Challenge), with deep U-Net network as the segmentation backbone.
- We test the effects of default DA method and strong DA method on the robustness of the network when faced with unknown domains.
- We adopt curriculum learning [11, 12] strategy to let the network gradually learn from easy to difficult scenes. Other techniques like Fourier-based data augmentation [13] have also been explored to further improve the segmentation performance.

The rest of this paper is organized as follows: Sect. 2 provides details about the method, including data pre-processing, our segmentation framework, loss function and post-processing. Section 3 presents experimental results and ablation studies. In Sect. 4, we conclude this work.

2   Methodologies

2.1   Dataset

We evaluated our method on task 2 of the LAScarQS 2022 challenge dataset [14–16], which contains 130 3D LGE MRI images for training. The training data are collected from 3 vendors, containing both pre-ablation data and post-ablation data, with two types of voxel size. The annotated area is left atrium (LA) cavity. The test data include 64 LGE MRI images with domains do not appear in the training data.

2.2   Data Pre-processing and Augmentation

The MRI images are firstly truncated to only keep the gray scale with frequency greater than 20. Then the three adjacent sequences are stacked to form a 3-channel input, with shape of $(B, 3, H, W)$, where H means height, W means width, B means the batch size, respectively. The images are normalized per slice by first subtracting the mean and then divided by the standard deviation for both training and testing stage.

Due to the unknown domains appear in test set, data enhancements are necessary to increase the robustness of the model. We have tested 2 groups of data augmentation strategies, which is shown in Table 1.

Table 1. Differences in data augmentation settings for normal and strong augmentation strategies. Both flip and shift operation is performed horizontally and vertically; the probability of random gamma augmentation is 0.5; the Gaussian noise is zero centered, with variance drawn from $U(0, 0.1)$.

Settings	Normal Augmentation	Strong Augmentation
Flips	p = 0.5	p = 0.5
Rotations	(-20°, 20°)	(-30°, 30°)
Zoom factor	(0.8, 1.2)	(0.7, 1.3)
Shift range	(0.1, 0.1)	(0.1, 0.1)
Gamma range	-	(0.7, 1.3)
Elastic deformations	-	p = 0.3
Random motion	-	p = 0.3
Gaussian noise	-	p = 0.15

Inspired by the curriculum Learning [11], we also perform multi-scale image cropping operations. In theory, a curriculum is a set of training criteria, each of which is related to a reweighting of the training distribution. In practice, the sizes we choose to crop images include: 192×192, 256×256, 384×384, 448×448. For sizes smaller than 350×350, we perform random cropping within the center area with size of 350×350 of the image, the offset factor is sampled uniformly from $(0, 350-W)$ or $(0, 350-H)$, where the H and W is the target size. For sizes bigger than 350×350, we perform central cropping. During training, in each epoch, we put the cropped images into the network in order of increasing size. Therefore, the portion occupied by the ventricle and the myocardium gradually changes from large to small, which helps the network learn from easy to difficult scenarios.

2.3 Model

We choose the 6 layers deep U-Net as the segmentation backbone, which is shown in Fig. 1. The max channel size is set to 512. The deep U-Net adopts a hierarchical feature representation with symmetrical encoder-decoder paths, those features include high-resolution positional features and low-resolution abstract features. Skip connections are added between encoder path and decoder path, to concatenate low-level and high-level information for better feature representation.

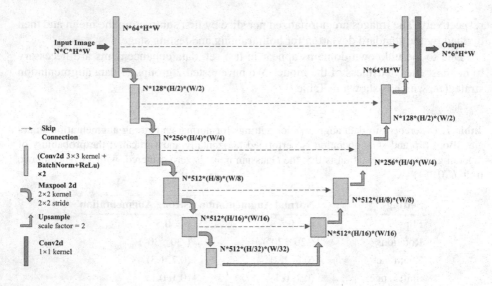

Fig. 1. The architecture of deep U-Net.

2.4   Loss Function and Post-processing

We choose weighted Cross Entropy loss and Dice loss for the deep U-net, which is defined as:

$$L_{seg} = L_{Dice} + L_{weightedCE} \qquad (1)$$

Since the input to the network is 3 adjacent CRM images, and each image responses to 2 classes, the output has a dimension of $(B, 6, H, W)$, then we convert the output into dimension of $(B, 3, 2, H, W)$. At the evaluation stage, three adjacent sequences stacked together and are predicted in a non-overlapping manner. We use 4 model ensemble method with majority voting strategy. The post-processing includes binary dilation and binary erosion with kernel radius of 6, we also use fill hole strategy and remove 2D regions smaller than 40 voxels.

3   Results

3.1   Implementation and Evaluation Metrics

All models are implemented in PyTorch, trained on a server with 2 Nvidia GTX1080Ti GPUs. We set SGD as the optimizer, the batch size is 16. The learning rate is first set to 1e-4, and then use cosine annealing as learning rate schedule. The training procedure ends after 600 epochs. We adopted 4-fold cross validation method, leave 32 cases for validation, and 98 cases for training. During the training stage, we stored one checkpoint with the lowest mean Dice loss of LA region on validation set.

The LAScarQS 2022 challenge used three metrics, i.e., the Dice coefficient, the average surface distance (ASD) and the Hausdorff distance for measuring the performance of algorithms. The dice coefficient provides a measure of the similarity of two objects, in a range of $[0, 1]$. Suppose X represents the ground truth mask, Y represents the predicted mask, the dice coefficient can be defined as:

$$dice(X, Y) = \frac{2|X \cap Y|}{|X| + |Y|} \tag{2}$$

The ASD is the average of all distances from points on the boundary of the predicted segmentation region to the ground truth boundary. The hausdorff distance describes the similarity between two sets, which is a function of the distance between the two sets of points. The definition of hausdorff distance between set A and set B is:

$$H(A, B) = \max(h(A, B), h(B, A)) \tag{3}$$

and $h(A, B)$ represents the hausdorff distance from set A to set B:

$$h(A, B) = \max_{a \in A} \left\{ \min_{b \in B} \{d(a, b)\} \right\} \tag{4}$$

where $d(a, b)$ stands for the Euclidian distance between two points in set A and set B. The smaller ASD and hausdorff distance values indicate the more precise segmentation results.

3.2 Results on 4-Folds Cross Validation Sets

Table 2 presents the performance comparison of different methods: normal data augmentation and strong data augmentation method as described in Sect. 2.2, MixStyle [17] which randomly shuffle the vector containing feature statistics information and mixes into original ones to increase the generalizability of the trained model, and the Fourier-based data augmentation [13] which converts an image into amplitude and phase components and then randomly mixes the amplitude component with component from other image. From Table 2 we can see that the mean dice score on 4-folds validation sets of strong data augmentation method is slightly lower than normal data augmentation, while the MixStyle and the Fourier-based methods adopt more aggressive approach for domain generation. We can see that the stronger the perturbation, the lower the accuracy on the 4-folds cross validation sets, but we still do not know the generalizability of each trained model.

3.3 Results on LAScarQS 2022 Challenge Validation Set

From Table 3 we can see that the MixStyle and Fourier-based methods are not suitable for this task. The failure of these two methods may be explained by the fact both methods mix information within the domain, while having the risk of amplifying noises. For example, as Fig. 2 shows, even mixing amplitude component from other image with relatively low weights (like 0.2) can corrode the brighter areas of the original image.

Table 2. Averaged Dice scores of LA cavity for each 4-folds comparing four data augmentation methods. The model used is Deep U-Net.

Method	Normal DA	Strong DA	MixStyle	Fourier Aug
Fold 1	**0.9166**	0.9165	0.9133	0.8951
Fold 2	**0.9184**	0.9178	0.9112	0.8988
Fold 3	**0.9204**	0.9185	0.9147	0.9019
Fold 4	0.9180	**0.9198**	0.9131	0.9083
Mean Dice	**0.9184**	0.9182	0.9131	0.9010

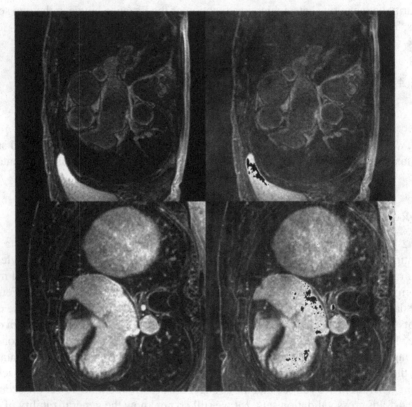

Fig. 2. The effect of Fourier-based data augmentation. The first column is the original LGE CMR images, the second column presents randomly mixing the amplitude component of original image with component from other image.

We have also tested the performance of Swin UNETR [18], which replaces the convolution block in the encoding path of the u-net with Swin Transformer Block and adds residual block in the skip-connection path. In practice, we take a two-stage method, by firstly using deep U-Net to get a coarse prediction of 3D target region with dimension of (320, 320, 48) or (320, 320, 48), depending on the spatial resolution of the training images. Then randomly crop the 3D image into size of (160, 160, 32) and send into the Swin UNETR. During the inference stage, we use sliding window inference with overlapping ratio of 0.5. As shown in Table 3, the Swin UNETR presents relatively weak domain-generation ability compared to deep U-Net. The experiment results indicate that with faster training speed and better generalization performance, CNNs is still hard to be replaced by Transformer. We can also see that the strong data augmentation method may cause a little drop of performance in cross-validation set, but it achieved best performance when facing unknown domains, with dice score of 0.8811 in vali-

Table 3. LAScarQS 2022 validation dataset benchmarks in terms of average dice score, the average surface distance (ASD) and the hausdorff distance (HD).

Method	Dice score	ASD	HD
Fourier Aug	0.8572	2.5920	26.5892
MixStyle	0.8702	2.0790	20.9350
Normal DA	0.8798	1.7953	**18.7546**
Strong DA	**0.8811**	**1.7815**	18.9708
Swin UNETR	0.8758	1.9476	20.3082

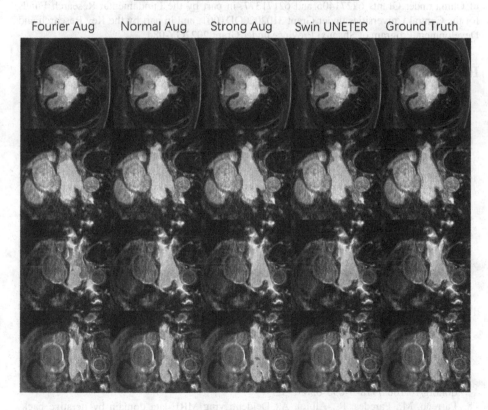

Fig. 3. Visual comparison of segmentation results of four models on the validation set. Left atrial is indicated in yellow. (Color figure online)

dation dataset. Furthermore, a visual comparison of the segmentation results of four models is presented in Fig. 3. It can be observed that deep U-Net network with normal or strong data augmentation gives the segmented left atrial regions that are closer to the ground truth labels.

4   Conclusion

In this work, we propose an efficient end-to-end segmentation method, for the task of segmenting 3D left atrial (LA) structures. We adopted deep U-Net with strong data augmentation method to learn the representative features from LGE CMR images. We further improved the learning strategy using curriculum learning to help the network gradually adapt to the difficult scenes. The experiment results indicate that the plain deep U-Net architecture beats Swin UNETR and achieves mean Dice score of 0.881 in the validation set of LAScarQS 2022 challenge. The experimental results are sufficient to demonstrate the effectiveness of curriculum learning and the powerful segmentation ability of deep U-Net.

Acknowledgment. The study was supported in part by the National Natural Science Foundation of China under Grants 62271405 and 62171377, in part by the Fundamental Research Funds for the Central Universities under Grant 3102020QD1001, and in part by the Key Research and Development Program of Shaanxi Province under Grant 2022GY-084.

References

1. Zhuang, Xiahai, et al.: Cardiac segmentation on late gadolinium enhancement MRI: a benchmark study from multi-sequence cardiac MR segmentation challenge. (2020) arXiv preprint arXiv:2006.12434
2. Liu, Y., Duan, Y., Zeng, T.: Learning multi-level structural information for small organ segmentation. Sig. Process. **193**, 108418 (2022)
3. Yueyun, L., Wang, Y., Duan, Y.: Effective 3D Boundary Learning via a Nonlocal Deformable Network. In: 2022 IEEE 19th International Symposium on Biomedical Imaging (ISBI). IEEE (2022)
4. Liu, L., et al.: Rician noise and intensity nonuniformity correction (NNC) model for MRI data. Biomed. Signal Process. Control **49**, 506–519 (2019)
5. Xia, Q., Yao, Y., Hu, Z., Hao, A.: Automatic 3D Atrial Segmentation from GE-MRIs Using Volumetric Fully Convolutional Networks. In: Pop, M., et al. (eds.) STACOM 2018. LNCS, vol. 11395, pp. 211–220. Springer, Cham (2019). https://doi.org/10.1007/978-3-030-12029-0_23
6. Yang, X., et al.: Combating Uncertainty with Novel Losses for Automatic Left Atrium Segmentation. In: Pop, M., et al. (eds.) STACOM 2018. LNCS, vol. 11395, pp. 246–254. Springer, Cham (2019). https://doi.org/10.1007/978-3-030-12029-0_27
7. Liu, Y., Zhang, M., Zhan, Q., Gu, D., Liu, G.: Two-Stage Method for Segmentation of the Myocardial Scars and Edema on Multi-sequence Cardiac Magnetic Resonance. In: Zhuang, X., Li, L. (eds.) MyoPS 2020. LNCS, vol. 12554, pp. 26–36. Springer, Cham (2020). https://doi.org/10.1007/978-3-030-65651-5_3
8. Parreño, M., Paredes, R., Albiol, A.: Deidentifying MRI data domain by iterative back-propagation. International Workshop on Statistical Atlases and Computational Models of the Heart, Springer, Cham (2020)

9. Scannell, C.M., Chiribiri, A., Veta, M.: Domain-adversarial learning for multi-Centre, multi-vendor, and multi-disease cardiac MR image segmentation. International Workshop on Statistical Atlases and Computational Models of the Heart, Springer, Cham (2020)

10. Liu, X., Thermos, S., O'Neil, A., Tsaftaris, S.A.: Semi-supervised Meta-learning with Disentanglement for Domain-Generalised Medical Image Segmentation. In: de Bruijne, M., et al. (eds.) MICCAI 2021. LNCS, vol. 12902, pp. 307–317. Springer, Cham (2021). https://doi.org/10.1007/978-3-030-87196-3_29

11. Yoshua, B., et al.: Curriculum learning In: Proceedings of the 26th annual international conference on machine learning 60, p. 6 (2009)

12. Hengfei, C., et al.: Deep U-Net architecture with curriculum learning for myocardial pathology segmentation in multi-sequence cardiac magnetic resonance images Knowl. Based Syst. 249, 108942 (2022)

13. Xu, Q., Zhang, R., Zhang, Y., Wang, Y., Tian, Q.: A fourier-based framework for domain generalization. In: Proceedings of the IEEE/CVF Conference on Computer Vision and Pattern Recognition, pp. 14383–14392 (2021)

14. Li, L., Veronika, A.Z., Schnabel, J.A., Zhuang, X.: AtrialJSQnet: a New Framework for Joint Segmentation and Quantification of Left Atrium and Scars Incorporating Spatial and Shape Information. Med. Image Anal. 76, 102303 (2022)

15. Li, L., Zimmer, V.A., Schnabel, J.A., Zhuang, X.: Medical Image Analysis on Left Atrial LGE MRI for Atrial Fibrillation Studies: A Review. Med. Image Anal. 77, 102360 (2022)

16. Lei Li, Zimmer, V.A., Schnabel, J.A., Zhuang, X.: AtrialGeneral: domain Generalization for Left Atrial Segmentation of Multi-Center LGE MRIs, MICCAI, 557–566 (2021)

17. Kaiyang, Z., et al.: Domain generalization with mix style. (2021) arXiv preprint arXiv:2104.02008

18. Hatamizadeh, A., et al.: SWIN UNETR: SWIN transformers for semantic segmentation of brain tumors in MRI images. (2022) arXiv preprint arXiv:2201.01266

Cross-Domain Segmentation of Left Atrium Based on Multi-scale Decision Level Fusion

Feiyan Li⬤ and Weisheng Li(✉)⬤

Chongqing Key Laboratory of Image Cognition, Chongqing University of Posts and Telecommunications, Chongqing, China
liws@cqupt.edu.cn

Abstract. The mortality rate of cardiovascular and cerebrovascular diseases has always been the highest in the world. As a common and frequent disease of cardiovascular disease, atrial fibrillation has been troubling patients. Therefore, modeling and analysis of atrial anatomical structure are very important for clinical diagnosis and treatment of atrial fibrillation. The segmentation of left atrium is the basis of atrial digital modeling. To solve the problem of cross-domain segmentation of left atrium, we proposed a segmentation method based on multi-scale decision level fusion strategy. Similar to most end-to-end segmentation networks, we also adopted 3D U-Net as the backbone network. However, in the decoder, we adopted multi-scale up-sampling to obtain multiple outputs, and fused the multiple outputs into one by means of multiplication. We used 130 cases with labels which provided by organizers of LAScarQS 2022 challenge for training and 20 cases without labels which also provided by them for testing. We uploaded the test results to the online test platform, which allowed each team to test up to 10 times, and the best result we achieved was Dice 0.88314, Hausdorff 20.88313mm and ASSD 1.79399mm.

Keywords: Left Atrium Segmentation · Multi-scale · Decision Level Fusion

1 Introduction

The mortality rate of cardiovascular and cerebrovascular diseases has always been the highest in the world. As a common and frequent disease of cardiovascular disease, atrial fibrillation has been troubling patients and seriously affecting patients' quality of life [1]. At present, the best treatment for atrial fibrillation is catheter ablation, but this method only responds well to a small number of patients. In order to screen patients suitable for this method, the volume and diameter [2] of the left atrium is often measured, and atrial segmentation is the basis of quantification of the atrium. In clinical practice, atrial quantification still adopts time-consuming and labor-intensive manual description method [3]. So automatic segmentation of left atrium (LA) is desired.

There are still many challenges in developing automated left atrial segmentation, such as changing atrial shape and poor image quality, as well as cross-domain problems in the clinic. In Fig. 1, the left atrial and scar quantification and segmentation challenge described cross-domain segmentation problem. The challenge provides 130 late

X. Zhuang et al. (Eds.): LAScarQS 2022, LNCS 13586, pp. 124–132, 2023.
https://doi.org/10.1007/978-3-031-31778-1_12

gadolinium enhanced (LGE) magnetic resonance imaging (MRIs) which are from three imaging centers for training and 20 LGE MRIs for testing.

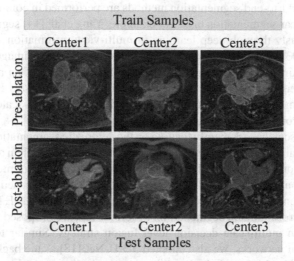

Fig. 1. Diagram of multi-center data. Center1 is University of Utah, Center2 is Beth Israel Deaconess Medical Center and Center3 is King's College London.

Actually, there are many studies on left atrium segmentation [4–7]. Catalina et al. [8] reported the benchmark of left atrium segmentation from 3D CT and MRI datasets as early as 2015, which summarized the left atrial segmentation challenge (LASC) carried out at the STACOM'13 workshop, in conjunction with MICCAI'13. In this challenge, region growing and multi-atlas were the dominant algorithms adopted by most teams. Since U-Net [9] was successfully applied to the medical image segmentation task in 2015, more and more researchers have adopted deep learning to solve the problems existing in the medical image segmentation task. Since then, the left atrium segmentation task has mainly adopted two solutions: one is the end-to-end deep learning method, the other is the combination of deep learning and traditional methods.

A representative end-to-end left atrium segmentation method proposed by Xiong et al. [10] which adopted a dual fully convolutional neural network to segment LGE MRIs and achieved Dice scores of 0.940 and 0.942 for the LA epicardium and endocardium. Another global benchmark [11] also proposed by Xiong et al. summarized the 2018 left atrium segmentation challenge, which showed the top method achieved a Dice scores of 93.2% and mean surface to surface distances of 0.7 mm. In 2018 left atrium segmentation challenge, most of the competition teams adopted the U-Net-based end-to-end segmentation method, and only two teams adopted the non-deep learning method. A number of researchers have continued to study it since the left atrial segmentation challenge. For example, Uslu et al. [12] proposed a multi-task network optimized to simultaneously generate left atrial segmentation and edge masks from LGE MRIs which achieved Hausdorff distances of 12.43mm and Dice scores of 0.92. In addition to U-Net, another representative network structure in medical image segmentation task is generative adversarial network (GAN). Chen et al. [13] proposed an inter-cascade generative adversarial network which named JAS-GAN, to segment the unbalanced atrial targets from LGE CMR images automatically and accurately in an end-to-end way. In addition, some end-to-end segmentation methods are performed in conjunction with the left atrium and scar segmentation task. For example, Yang et al. [14] segmented LA and scar simultaneously through deep learning in multi-view information which obtained Dice scores of 93% for LA anatomy and 87% for scar. Medical image segmentation schemes combining deep learning with traditional methods are often adopted. Zhang et al. [15] adopted deep convolutional neural network with unscented Kalman filter to segment LA from long-axis MRIs. Li et al. [16] designed a multi-scale convolutional neural network combined graph-cut to quantify atrial scar.

The above research work mainly focused on the automatic segmentation of left atrium and the quantification of scar, but few studies aimed to solve the problem of cross-domain atrial segmentation. Only Li et al. [17] discussed LA segmentation of multi-center LGE MRIs. To better align with real clinical needs, the challenge proposed two tasks: LA scar quantification and left atrial segmentation from multi-center LGE MRIs. To solve the problem of cross-domain segmentation of left atrium, we proposed a segmentation method based on multi-scale decision level fusion strategy. Similar to most end-to-end segmentation networks, we also adopted 3D U-Net [18] as the backbone network. However, in the decoder, we adopted multi-scale up-sampling to obtain multiple outputs, and fused the multiple outputs into one by means of multiplication.

2   Methodology

2.1   Data Preprocessing

The task 2 of left atrial scar quantification & segmentation challenge provides us 130 LGE MRIs which are from real clinical environment [19, 20]. All 130 cases are manually marked by specialists in the left atrium. In addition, the challenge organizers have provided 20 un-labelled cases for online platform testing. These cases presented in the challenge all have atrial fibrillation and are from multiple centers. Moreover, there is unknown domain data in the test set that is not in the train set.

In order to facilitate training and testing, we carried out data preprocessing operations as shown in Fig. 2. For any raw data $\mathcal{F}_{original}$, we zoomed it to $n \times n \times 80$ where 80 represents the number of slices and n can be selected based on the size of the raw data. In this paper, we selected $n = 350, 400, 450, 500$. Then we cropped the center area to $160 \times 160 \times 80$ and made sure we covered the entire heart chamber. We know that for segmentation task, boundary has a great influence on segmentation accuracy. There is unknown domain data in test set. In order to ensure the unification of prior knowledge during training and testing as much as possible, we used edge detection operator Prewitt to extract the edge of the image after cropping, and then added the edge and the image after cropping to get $\mathcal{F}_{input}$. It is obvious that the edge of the image $\mathcal{F}_{input}$ is enhanced. The label corresponding to the original image was also preprocessed in the same way.

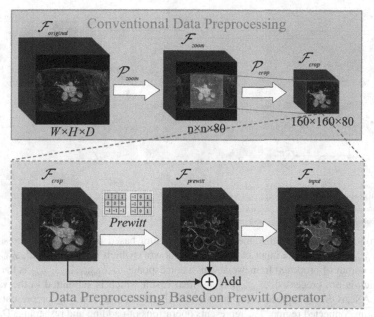

Fig. 2. Schematic diagram of data preprocessing. $\mathcal{F}_{original}$ is the original image which is not processed, $\mathcal{F}_{input}$ represents the input of proposed framework which is preprocessed, $\mathcal{F}_{zoom}$ represents the image which is zoomed, $\mathcal{F}_{crop}$ represents the image which is cropped, and $\mathcal{F}_{prewitt}$ represents the edge image extracted by the edge operator Prewitt. $\mathcal{P}_{zoom}$ and $\mathcal{P}_{crop}$ represent zooming operation and cropping operation, separately.

2.2 Proposed Method

Figure 3 shows proposed segmentation framework of left atrium based on multi-scale decision level fusion. The preprocessed $\mathcal{F}_{input}$ has been described in Fig. 2. The shape of input $\mathcal{F}_{input}$ is $160 \times 160 \times 80$, and the shape of output $\mathcal{F}_{output}$ is also $160 \times 160 \times 80$. The output $\mathcal{F}_{output}$ needs to be uploaded to the online test platform, the output $\mathcal{F}_{output}$ needs to be conducted $\mathcal{P}_{pr}$ operation (padding and reshaping) to make sure it matches the shape of original image $\mathcal{F}_{original}$. The backbone of proposed framework is based on 3D U-Net, but the details of each layer is different from it. Each blue block in Fig. 3 represent a combination of dilation convolution. The function of dilation convolution is to increase the receptive field without increasing the number of parameters, so as to obtain more features. The DilationConv3D block is composed of three continuous dilation convolutional layers. The input of DilationConv3D block is $\mathcal{D}_{input}$ and the output of DilationConv3D block is $\mathcal{D}_{output}$, the middle three outputs of consecutive dilation convolution are $\mathcal{D}_{o1}$, $\mathcal{D}_{o2}$ and $\mathcal{D}_{o3}$, respectively. To enhance feature representation, we add three consecutive dilation convolutions, the description of DilationConv3D block is as follows:

$$\mathcal{D}_{output} = \mathcal{D}_{o1}(\mathcal{D}_{input}) \oplus \mathcal{D}_{o2}(\mathcal{D}_{o1}(\mathcal{D}_{input})) \oplus \mathcal{D}_{o3}(\mathcal{D}_{o2}(\mathcal{D}_{o1}(\mathcal{D}_{input}))) \tag{1}$$

where $\oplus$ represents addition of mathematics.

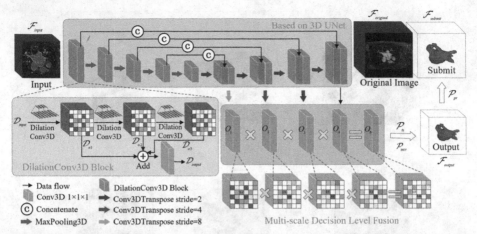

Fig. 3. Proposed segmentation framework of left atrium based on multi-scale decision level fusion. $\mathcal{F}_{input}$ represents the input of proposed framework which is preprocessed, $\mathcal{F}_{output}$ represents the output of proposed framework which corresponds to $\mathcal{F}_{input}$, $\mathcal{F}_{original}$ is the original image which is not processed. $\mathcal{F}_{submit}$ is the final result which is submitted to the validation phase of LAScarQS. $\mathcal{P}_{ts}$ represents the operation of threshold selection, $\mathcal{P}_{mcr}$ represents finding the maximum connected region, $\mathcal{P}_{pr}$ represents operations of padding and reshaping. $\mathcal{D}_{input}$ and $\mathcal{D}_{output}$ represents the input and output of dilation convolution block, respectively. $\mathcal{D}_{o1}$, $\mathcal{D}_{o2}$ and $\mathcal{D}_{o3}$ represent the output of different stage. O_1, O_2 and O_3 represent the output of different stride in up-sampling.

Usually, there is only one output in 3D UNet like O_4 in Fig. 3. In order to solve the problem that cross-domain segmentation is not robust enough, we propose a multi-scale decision level fusion approach to achieve left atrium segmentation. O_1, O_2 and O_3 represent the output of stride = 8,4,2 in up-sampling, respectively. O_1, O_2 and O_3 represent different predicted results. So the combination of O_1, O_2 and O_3 is called decision level fusion. The multi-scale decision level fusion can be described as follows:

$$O_5 = O_1 \times O_2 \times O_3 \times O_4 \tag{2}$$

where $\times$ represents multiplication of mathematics. O_5 is the result of the joint decision of the four predicted results. In other words, only when the prediction results of each scale are close enough to the ground truth, the final prediction results can be more accurate. $\mathcal{F}_{output}$ is obtained when O_5 is conducted $\mathcal{P}_{ts}$ operation and $\mathcal{P}_{mcr}$ operation.

3 Experimental Results and Analysis

We conducted experiments on device of Nvidia Geforce RTX 2080Ti. The average running time of each case is about 20s. In experiments, we adopted 130 patients with atrial fibrillation for training which were from three centers. And we adopted 20 patients for testing which were from four centers. We submitted our results to online test platform. Table 1 shows the best test result of each team published by the online test platform. As Table 1 shows, not every team participating in the challenge submitted their test results. There are three metrics used to measure the performance of different methods: Dice coefficient, Hausdorff distance and average symmetric surface distance (ASSD). In Table 1, Team79 achieves the highest Dice score which is above 0.89, the shortest ASSD and the shortest Hausdorff distance. In fact, each of the top ten teams achieved a Dice score greater than 0.88, which is a third decimal point difference. Team9 is proposed method which achieves 0.883 of Dice score, 20.883 of Hausdorff distance and 1.794 of ASSD.

Table 1. Test results on online test platform.

Method	Dice	Hausdorff(mm)	ASSD(mm)
Team79	0.893	15.863	1.612
Team29	0.890	17.124	1.706
Team52	0.890	16.448	1.715
Team28	0.889	17.203	1.747
Team60	0.886	17.257	1.780
Team44	0.886	17.226	1.763
Team76	0.886	16.996	1.786
Team38	0.886	18.389	1.813
Team9 (Proposed)	0.883	20.883	1.794
Team25	0.881	18.971	1.781
Team41	0.879	21.199	1.900
Team71	0.878	19.796	1.981
Team64	0.877	17.087	1.933
Team44	0.875	28.227	2.383
Team1	0.873	36.351	2.134
Team14	0.868	19.106	2.063
Team26	0.864	33.489	2.026
Team37	0.858	25.553	2.396
Team39	0.853	23.425	2.137
Team46	0.847	105.794	3.395
Team8	0.784	28.259	3.831
Team11	0.775	52.084	5.045
Team56	0.629	43.922	6.690
Team49	0.580	93.419	10.891

The subjective test results corresponding to Table 1 are shown in Fig. 4. It is obvious that cases with a Dice coefficient greater than 90% have smooth surface and complete shape, while the cases with Dice coefficient lower than 90% have serrated surface and uneven surface. Overall, the segmentation results of left atrium are intact in all 20 patients. Furthermore, the proposed method in this paper is not completely unpredictable because of unknown domain in the test set, indicating that the proposed framework is useful for cross-domain segmentation of left atrium.

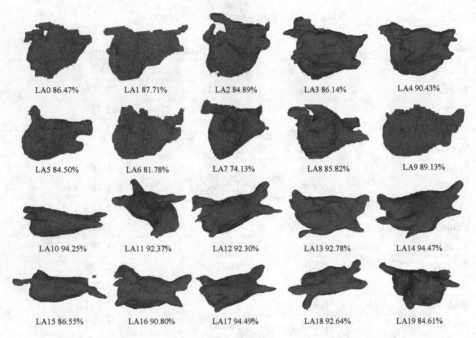

Fig. 4. Subjective experimental results of proposed method on test phase.

To prove that the proposed multi-scale decision level fusion strategy was useful for atrial segmentation, we performed ablation experiments on different decision levels. The challenge organizers provided 130 cases with labels, of which 100 cases were randomly selected for training and the remaining 30 cases for testing in ablation experiments. Data augmentation and preprocessing are the same as the previous experiment. The ablation experimental results are shown in Table 2. O_1, O_2 and O_3 are described in Fig. 3. The proposed method achieved highest Dice score, the shortest Hausdorff distance and the shortest ASSD. The proposed method without O_1, O_2 and O_3 are inferior to the proposed method. It can be seen that each branch is important for backbone network.

w/o: without.

Table 2. Ablation experimental results.

Method	Dice(%)	Hausdorff(mm)	ASSD(mm)
Proposed w/o O_1	91.342 ± 2.234	9.429 ± 2.666	0.985 ± 0.380
Proposed w/o O_2	91.179 ± 2.274	9.475 ± 2.642	0.971 ± 0.383
Proposed w/o O_3	91.314 ± 2.147	9.894 ± 2.727	0.937 ± 0.308
Proposed w/o O_{123}	91.275 ± 2.291	9.383 ± 2.297	0.949 ± 0.318
Proposed	91.486 ± 2.150	9.315 ± 2.584	0.930 ± 0.345

4   Conclusion

In this work, in order to segment left atrium from multi-center LGE MRIs and predict unknown domain data, we proposed a framework based on multi-scale decision level fusion strategy. Similar to most end-to-end segmentation networks, we also adopted 3D U-Net as the backbone network. However, in the decoder, we adopted multi-scale up-sampling to obtain multiple outputs, and fused the multiple outputs into one by means of multiplication. In the stage of data preprocessing, edge detection operator Prewitt was used to extract latent features of source domain and target domain. We adopted 130 cases for training and 20 cases for testing and obtained Dice 0.88314, Hausdorff 20.88313mm and ASSD 1.79399mm.

Acknowledgment. This work was supported by the National Key Research and Development Program of China [2019YFE0110800, 2016YFC1000307–3], National Natural Science Foundation of China [61972060, U1713213, 62027827], the Natural Science Foundation of Chongqing [cstc2020jcyj-zdxmX0025, cstc2019cxcyljrc-td0270, cstc2019jcyj-cxttX0002], Chongqing University of Posts and Telecommunications Ph.D. Innovative Talents Project [BYJS202110].

References

1. Chugh, S. S., et al.: Worldwide epidemiology of atrial fibrillation: a global burden of disease 2010 study. Circulation **129**(8), 837--847 (2014).
2. Berruezo, A., et al.: Preprocedural predictors of atrial fibrillation recurrence after circumferential pulmonary vein ablation. Eur. Heart J. **28**(7), 836–841 (2007)
3. Karim, R., et al.: Algorithms for left atrial wall segmentation and thickness–evaluation on an open-source ct and mri image database. Med. Image Anal. **50**, 36–53 (2018)
4. Yang, X., et al.: Combating Uncertainty with Novel Losses for Automatic Left Atrium Segmentation. In: Pop, M., et al. (eds.) STACOM 2018. LNCS, vol. 11395, pp. 246–254. Springer, Cham (2019). https://doi.org/10.1007/978-3-030-12029-0_27
5. Mortazi, A., Karim, R., Rhode, K., Burt, J., Bagci, U.: CardiacNET: Segmentation of Left Atrium and Proximal Pulmonary Veins from MRI Using Multi-view CNN. In: Descoteaux, M., Maier-Hein, L., Franz, A., Jannin, P., Collins, D.L., Duchesne, S. (eds.) MICCAI 2017. LNCS, vol. 10434, pp. 377–385. Springer, Cham (2017). https://doi.org/10.1007/978-3-319-66185-8_43

6. Jamart, K., Xiong, Z., Talou, G. D. M., Stiles, M. K., Zhao, J.: Mini review: deep learning for atrial segmentation from late gadoliniumenhanced MRIs. Front. Cardiovas. Med. **7**, 86 (2020)

7. Chen, J., et al.: Multiview Two-Task Recursive Attention Model for Left Atrium and Atrial Scars Segmentation. In: Frangi, A.F., Schnabel, J.A., Davatzikos, C., Alberola-López, C., Fichtinger, G. (eds.) MICCAI 2018. LNCS, vol. 11071, pp. 455–463. Springer, Cham (2018). https://doi.org/10.1007/978-3-030-00934-2_51

8. Tobon-Gomez, C., Geers, A.J., Peters, J., et al.: Benchmark for algorithms segmenting the left atrium from 3D CT and MRI datasets. IEEE Trans. Med. Imaging **34**(7), 1460–1473 (2015)

9. Ronneberger, O., Fischer, P., Brox, T.: U-Net: Convolutional Networks for Biomedical Image Segmentation. In: Navab, N., Hornegger, J., Wells, W.M., Frangi, A.F. (eds.) MICCAI 2015. LNCS, vol. 9351, pp. 234–241. Springer, Cham (2015). https://doi.org/10.1007/978-3-319-24574-4_28

10. Xiong, Z., Fedorov, V.V., Fu, X., Cheng, E., Macleod, R., Zhao, J.: Fully automatic left atrium segmentation from late gadolinium enhanced magnetic resonance imaging using a dual fully convolutional neural network. IEEE Trans. Med. Imaging **38**(2), 515–524 (2019)

11. Xiong, Z., Xia, Q., Hu, Z., et al.: A global benchmark of algorithms for segmenting the left atrium from late gadolinium-enhanced cardiac magnetic resonance imaging. Med. Image Anal. **67**, 101832 (2021)

12. Uslu, F., Varela, M., Boniface, G., Mahenthran, T., Chubb, H., Bharath, A.A.: LA-Net: a multi-task deep network for the segmentation of the left atrium. IEEE Trans. Med. Imaging **41**(2), 456–464 (2022)

13. Chen, J., et al.: JAS-GAN: Generative adversarial network based joint atrium and scar segmentations on unbalanced atrial targets. IEEE J. Biomed. Health Inform. **26**(1), 103–114 (2021)

14. Yang, G., et al.: Simultaneous left atrium anatomy and scar segmentations via deep learning in multiview information with attention. Futur. Gener. Comput. Syst. **107**, 215–228 (2020)

15. Zhang, X., Noga, M., Martin, D.G., Punithakumar, K.: Fully automated left atrium segmentation from anatomical cine long-axis MRI sequences using deep convolutional neural network with unscented Kalman filter. Med. Image Anal. **68**, 101916 (2021)

16. Li, L., et al.: Atrial scar quantification via multi-scale CNN in the graph-cuts framework. Med. Image Anal. **60**, 101595 (2020)

17. Li, L., Zimmer, V.A., Schnabel, J.A., Zhuang, X.: AtrialGeneral: Domain Generalization for Left Atrial Segmentation of Multi-center LGE MRIs. In: de Bruijne, M., et al. (eds.) MICCAI 2021. LNCS, vol. 12906, pp. 557–566. Springer, Cham (2021). https://doi.org/10.1007/978-3-030-87231-1_54

18. Çiçek, Ö., Abdulkadir, A., Lienkamp, S.S., Brox, T., Ronneberger, O.: 3D U-Net: Learning Dense Volumetric Segmentation from Sparse Annotation. In: Ourselin, S., Joskowicz, L., Sabuncu, M.R., Unal, G., Wells, W. (eds.) MICCAI 2016. LNCS, vol. 9901, pp. 424–432. Springer, Cham (2016). https://doi.org/10.1007/978-3-319-46723-8_49

19. Li, L., Zimmer, V.A., Schnabel, J.A., Zhuang, X.: AtrialJSQnet: a new framework for joint segmentation and quantification of left atrium and scars incorporating spatial and shape information. Med. Image Anal. **76**, 102303 (2022)

20. Li, L., Zimmer, V.A., Schnabel, J.A., Zhuang, X.: Medical image analysis on left atrial LGE MRI for atrial fibrillation studies: a review. Med. Image Anal. **77**, 102360 (2022)

Using Polynomial Loss and Uncertainty Information for Robust Left Atrial and Scar Quantification and Segmentation

Tewodros Weldebirhan Arega(✉), Stéphanie Bricq, and Fabrice Meriaudeau

ImViA Laboratory, Université Bourgogne Franche-Comté, Dijon, France
tewdrosw@gmail.com

Abstract. Automatic and accurate segmentation of the left atrial (LA) cavity and scar can be helpful for the diagnosis and prognosis of patients with atrial fibrillation. However, automating the segmentation can be difficult due to the poor image quality, variable LA shapes, and small discrete regions of LA scars. In this paper, we proposed a fully-automatic method to segment LA cavity and scar from Late Gadolinium Enhancement (LGE) MRIs. For the loss functions, we propose two different losses for each task. To enhance the segmentation of LA cavity from the multi-center dataset, we present a hybrid loss that leverages Dice loss with a polynomial version of cross-entropy loss (PolyCE). We also utilize different data augmentations that include histogram matching to increase the variety of the dataset. For the more difficult LA scar segmentation, we propose a loss function that uses uncertainty information to improve the uncertain and inaccurate scar segmentation results. We evaluate the proposed method on the Left Atrial and Scar Quantification and Segmentation (LAScarQS 2022) Challenge dataset. It achieves a Dice score of 0.8897 and a Hausdorff distance (HD) of 16.91 mm for LA cavity and a Dice score of 0.6406 and sensitivity of 0.5853 for LA scar. From the results, we notice that for LA scar segmentation, which has small and irregular shapes, the proposed loss that utilizes the uncertainty estimates generated by the scar yields the best result compared to the other loss functions. For the multi-center LA cavity segmentation, we observe that combining the region-based Dice loss with the pixelwise PolyCE can achieve a good result by enhancing the segmentation result in terms of both Dice score and HD. Furthermore, using moderate-level data augmentation with histogram matching improves the model's generalization capability.

Keywords: Cardiac MRI · Late Gadolinium Enhancement MRI · Left Atrium · Scar quantification · Segmentation · Deep learning · PolyLoss · Uncertainty

1 Introduction

Atrial fibrillation (AF) is an irregular and often very rapid heart rhythm (arrhythmia). During atrial fibrillation, the heart's upper chambers (the atria)

X. Zhuang et al. (Eds.): LAScarQS 2022, LNCS 13586, pp. 133–144, 2023.
https://doi.org/10.1007/978-3-031-31778-1_13

beat irregularly and out of synchronization with the heart's lower chambers (the ventricles). AF increases the risk of stroke, heart failure, and other heart-related complications [6]. One of the most commonly used techniques to treat AF patients is radio-frequency catheter ablation using the pulmonary vein (PV) isolation [27].

Late Gadolinium Enhancement (LGE), sometimes called delayed-enhancement MRI, is a gold standard imaging technique to visualize and quantify the left atrial (LA) scars. In a clinical routine, human experts generally segment the LA anatomy and LA scars manually. Manual segmentation is time-consuming and suffers from intra- and inter-observer variability. This problem can be addressed by automating the segmentation. However, automatic segmentation of LA anatomy and LA scars from LGE MRI is still challenging due to poor image quality, variable LA shapes, thin LA walls, and small isolated regions of the LA scars [16].

Few studies have been proposed to segment LA cavity from LGE MR images. Gao et al. (2010) [7] and Zhu et al. (2013) [32] utilized region-based active-contour and variational region growing with shape prior respectively to segment LA cavity. Tao et al. (2016) [25] used atlas-based methods leveraging auxiliary images with better anatomical information to help the LA cavity segmentation from LGE MRI [17]. However, accurately segmenting LA cavity using these conventional methods depend on additional information such as shape prior or auxiliary images [17]. Recently, deep learning-based algorithms have been successfully applied to segment LA cavity from LGE MRI. Vesal et al. (2018) [26] proposed a 3D U-Net with dilated convolutions at the bottleneck of the network and residual connections between the encoder blocks to incorporate local and global information. Chen et al. (2018) [5] adopted multi-task learning to perform both LA cavity segmentation and pre/post ablation classification. Other works [10,28,30] utilized a two-stage cascaded segmentation framework to first locate the region of interest (ROI) that covers the atrial cavity, then used a second network to segment LA cavity from the cropped ROI. The main problem with these cascaded approaches is that they can be time- and resource-intensive.

Recently, semi-automatic and fully-automatic deep learning based methods have been widely used to segment scar [1,21,31]. For LA scar segmentation, some studies proposed to use non-deep learning based methods such as thresholding [22,24], clustering [23], deformable and graph-based methods [11,12]. Although these conventional methods have shown encouraging results, they rely on initial manual segmentation of the LA cavity. Deep learning methods have been presented to automatically segment LA scar from LGE MRIs. Li et al. [14] proposed to use graph-cuts with multi-scale CNNs to automatically segment LA scar. Other works utilized multi-task learning to jointly segment LA cavity and scar [16,29].

In this paper, we proposed a fully automatic deep learning based method that leverages a polynomial loss and an uncertainty based loss to segment LA cavity from multi-center LGE MRIs and LA scar from single-center LGE MRIs, respectively. To increase the variety of the dataset, we also employ various data augmentation techniques, including histogram matching. We evaluated our method on Left Atrial and Scar Quantification and Segmentation (LAScarQS 2022) Challenge dataset. The proposed losses achieve the best result compared to other losses in both the multi-center LA cavity segmentation and the highly imbalanced LA scar segmentation. In addition, the employed data augmentation techniques improve the model's generalization on the LA cavity segmentation from multi-center images.

2   Dataset

The Left Atrial and Scar Quantification and Segmentation Challenge (LAScarQS 2022)[1] consists of 200 LGE MRIs acquired in a real clinical environment from patients suffering Atrial fibrillation (AF). All the LGE MRIs were collected from three different clinical centers. The images from the first center (University of Utah) were acquired using Siemens Avanto 1.5T or Vario 3T. The voxel resolution of the images was $1.25 \times 1.25 \times 2.5$ mm. The LGE MRIs from the second center (Beth Israel Deaconess Medical Center) were acquired with Philips Achieva 1.5T. The spatial resolution of the images was $1.4 \times 1.4 \times 1.4$ mm. Similar to the second center, the images from the third center (King's College London) were acquired with a Philips Achieva 1.5T. The spatial resolution of the LGE MRI scan was $1.3 \times 1.3 \times 4.0$ mm. The challenge has two tasks. The first one focuses on left atrial blood pool segmentation from multi-center LGE MRIs. The second task focuses on segmentation of left atrial scar [15–17]. We declare that the segmentation method implemented for participation in the LAScarQS 2022 challenge has not used any pre-trained models nor extra MRI datasets other than those given by the organizers.

3   Methods

3.1   Network Architecture

For both LA cavity and LA scar segmentation, we employed a 3D segmentation network. The network architecture is based on 3D nnU-Net framework [9]. As demonstrated in Fig. 1, we altered the standard nnU-Net network architecture by adding Dropout at the network's middle layers [3] to lessen overfitting and improve generalization. The U-Net's encoder and decoder consist of 10 convolutional layers where each convolution is followed by instance normalization and Leaky ReLU (negative slope of 0.01) activation function. The kernel size of the convolution is $3 \times 3 \times 3$. During pre-processing, we resampled all the volumes to 0.625 mm $\times 0.625$ mm $\times 1.0$ mm and 0.625 mm $\times 0.625$ mm $\times 2.5$ mm for LA cavity segmentation and LA scar segmentation respectively (the median voxel spacing of the training cases). The intensity of every volume was normalized to have zero-mean and unit-variance.

---

[1] https://zmic.fudan.edu.cn/lascarqs22.

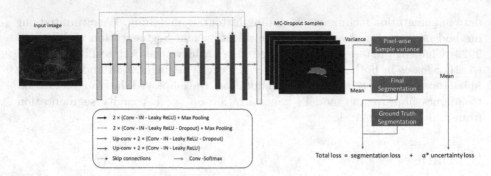

Fig. 1. Overview of the network architecture.

3.2   Loss Functions

Recently, Leng et al. (2022) [13] proposed PolyLoss, a new loss function that expresses the commonly used loss functions such as cross-entropy (Eq. 1) and focal loss (Eq. 3) as a linear combination of polynomial functions. Using Taylor expansion, cross-entropy can be represented as sum of polynomial bases $(1-p)^j$, as shown in Eq. 2, where p is the prediction probability of the target class [13]. By dropping the higher-order polynomials and adding terms that perturb the polynomial coefficients, they came up with a simplified version of the polynomial loss called Poly-1. This loss function modifies the cross-entropy by only adding one hyper-parameter (ϵ) [13], as can be seen in Eq. 2. PolyLoss has shown good performance on computer vision tasks by outperforming cross-entropy and focal losses [13].

Inspired by [13], in this paper, we proposed a loss function that uses Dice loss with PolyLoss (Eq. 5) for a LA cavity and scar segmentation. Dice loss is a region based loss that directly optimizes the Dice coefficient metric as shown in Eq. 4. We hypothesized that by combining the region based Dice loss with the polynomial version of the cross-entropy (PolyCE) (Eq. 5) can improve the segmentation of LA cavity from multi-center LGE MRIs.

$$L_{CE} = -log(p) = \sum_{n=1}^{\infty} \frac{1}{n}(1-p)^n, \tag{1}$$

$$L_{PolyCE} = L_{CE} + \epsilon(1-p), \tag{2}$$

$$L_{Focal} = -(1-p)^{\gamma} log(p), \tag{3}$$

$$L_{Dice} = 1 - \frac{2|Y \cap G|}{|Y| + |G|}, \tag{4}$$

$$L_{DicePolyCE} = L_{Dice} + L_{PolyCE}, \tag{5}$$

where Y and G represent the predicted and manual segmentation maps, respectively.

Arega et al. (2021) [2] proposed a segmentation model that generates uncertainty estimates (sample variance) during training using the Monte-Carlo-dropout Bayesian method and utilizes the uncertainty information to enhance the segmentation results by incorporating it into the segmentation loss function [2]. During training, the model is sampled N times, and the mean of these samples is used as the final segmentation. The sample variance (uncertainty) (σ_i) is computed as a variance of the N Monte-Carlo prediction samples of each pixel i [2]. Since sample variance is a pixel-wise uncertainty measure, to determine the image-level uncertainty the mean of the pixel-wise uncertainty values is computed as shown in Eq. 7, where I is the total number of pixels of the image [2]. This image-level uncertainty is considered as uncertainty loss. Then, it is added to a segmentation loss with a hyper-parameter value alpha (α) that controls the contribution of the uncertainty loss to the total loss as shown in Eq. 8. They have shown that uncertainty information can be advantageous, particularly to improve the segmentation of semantically and visually challenging pathologies such as scars which generate higher epistemic uncertainty [2].

In this paper, we proposed to adopt the uncertainty loss in combination with the hybrid loss of Dice and Focal (DiceFocal) loss [33] (Eq. 6) for LA scar segmentation. We hypothesized that by fusing DiceFocal loss, which has shown good performance on highly imbalanced dataset [20], with the uncertainty loss (Uncertainty DiceFocal Loss) (Eq. 8) can enhance the segmentation of the more challenging LA scar segmentation.

$$L_{Seg(DiceFocal)} = L_{Dice} + L_{Focal}, \tag{6}$$

$$L_{Uncertainty} = \frac{1}{I}\sum_i(\sigma_i^2), \tag{7}$$

$$L_{Total(UncertaintyDiceFocalLoss)} = L_{Seg(DiceFocal)} + \alpha \times L_{Uncertainty}, \tag{8}$$

3.3   Data Augmentations

We applied a variety of data augmentations to improve the generalization and robustness of the models in the multi-center dataset, including intensity-based data augmentation, spatial data augmentation, and histogram matching augmentation [3,9]. Histogram matching is the transformation of an image so that the histogram of a source image matches the histogram of a reference image [8]. Mathematically, it is the process of altering one image so that the cumulative distribution function (CDF) of values in each band corresponds to the CDF of bands in another image. Some examples of the source, reference, and matched images are shown in Fig. 2.

In the LAScarQS 2022 challenge, there was no specific information about each training image regarding the clinical center from which they came from. In this work, we used histogram matching by taking random training images and matching them to a selected low performing training images which had the worst performance in terms of Dice. The matched images were then added to the training dataset to enhance the generalizability of the model on LA cavity segmentation from multi-Center LGE MRIs.

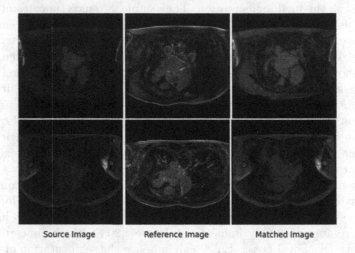

Source Image   Reference Image   Matched Image

Fig. 2. Examples showing histogram matching based data augmentations on LA cavity segmentation dataset.

3.4   Training

The segmentation models were trained for 1000 epochs in a 5-fold cross-validation scheme. Stochastic gradient descent (SGD) with Nesterov momentum ($\mu = 0.99$) with an initial learning rate of 0.01 was used to optimize the network's weights. The learning rate was decayed using the "poly" learning rate policy [9]. We employed a mini-batch size of 2. We used a value of 1 for epsilon (ϵ) in PolyLoss (Eq. 2) and a value of 2 for gamma (γ) in Focal loss (Eq. 3). For the uncertainty loss, the weighting factor (α) (in Eq. 8) is empirically selected to be 2.0. For histogram matching, we utilized Simple ITK's python library [19]. The training was done on NVIDIA GPUs using Pytorch deep learning framework based on nnU-Net implementation [9].

4   Results and Discussion

To evaluate LA cavity segmentation, Dice coefficient, average surface distance (ASD) and Hausdorff distance (HD) metrics were used. For LA scar segmentation and quantification, accuracy, specificity, sensitivity, Dice coefficient of the scar, and generalized Dice score of the cavity and scar were used [16]. All the comparisons were done on the validation set provided by the challenge. The validation dataset for LA scar segmentation consists of 10 cases from center 1, the same center as the training dataset. For LA cavity segmentation which focuses on a multi-center problem, the validation dataset contains 10 cases from center 1, the same center as the training dataset, and 10 cases from center 2.

The baseline method is the standard nnU-Net network [9] with Dropout layers added at the middle layers of the segmentation network as mentioned in Sect. 3.1. It uses light data augmentation that includes rotation, scaling, Gaussian blur and noise. In terms of the loss function, the baseline method employs a hybrid loss of Dice loss with cross-entropy Loss (DiceCE).

Regarding the data augmentation, we separated the experiments into light data augmentation (baseline), moderate data augmentation and histogram matching augmentation. The same network architecture was used during the comparison. The moderate data augmentation uses elastic deformation, rotation, scaling, mirroring, additive brightness, Gaussian noise and blurring. For histogram matching (HM) augmentation, the matched images were added to the training dataset as mentioned in Sect. 3.3.

Comparing the data augmentation experiments' performance in Table 1, it can be observed that moderate data augmentation improved the segmentation performance from 17.1836 mm to 16.8721 mm in terms of HD. However, it yielded a bit worse result in both Dice and ASD compared to the baseline (light data augmentation). Similarly, the histogram matching-based data augmentation significantly decreased the HD from 17.1836 mm to 16.6851 mm. However, its performance was slightly lower in terms of Dice score and ASD.

Comparing the performance of the loss functions on the segmentation of LA cavity, the proposed loss outperformed the other loss functions as shown in Table 1. The baseline (DiceCE loss) yielded a Dice score of 0.8884, ASD of 1.74629 and HD of 17.18363 mm whereas DiceFocal loss achieved a Dice score of 0.8885, ASD of 1.7474 and HD of 17.2035 mm. Using only the polynomial version of cross-entropy loss (PolyCE) enhanced the segmentation result mainly in terms of Dice score and HD. When PolyCE is combined with Dice loss, the segmentation result of LA cavity was improved further from 0.8884 to 0.8897, from 1.7463 to 1.7203, and from 17.1836 to 16.9067 mm in terms of Dice score, ASD and HD respectively compared to the baseline which uses DiceCE loss.

Table 2 shows the comparison of the different loss functions on LA scar segmentation. Compared to LA cavity segmentation, it has imbalanced classes because the scar is very small compared to the cavity. Due to this, we have compared the proposed loss not only to the baseline but also to other loss functions which are commonly used for imbalanced segmentation. For example, hybrid loss functions such as DiceFocal loss [33], and DiceTopK loss [4] which combines Dice loss with Focal loss and TopK loss respectively to mitigate class imbalance [20]. In the comparison, we have also included Focal loss [18], a loss function that was designed to deal with foreground-background class imbalance by focusing more on the hard examples.

Table 1. Comparison of LA cavity segmentation performance using various data augmentations and compound loss functions on validation set ($n = 20$) of the challenge. Dice: Dice score, ASD: average surface distance, HD: Hausdorff distance. The bold values are the best.

Method	Dice	ASD	HD (mm)
Baseline	0.8884	1.7463	17.1836
Moderate DataAug	0.8868	1.7755	16.8721
HM DataAug	0.8867	1.7536	**16.6851**
DiceFocal	0.8885	1.7474	17.2035
OnlyPolyCE	0.8893	1.7413	17.0053
Proposed (DicePolyCE)	**0.8897**	**1.7203**	16.9067

As shown in Table 2, the baseline, which combines Dice loss with cross-entropy loss (DiceCE) [9], yielded an accuracy of 0.7764, sensitivity of 0.5529, Dice score of 0.6258 and generalized Dice score 0.9187 for scar segmentation. The DicePolyCE loss enhanced the performance of baseline as it increased the accuracy, sensitivity, Dice and generalized Dice of scar by 22%, 1%, 0.5%, 0.01%, respectively. DiceTopK loss [4] achieved an accuracy of 0.7751, sensitivity of 0.5503, Dice score of 0.6222 and generalized Dice score 0.9183 which is lower than the baseline. Using only Focal loss [18] achieved the worst result as can be seen in Table 2. The other commonly used loss function for an imbalanced dataset that is DiceFocal loss [33] yielded much better result compared to the baseline, DicePolyCE and DiceTopK loss with an accuracy of 0.9999, sensitivity of 0.5749, Dice score of 0.6363 and generalized Dice score 0.9199. The proposed loss, where uncertainty loss is combined with DiceFocal loss achieved the best result outperforming the other loss functions. In terms of specificity, all the loss functions achieved a similar score of 0.9999.

From the results, we observed that a compound loss that utilizes Dice loss with the polynomial version of cross-entropy loss (DicePolyCE) consistently improves the performance of the most common compound loss that combines Dice loss with cross-entropy loss. The performance enhancement was in both the mildly imbalanced LA cavity segmentation and the highly imbalanced LA scar segmentation. This shows the robustness of the proposed loss in LA cavity and scar segmentation.

In LA scar segmentation, the second proposed loss function which utilizes uncertainty information outperformed the commonly used loss functions for highly imbalanced segmentation such as DiceTopK [4] and Focal loss [18] functions [20], DiceFocal loss [33]. This confirms the importance of incorporating uncertainty information as part of the learning process to enhance particularly the segmentation of pathologies with irregular structures like scars.

Table 2. Comparison of LA scar segmentation performance using different compound loss functions on validation set ($n = 10$) of the challenge. GDice: generalized Dice score of cavity and scar. The bold values are the best.

Method	Accuracy	Specificity	Sensitivity	Dice	GDice
Baseline	0.7764	0.9999	0.5529	0.6258	0.9187
DiceTopK Loss	0.7751	0.9999	0.5503	0.6222	0.9183
DiceFocal Loss	0.9999	0.9999	0.5749	0.6363	0.9199
Focal Loss	0.9999	0.9999	0.5095	0.6047	0.9139
DicePolyCE Loss	0.9999	0.9999	0.5605	0.6301	0.9187
Proposed (Uncertainty+ DiceFocal Loss)	**0.9999**	**0.9999**	**0.5853**	**0.6406**	**0.9205**

In terms of data augmentation, the experiments were mainly focused on the multi-center LA cavity segmentation. From the results, we can say that using moderate data augmentation and histogram matching can enhance the model's generalization as it improved the segmentation result, particularly in terms of HD compared to the light data augmentation.

5   Conclusion

In this paper, we proposed a fully automatic deep learning method that utilizes a novel hybrid loss function that combines Dice loss with a polynomial version of cross-entropy loss to segment LA cavity from multi-center LGE MRIs and an uncertainty-based loss function to segment scar from single-center LGE MRIs. We also employed various data augmentation techniques, which include histogram matching, to increase the size and variety of the training dataset. In the experiments, we have compared the proposed loss function with the commonly used losses in the multi-center LA cavity segmentation and in the highly imbalanced LA scar segmentation. We observe that the proposed losses yield the best result outperforming the other losses in both LA cavity and scar segmentation. From the results, we can say that using the polynomial version of cross-entropy in combination with Dice loss can be a better alternative loss function for anatomical segmentation such as LA cavity. For segmentation such as LA scar, which generates high epistemic uncertainty due to its small and complex structure, utilizing a loss function that incorporates uncertainty information can be useful for robust segmentation. Additionally, applying moderate-level data augmentation with histogram matching can improve the results and increase the model's generalization capability.

Acknowledgements. This work was supported by the French National Research Agency (ANR), with reference ANR-19-CE45-0001-01-ACCECIT. Calculations were performed using HPC resources from DNUM CCUB (Centre de Calcul de l'Université de Bourgogne) and from GENCI-IDRIS (Grant 2022-AD011013506). We also thank the Mesocentre of Franche-Comté for the computing facilities.

References

1. Arega, T.W., Bricq, S.: Automatic myocardial scar segmentation from multi-sequence cardiac MRI using fully convolutional densenet with inception and squeeze-excitation module. In: Zhuang, X., Li, L. (eds.) MyoPS 2020. LNCS, vol. 12554, pp. 102–117. Springer, Cham (2020). https://doi.org/10.1007/978-3-030-65651-5_10

2. Arega, T.W., Bricq, S., Meriaudeau, F.: Leveraging uncertainty estimates to improve segmentation performance in cardiac MR. In: Sudre, C.H., et al. (eds.) UNSURE/PIPPI -2021. LNCS, vol. 12959, pp. 24–33. Springer, Cham (2021). https://doi.org/10.1007/978-3-030-87735-4_3

3. Arega, T.W., Legrand, F., Bricq, S., Meriaudeau, F.: Using MRI-specific data augmentation to enhance the segmentation of right ventricle in multi-disease, multi-center and multi-view cardiac MRI. In: Puyol Antón, E., et al. (eds.) STACOM 2021. LNCS, vol. 13131, pp. 250–258. Springer, Cham (2022). https://doi.org/10.1007/978-3-030-93722-5_27

4. Brugnara, G., et al.: Automated volumetric assessment with artificial neural networks might enable a more accurate assessment of disease burden in patients with multiple sclerosis. Eur. Radiol. **30**(4), 2356–2364 (2020). https://doi.org/10.1007/s00330-019-06593-y

5. Chen, C., Bai, W., Rueckert, D.: Multi-task learning for left atrial segmentation on GE-MRI. In: Pop, M., et al. (eds.) STACOM 2018. LNCS, vol. 11395, pp. 292–301. Springer, Cham (2019). https://doi.org/10.1007/978-3-030-12029-0_32

6. Clinic, M.: Atrial fibrillation - symptoms and causes (2021). https://www.mayoclinic.org/diseases-conditions/atrial-fibrillation/symptoms-causes/syc-20350624

7. Gao, Y., Gholami, B., Macleod, R., Blauer, J.J.E., Haddad, W.M., Tannenbaum, A.R.: Segmentation of the endocardial wall of the left atrium using local region-based active contours and statistical shape learning. In: Medical Imaging (2010)

8. Gorelick, N.: Histogram matching (2021). https://medium.com/google-earth/histogram-matching-c7153c85066d

9. Isensee, F., Jaeger, P., Kohl, S., Petersen, J., Maier-Hein, K.: nnU-Net: a self-configuring method for deep learning-based biomedical image segmentation. Nat. Methods **18**, 1–9 (2021). https://doi.org/10.1038/s41592-020-01008-z

10. Jamart, K., Xiong, Z., Talou, G.M., Stiles, M.K., Zhao, J.: Two-stage 2D CNN for automatic atrial segmentation from LGE-MRIs. In: Pop, M., et al. (eds.) STACOM 2019. LNCS, vol. 12009, pp. 81–89. Springer, Cham (2020). https://doi.org/10.1007/978-3-030-39074-7_9

11. Karim, R., et al.: A method to standardize quantification of left atrial scar from delayed-enhancement MR images. IEEE J. Transl. Eng. Health Med. **2**, 1–15 (2014)

12. Karim, R., et al.: Evaluation of current algorithms for segmentation of scar tissue from late gadolinium enhancement cardiovascular magnetic resonance of the left atrium: an open-access grand challenge. J. Cardiovasc. Magn. Reson. **15**, 105–105 (2013)

13. Leng, Z., et al.: Polyloss: a polynomial expansion perspective of classification loss functions. arXiv abs/2204.12511 (2022)

14. Li, L., et al.: Atrial scar quantification via multi-scale CNN in the graph-cuts framework. Med. Image Anal. **60**, 101595 (2020)

15. Li, L., Zimmer, V.A., Schnabel, J.A., Zhuang, X.: AtrialGeneral: domain generalization for left atrial segmentation of multi-center LGE MRIs. In: de Bruijne, M., et al. (eds.) MICCAI 2021. LNCS, vol. 12906, pp. 557–566. Springer, Cham (2021). https://doi.org/10.1007/978-3-030-87231-1_54
16. Li, L., Zimmer, V.A.M., Schnabel, J.A., Zhuang, X.: Atrialjsqnet: a new framework for joint segmentation and quantification of left atrium and scars incorporating spatial and shape information. Med. Image Anal. **76**, 102303 (2022)
17. Li, L., Zimmer, V.A.M., Schnabel, J.A., Zhuang, X.: Medical image analysis on left atrial LGE MRI for atrial fibrillation studies: A review. Med. Image Anal. **77**, 102360 (2022)
18. Lin, T.Y., Goyal, P., Girshick, R., He, K., Dollár, P.: Focal loss for dense object detection. In: Proceedings of the IEEE International Conference on Computer Vision, pp. 2980–2988 (2017)
19. Lowekamp, B.C., Chen, D.T., Ibáñez, L., Blezek, D.J.: The design of simpleitk. Front. Neuroinform. **7** (2013)
20. Ma, J., et al.: Loss odyssey in medical image segmentation. Med. Image Anal. **71**, 102035 (2021)
21. Moccia, S., et al.: Development and testing of a deep learning-based strategy for scar segmentation on CMR-LGE images. Magn. Reson. Mater. Phys. Biol. Med. **32**, 187–195 (2018)
22. Oakes, R.S., et al.: Detection and quantification of left atrial structural remodeling using delayed enhancement MRI in patients with atrial fibrillation (2009)
23. Perry, D., Morris, A.K., Burgon, N., McGann, C., Macleod, R., Cates, J.E.: Automatic classification of scar tissue in late gadolinium enhancement cardiac MRI for the assessment of left-atrial wall injury after radiofrequency ablation. In: Medical Imaging (2012)
24. Ravanelli, D., et al.: A novel skeleton based quantification and 3-D volumetric visualization of left atrium fibrosis using late gadolinium enhancement magnetic resonance imaging. IEEE Trans. Med. Imaging **33**, 566–576 (2014)
25. Tao, Q., Ipek, E.G., Shahzad, R.K., Berendsen, F.F., Nazarian, S., van der Geest, R.J.: Fully automatic segmentation of left atrium and pulmonary veins in late gadolinium-enhanced MRI: towards objective atrial scar assessment. J. Magn. Resonan. Imaging **44** (2016)
26. Vesal, S., Ravikumar, N., Maier, A.K.: Dilated convolutions in neural networks for left atrial segmentation in 3D gadolinium enhanced-MRI. arXiv abs/1808.01673 (2018)
27. Wilber, D.J., et al.: Comparison of antiarrhythmic drug therapy and radiofrequency catheter ablation in patients with paroxysmal atrial fibrillation: a randomized controlled trial. JAMA **303**(4), 333–40 (2010)
28. Xia, Q., Yao, Y., Hu, Z., Hao, A.: Automatic 3D atrial segmentation from GE-MRIs using volumetric fully convolutional networks. In: Pop, M., et al. (eds.) STACOM 2018. LNCS, vol. 11395, pp. 211–220. Springer, Cham (2019). https://doi.org/10.1007/978-3-030-12029-0_23
29. Yang, G., et al.: Simultaneous left atrium anatomy and scar segmentations via deep learning in multiview information with attention. Future Gener . Comput. Syst. **107**, 215–228 (2020)
30. Yang, X., et al.: Combating uncertainty with novel losses for automatic left atrium segmentation. arXiv abs/1812.05807 (2018)
31. Zabihollahy, F., White, J.A., Ukwatta, E.: Myocardial scar segmentation from magnetic resonance images using convolutional neural network. In: Medical Imaging (2018)

32. Zhu, L., Gao, Y., Yezzi, A.J., Tannenbaum, A.R.: Automatic segmentation of the left atrium from MR images via variational region growing with a moments-based shape prior. IEEE Trans. Image Process. **22**, 5111–5122 (2013)
33. Zhu, W., et al.: Anatomynet: deep learning for fast and fully automated whole-volume segmentation of head and neck anatomy. Med. Phys. **46**, 576–589 (2019)

Automated Segmentation of the Left Atrium and Scar Using Deep Convolutional Neural Networks

Kumaradevan Punithakumar[1,2(✉)] and Michelle Noga[1,2]

[1] Department of Radiology and Diagnostic Imaging, University of Alberta, Edmonton, Canada
[2] Servier Virtual Cardiac Centre, Mazankowski Alberta Heart Institute, Edmonton, Canada
punithak@ualberta.ca

Abstract. Atrial fibrillation (AF) causes irregular heart rhythm, and its incidence and prevalence are increasing worldwide. It was estimated that 46.3 million individuals were living with AF in 2016. Late gadolinium enhancement (LGE) magnetic resonance imaging (MRI) offers an option to image the left atrium (LA) and detect scars in the chamber, which play a central role in the treatment of AF in patients. This study proposes a deep convolutional neural network approach to automate segmentation of the LA for LGE MRI images and quantify the scars in the chamber, which are otherwise tedious and time-consuming tasks to be performed manually. The proposed method was trained and evaluated using the datasets provided by the LAScarQS 2022 challenge organizers. A total of 194 LGE MRI datasets were used in this study which were acquired from three different clinical centers. The challenge is divided into two tasks. For the first task, only the post-ablation LGE MRI scans are considered where the objective is to delineate the LA and scar. The second task considers both pre and post-ablation scans where the objective is to segment the LA. The performance of the algorithm is evaluated using Dice similarity (DM), average surface distance (ASD) and Hausdorff distance (HD) metrics. For the first task, the proposed approach yielded 90.71%, 1.681, and 21.45 for average DM, ASD and HD values for the segmentation of LA from the validation set. The corresponding values for the second task are 89.32%, 1.613, and 15.86, respectively. The proposed method yielded an average DM of 63.31% for the delineation of LA scar from the validation set.

Keywords: Atrial fibrillation · Magnetic resonance imaging · Deep convolutional neural network · Left atrium · Late gadolinium enhancement

1 Introduction

The incidence and prevalence of atrial fibrillation (AF), a cardiac condition that causes irregular heart rhythm, are increasing worldwide [3]. One option to diag-

X. Zhuang et al. (Eds.): LAScarQS 2022, LNCS 13586, pp. 145–152, 2023.
https://doi.org/10.1007/978-3-031-31778-1_14

nose AF is to image the left atrium (LA) using late gadolinium enhancement (LGE) magnetic resonance imaging (MRI) [5]. The manual assessment of the LGE MRI scans is tedious due to the large number of images produced by MRI scanners in each scan, and there has been increasing research interest in the development of automated methods to assess the LA from LGE MRI scans [4].

Earlier methods to delineate the LA from MRI images were based on traditional segmentation techniques such as salient feature and contour evolution [12]. Recently, the deep convolutional neural network based techniques have become the dominant approaches to delineate the LA from MRI scans [7,11]. The research interest in automated segmentation approaches is evident by the public segmentation challenge to delineate the chamber from LGE 3D MRI sequences which was hosted at the Statistical Atlases and Computational Models of the Heart (STACOM) workshop in the Medical Image Computing and Computer Assisted Intervention (MICCAI) conference in 2018 [8]. A V-net [6] based convolutional neural network approach [10] yielded the best performance among more than 15 research teams that participated in the challenge. A review of medical image computing techniques related to the LA assessment using LGE MRI could be found at [5].

This study proposes a deep convolutional neural network approach, known as nnU-Net [1], to delineate the LA cavity and scar from LGE MRI scans. Trained from scratch, the proposed approach was evaluated using the datasets provided by the LAScarQS 2022 challenge hosted by MICCAI 2022. The challenge consists of two tasks. The first task is to delineate the LA cavity and scar from LGE MRI scans acquired from patients at pre-ablation. The second task is to delineate the LA cavity from LGE MRI scans acquired from patients at pre and post-ablation. Instead of using the LGE MRI datasets in their original orientation, the proposed method first aligns them along the coordinate axes. The preprocessing was applied to both the image datasets and annotated labels. The preprocessed datasets were then used for training the neural networks. Upon trained, the neural networks were applied for the prediction of the segmented LA cavity and scar regions which were then reoriented to match the original image scans.

2   Methodology

In this study, we trained the nnU-Net approach [1] with a modification to the geometric orientation of the input images and labels. The nnU-Net approach uses U-Net [9] as the neural network architecture. The overall approach used for neural network training and inference is given in Fig. 1. The LAScarQS 2022 challenge consists of two tasks. The aim of Task 1 is to delineate both the LA cavity and scar. The aim of Task 2 is to delineate the LA cavity from scans acquired at pre and post-ablation. Separate neural networks were trained from scratch for Task 1 and Task 2.

Training

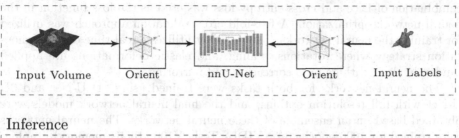

Inference

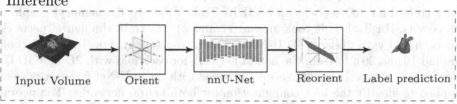

Fig. 1. The proposed neural network based solution to segment the LA cavity and scar from the LGE MRI volumes.

2.1 Data

The dataset shared by the LAScarQS 2022 challenge organizers consists of 194 LGE MRIs acquired from three different centers, namely, the University of Utah, Beth Israel Deaconess Medical Center and King's College London. The images were acquired using Siemens Avanto 1.5T, Siemens Vario 3T, or Philips Acheiva 1.5T scanners. All scans were acquired using free-breathing with navigator-gating or navigator-gating with fat suppression option. All scans were acquired as three-dimensional images with the spatial resolution of $1.25 \times 1.25 \times 2.5$, $1.4 \times 1.4 \times 1.4$ or $1.3 \times 1.3 \times 4.0$ mm. The patients underwent the MRI examinations prior to ablation or one month to six months after ablation.

Task 1: The training set for the Task 1 consists of 60 LGE MRI scans with ground truth delineations of the LA cavity and scar saved in separate files in NIFTI format. The validation set consists of 10 LGE MRI scans.

Task 2: The training set for the Task 2 consists of 130 LGE MRI scans with ground truth delineations of the LA cavity. The validation set consists of Task 2 consists of 20 LGE MRI scans.

2.2 Neural Network Training

Two separate nnU-Net [1] frameworks were used for Task 1 and Task 2. The nnU-Net approach for Task 1 was trained using a multi-label input where separate label values were used for LA cavity, LA scar and background. The nnU-Net for Task 2 was trained using the labelling corresponding to LA cavity and background only. We used the default nnU-Net configurations for both tasks. A combination of Dice and cross-entropy loss was used as the loss function in the neural network optimization. A five-fold cross validation approach was utilized for training the neural networks. The nnU-Net utilizes a real-time data augmentation strategy where rotations, scaling, and elastic deformations are applied randomly along with gamma correction and mirroring.

The neural networks for both tasks were trained using 2D U-Net and 3D U-Net with full resolution options, and the final neural network models were obtained based on an ensemble of these neural networks. The neural networks were trained for 1000 epochs on NVIDIA Tesla V100 (16GB memory) graphics processors. For Task 1, it took around 17 and 24 h to train the neural network for each fold with 2D and 3D U-Net options, respectively. For Task 2, it took around 16 and 20 h to train the neural network for each fold with 2D and 3D U-Net options, respectively. The scripts provided with the nnU-Net framework were applied to identify the best configuration for both neural networks. The neural network model for the nnU-Net was implemented using the PyTorch module.

3   Results

The proposed method was evaluated quantitatively over the validation sets shared by the LAScarQS 2022 challenge organizers for Task 1 and Task 2 using an automated online system. The ground truth labels for the validation sets were blinded to the participants.

The proposed approach yielded Dice, average surface distance (ASD) and Hausdorff distance (HD) metric values of 90.71%, 1.681 and 21.45 for the delineation of the LA cavity in Task 1, respectively. The corresponding values for Task 2 are 89.32%, 1.613 and 15.86. For LA scar segmentation in Task 1, the proposed method yielded a Dice metric value of 63.31%. The accuracy, specificity and sensitivity values of the scar segmentation in Task 1 are 0.99995, 0.99998 and 0.56994, respectively. The quantitative evaluation scores obtained for the delineation of the LA cavity and scar from Task 1 and Task 2 are reported in Table 1.

The segmentation results for the LA cavity and scar from an example validation dataset from Task 1 are shown in Fig. 2 where the predictions for the cavity and scar are shown using green and red labels. Figure 3 shows the 3D rendered predictions of the cavity and scar using the same colours against the multi-planar view of the original LGE MRI data.

A 3D rendered results of the predicted labels corresponding to the LA cavity and scar using 3D Slicer[2] in green and red colors are shown in Fig. 4.

The segmentation results for the LA cavity from an example validation dataset from Task 2 are shown in Fig. 5 where the predictions for the cavity are shown using the green label. Figure 6 shows the 3D rendered prediction of the cavity against the multi-planar view of the original LGE MRI data.

Table 1. Overall performance of the proposed fully automated method evaluated over validation LGE MRI datasets acquired from 10 and 20 patients for tasks 1 and 2, respectively. The evaluations were performed by comparing ground truth delineations of the LA cavity and scar for Task 1. For Task 2, ground truth delineations were available only for the LA cavity.

Metric	Task 1 (LA cavity)	Task 1 (LA scar)	Task 2 (LA cavity)
Dice (%)	90.71	63.31	89.32
ASD	1.681	–	1.613
HD	21.45	–	15.86
GDice (%)	–	92.14	–
Accuracy	–	0.99995	–
Specificity	–	0.99998	–
Sensitivity	–	0.56994	–

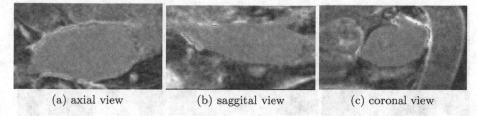

(a) axial view   (b) saggital view   (c) coronal view

Fig. 2. The neural network predicted segmentation results for the LA cavity (green) and scar (red) for an example image volume from Task 1 datasets. (Color figure online)

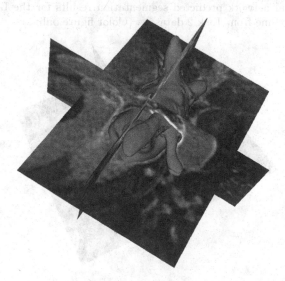

Fig. 3. The neural network predicted segmentation results of LA cavity (green) and scar (red) for an example image volume from Task 1 datasets rendered on the multi-planar view of the original data. (Color figure online)

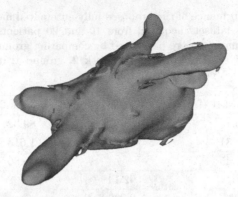

Fig. 4. The neural network predicted segmentation results of LA cavity (green) and scar (red) for an example image volume from Task 1 datasets rendered using 3D Slicer. (Color figure online)

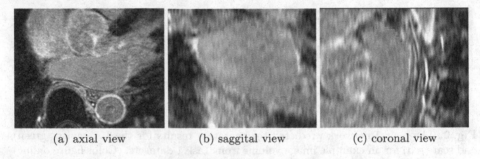

(a) axial view   (b) saggital view   (c) coronal view

Fig. 5. The neural network predicted segmentation results for the LA cavity for an example image volume from Task 2 datasets. (Color figure online)

Fig. 6. The neural network predicted segmentation results of the LA cavity for an example image volume from Task 2 validation dataset rendered on the multi-planar view of the original data.

4 Conclusion

In this study, we utilized a deep convolutional neural network approach known as nnU-Net to delineate the left atrial cavity and scar from late gadolinium enhancement magnetic resonance imaging as a part of the LAScarQS 2022 segmentation challenge. Instead of using the scans in their original orientation, we first aligned them along the coordinate axes and input them into the neural network. The proposed method was trained using 60 and 130 datasets for tasks 1 and 2, respectively. The predicted segmentation results were reoriented to match the corresponding image data. The proposed method yielded Dice score values of 90.71% and 89.32% for the delineation of the LA cavity over the validation sets of tasks 1 and 2, respectively. The corresponding value for the LA scar from task 1 is 63.31%.

Acknowledgment. The authors wish to thank the challenge organizers for providing train and test datasets as well as performing the algorithm evaluation. The authors of this paper declare that the segmentation method they implemented for participation in the LAScarQS 2022 challenge has not used any pre-trained models nor additional datasets other than those provided by the organizers. This research was enabled in part by support provided by WestGrid (www.westgrid.ca) and the Digital Research Alliance of Canada (alliancecan.ca).

References

1. Isensee, F., Jaeger, P.F., Kohl, S.A.A., Petersen, J., Maier-Hein, K.H.: nnU-Net: a self-configuring method for deep learning-based biomedical image segmentation. Nat. Methods **18**(2), 203–211 (2021)
2. Kikinis, R., Pieper, S.D., Vosburgh, K.G.: 3D slicer: a platform for subject-specific image analysis, visualization, and clinical support. In: Jolesz, F.A. (ed.) Intraoperative Imaging and Image-Guided Therapy, pp. 277–289. Springer, New York (2014). https://doi.org/10.1007/978-1-4614-7657-3_19
3. Kornej, J., Börschel, C.S., Benjamin, E.J., Schnabel, R.B.: Epidemiology of atrial fibrillation in the 21st century: novel methods and new insights. Circ. Res. **127**(1), 4–20 (2020)
4. Li, L., Zimmer, V.A., Schnabel, J.A., Zhuang, X.: AtrialGeneral: domain generalization for left atrial segmentation of multi-center LGE MRIs. In: de Bruijne, M., et al. (eds.) MICCAI 2021. LNCS, vol. 12906, pp. 557–566. Springer, Cham (2021). https://doi.org/10.1007/978-3-030-87231-1_54
5. Li, L., Zimmer, V.A., Schnabel, J.A., Zhuang, X.: AtrialJSQnet: a new framework for joint segmentation and quantification of left atrium and scars incorporating spatial and shape information. Med. Image Anal. **76**, 102303 (2022)
6. Milletari, F., Navab, N., Ahmadi, S.: V-net: fully convolutional neural networks for volumetric medical image segmentation. In: 2016 Fourth International Conference on 3D Vision (3DV), pp. 565–571 (Oct 2016)
7. Mortazi, A., Karim, R., Rhode, K., Burt, J., Bagci, U.: *CardiacNET*: segmentation of left atrium and proximal pulmonary veins from MRI using multi-view CNN. In: Descoteaux, M., Maier-Hein, L., Franz, A., Jannin, P., Collins, D.L., Duchesne, S. (eds.) MICCAI 2017. LNCS, vol. 10434, pp. 377–385. Springer, Cham (2017). https://doi.org/10.1007/978-3-319-66185-8_43

8. Pop, M., et al.: Statistical Atlases and Computational Models of the Heart: Atrial Segmentation and LV Quantification Challenges: 9th International Workshop, STACOM 2018, Held in Conjunction with MICCAI 2018, Granada, Spain, 16 September 2018, Revised Selected Papers, vol. 11395. Springer, Cham (2019). https://doi.org/10.1007/978-3-030-12029-0

9. Ronneberger, O., Fischer, P., Brox, T.: U-net: convolutional networks for biomedical image segmentation. In: Navab, N., Hornegger, J., Wells, W.M., Frangi, A.F. (eds.) MICCAI 2015. LNCS, vol. 9351, pp. 234–241. Springer, Cham (2015). https://doi.org/10.1007/978-3-319-24574-4_28

10. Xia, Q., Yao, Y., Hu, Z., Hao, A.: Automatic 3D atrial segmentation from GE-MRIs using volumetric fully convolutional networks. In: Pop, M., et al. (eds.) STACOM 2018. LNCS, vol. 11395, pp. 211–220. Springer, Cham (2019). https://doi.org/10.1007/978-3-030-12029-0_23

11. Zhang, X., Noga, M., Martin, D., Punithakumar, K.: Fully automated left atrium segmentation from anatomical cine long-axis MRI sequences using deep convolutional neural network with unscented Kalman filter. Med. Image Anal. **68** (2021)

12. Zhu, L., Gao, Y., Yezzi, A., MacLeod, R., Cates, J., Tannenbaum, A.: Automatic segmentation of the left atrium from MRI images using salient feature and contour evolution. In: 2012 Annual International Conference of the IEEE Engineering in Medicine and Biology Society (EMBC), pp. 3211–3214. IEEE (2012)

Automatic Semi-supervised Left Atrial Segmentation Using Deep-Supervision 3DResUnet with Pseudo Labeling Approach for LAScarQS 2022 Challenge

Moona Mazher[1], Abdul Qayyum[2(✉)], Mohamed Abdel-Nasser[1,3], and Domenec Puig[1]

[1] Department of Computer Engineering and Mathematics, University Rovira i Virgili, Tarragona, Spain
[2] ENIB, UMR CNRS 6285 LabSTICC, 29238 Brest, France
qayyum@enib.fr
[3] Faculty of Engineering, Department of Electrical Engineering, Aswan University, Aswan, Egypt

Abstract. Left atrial (LA) and atrial scar segmentation from late gadolinium-enhanced magnetic resonance imaging (LGE MRI) is an important task in clinical practice. Late gadolinium enhancement magnetic resonance imaging (LGE MRI) is commonly used to visualize and quantify left atrial (LA) scars. The position and extent of LA scars provide important information on the pathophysiology and progression of atrial fibrillation (AF). LAScarQS 2022: Left Atrial and Scar Quantification & Segmentation Challenge provided the dataset to evaluate the segmentation model to segment the LA and scars. In this paper, we have developed a semi-supervised segmentation approach using the pseudo labeling approach. We have trained two different models for LA segmentation. In the first model, we have trained 3DResUnet with deep supervision techniques to get the pseudo label using training and validation datasets and in the second model, we have trained the nnUNet model that uses the pseudo segmentation labels of the first model with true labels for LA segmentation. The proposed solution provides optimal performance for the LA segmentation task and achieved a 0.88 Dice score on the validation dataset. The source code will be publicly available at https://github.com/RespectKnowledge/Semi-supervised_Segmentation_LAS-carQS-2022-Challenge.

Keywords: Semi-supervised · LA segmentation · 3DResUNet · Deep Supervision · nnUNet · Semi-supervised · Pseudo labeling

1 Introduction

The segmentation and quantification of left atrial (LA) and scars from LGE MRI provide reliable information for patient selection, treatment stratification, and clinical diagnosis [1]. Automatic segmentation of LA and scars from LGE MRI is highly desired as manual delineations of LA and scars are time-consuming and prone to be subjective.

© The Author(s), under exclusive license to Springer Nature Switzerland AG 2023
X. Zhuang et al. (Eds.): LAScarQS 2022, LNCS 13586, pp. 153–161, 2023.
https://doi.org/10.1007/978-3-031-31778-1_15

Automatic methods. However, the development of automatic techniques remains challenging, mainly due to poor image quality, various LA shapes, thin LA walls, and enhanced noise from the surrounding. The challenges for automatic LA cavity segmentation are mainly from the large variations in terms of LA shape, intensity range as well as poor image quality.

In the past various challenges have been introduced for Left Atrial Segmentation. In Left Atrial Segmentation Challenge 2013 (LASC 2013) [2], 30 CT and 30 MRI are provided and various atlas-based methods, such as region growing, statistical shape models (SSM), and multi-atlas segmentation (MAS) are proposed for LA segmentation. However, it could be difficult to obtain a reasonable result when applying atlas-based methods to LGE MRI directly, because in general LGE MRI has relatively poor quality. A common way to solve this problem is to combine LGE MRI with additional balanced steady-state free precession (bSSFP) MRI images to incorporate shape prior [3, 4]. In 2020, various deep learning models have been proposed to segment LA from LGE MRI using 154 LGE MRIs images for the LA segmentation challenge [5]. In this challenge, the results of deep learning-based methods were significantly better than that of traditional atlas-based methods. For instance, the Chen et al. [6] proposed a two-task network for LA segmentation and patient classification. Yang et al. [3] presented a deep network using transfer learning and employed a deep supervision strategy for LA segmentation. Currently, LAScarQS 2022 (Left Atrial and Scar Quantification & Segmentation Challenge) provides more than 200 LGE MRIs that were acquired in a real clinical environment from patients suffering from Atrial fibrillation (AF). The target of this challenge is to develop (semi-) automatically segment the LA cavity and quantify LA scars from LGE MRI. This is however still challenging due to the poor image quality of LGE MRI, the prior model of scars is hard to construct on account of the various LA shapes, the thin wall, the surrounding enhanced regions, and the complex patterns of scars in AF patients. To solve the issues for LA segmentation, we need a robust solution for LA segmentation using LGE MRI. We have been inspired by semi-supervised methods that exist in the literature [7–11] however.

The main findings of this paper are as follows:

1. We have proposed a semi-supervised two-stage solution for LA segmentation. In the first stage, an efficient 3DResUnet model with deep supervision was proposed to train on the training dataset and produced pseudo labels using the sub-training and validation dataset.
2. The nnUNet [10] state-of-the-Art segmentation model has been trained using a sub-training and full training dataset to generate pseudo labeling with a validation dataset. An extensive experiment has been performed to test the proposed two-stages technique for LA segmentation.

A detailed description of the proposed model is shown in Fig. 1.

2   Material and Methods

2.1   LAScarQS 2022 Dataset Descriptions

The challenge provided an LGE MRI dataset from multiple imaging centers around the world. The dataset has been collected from three different centers such as Center 1 (University of Utah), Center 2 (Beth Israel Deaconess Medical Center), and Center 3 (King's College London). The clinical images were acquired from Siemens Avanto 1.5T or Vario 3T using free-breathing (FB), Philips Acheiva 1.5T using FB and navigator-gating with fat suppression, and Philips Acheiva 1.5T using FB and navigator-gating with fat suppression. The spatial resolution of one 3D LGE MRI scan was $1.25 \times 1.25 \times 2.5$ mm using center1 data, $1.4 \times 1.4 \times 1.4$ mm using center 2, and $1.3 \times 1.3 \times 4.0$ mm using center 3. A detailed description of the challenge dataset can be found [13–15]. We participated in task 2 and task 2 datasets consisting of 130 LGE MRIs training and validation cases. Moreover, 64 LGE MRI unseen testing cases including an unknown domain do not appear in the training data. The training dataset has been divided into two parts and these two training parts are used for training and validation of the proposed approach.

2.2   Proposed Method

Proposed Model. Our proposed model consisted of two stages. In the first stage, we proposed 3DResUNet with a deep supervision technique. The proposed model was trained on the training dataset and validation dataset used to predict the labels. These labels are called pseudo labels. In the second stage, the nnUNet model was trained using pseudo and training datasets. The pseudo labels with validation cases were used in the second stage with the original training dataset to train the nnUNet.

3D-ResUnet with Deep Supervision: A framework of the proposed model is presented as an encoder, a decoder, and a baseline module. The 1×1 convolutional layer with softmax function has been used at the end of the proposed model. The 3D strides convolutional layer has been used to reduce the input image spatial size. The convolutional block consists of convolutional layers with Batch-Normalization and ReLU activation functions to extract the different feature maps from each block on the encoder side. In the encoder block, the spatial input size has been reduced with an increasing number of feature maps and on the decoder side, the input image spatial size will increase using a 3D Conv-Transpose layer. The input features' maps that are obtained from every encoder block are concatenated with every decoder block feature map to reconstruct the semantic information. The convolutional (3x3x3conv-BN-ReLu) layer used the input feature maps extracted from every convolutional block on the encoder side and further passed these feature maps into the proposed residual module. The spatial size doubled at every decoder block and feature maps are halved at each decoder stage of the proposed model. The residual block has been inserted at each encoder block with a skip connection. The feature concatenation has been done at every encoder and decoder block except the last 1x1 convolutional layer. The three-level deep-supervision technique is applied to get the aggregate loss between ground truth and prediction. The nnUNet has been modified for training and optimization parameters as compared to the original nnUNet. The batch size in uuUNet was $40 \times 256 \times 224$ using 500 epochs.

Training and Optimization. The proposed deep learning model is implemented in PyTorch and other libraries based on python are used for pre-processing and analysis of the datasets. The SimpleITK is used for reading and writing the nifty data volume. The ITK-SNAP is used for data visualization. The learning rate of 0.0004 with Adam optimizer has been for training the proposed model. The binary cross-entropy function is used as a loss function between the output of the model and the ground-truth sample. 2 batch-size with 200 epochs has been used with 20 early stopping steps. The best model weights have been saved for prediction in the validation phase. The $256 \times 256 \times 16$ input image size was used for training. The Pytorch library is used for model development, training, optimization, and testing. The V100 tesla NVIDIA-GPU machine is used for training and testing the proposed model. The total training time was 18 h using a single GPU V100 tesla machine. The data augmentation methods such as horizontal flipping (p = 0.5), vertical flip (p = 0.5), and RandomGamma (p = 0.8) were used to augment the dataset for training the proposed model. The dataset cases have different intensity ranges. The dataset is normalized between 0 and 1 using the maximal and min intensity normalization method. The training shape of each volume is fixed ($256 \times 256 \times 16$) and resample the prediction mask to the original shape for each validation volume using the linear interpolation method. The prediction mask produced by our proposed model has been resampled such that it has the same size and spacing as the original image and copies all of the meta-data, i.e., origin, direction, orientation, etc.

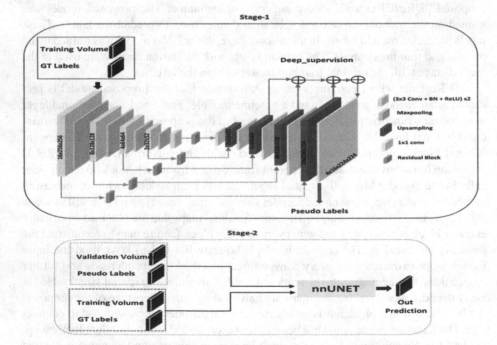

Fig. 1. Proposed model for segmentation using the LAScarQS 2022 dataset.

3   Results and Discussion

3.1   Quantitative Results

The performance of our proposed model on unseen validation datasets in terms of Dice, ASD, and HD is shown in Table 1. This performance is measured by the challenge organizer using 20 validation cases. The average performance using the validation dataset of the proposed model with validation-based pseudo labels, training set-based pseudo labels, nnUNet, 3DResUnet, 3DDenseUnet, and base 3DUnet is shown in Table 1. The 80% training dataset used to train the proposed 3DResUnet and nnUNet model used with pseudo labels generation by 3DResUNet. The proposed model with unlabeled validation samples achieved the highest performance as compared to using fewer training samples. The proposed pseudo-label model produced more generalized performance even with a smaller number of training samples. The Dice score is almost near to the full supervised training dataset when 80% of semi-supervised sub-training samples were used in 3DResUnet to produce pseudo labels. However, the HD produced by 3DResUnet based on an 80% training set in the semi-supervised setting is higher when we used full training samples with validation samples for a pseudo-label generation. It concluded that we can use a few training samples with a pseudo label to achieve optimal performance.

Table 1. Performance comparison of the proposed solution with different configurations on the validation dataset. Where Full-proposed with PLVal is pseudo label using validation and full supervised training dataset. PLTr is a pseudo label using a semi-supervised sub-training dataset.

Models	LAcavity_Dice	LAcavity_ASD	LAcavity_HD
Full-proposedwithPLVal	0.88550	1.81263	18.38903
Semi-proposedwithPLTr	0.881289	2.83415	66.90356
nnUNet model	0.862269	8.801397	138.4065
3DResUnet model	0.845154	4.694311	106.6657
3DDenseUnet model	0.829744	7.444355	116.2937
3Dunet model	0.81657	12.34645	130.0478

The 3DResUnet produced a better performance as compared to 3DDenseUnet and base 3DUnet is shown in Table 1. The Residual module has many advantages such as alleviating the vanishing-gradient problem, strengthening feature propagation, encouraging feature reuse, and substantially reducing the number of parameters. The performance analysis for proposed full supervised data with the pseudo label, semi-supervised, and existing deep learning models for 20 validation subjects is shown in Fig. 2. The result on unseen test dataset is shown in Table 2.

3.2   Qualitative Results

Figure 3 shows the prediction produced by the proposed model on some validation subjects (subj_12, subj_15, sub_18). The model somehow predicted the correct segmentation mask. In subj_18, the proposed model produced a little distorted predicted segmentation mask as compared to the ground-truth segmentation mask while in subjects 12 and 15, the predicted mask almost has a similar shape as compared to ground-truth segmentation masks.

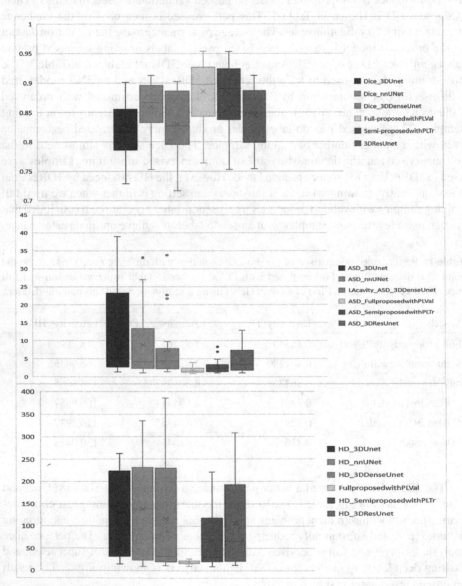

Fig. 2. Performance analysis of proposed and existing deep learning models using 20 validation subjects.

Variability of atrial shapes and poor quality and complex intensity distribution of LGE MRI make it challenging for automatic LGE MRI-based LA segmentation. Another

Table 2. Performance comparison of the proposed solution using Full-proposedwithPLVal on unseen test dataset

Models	LAcavity_Dice	LAcavity_ASD	LAcavity_HD
Full-proposedwithPLVal	0.939741	1.256029	30.09369

problem is the lack of model generalization ability even for the dataset collected from the same center. We have trained various supervised 3D encoder and decoder-based deep learning models using full spatial resolution and patch-based approaches to tackle the LA segmentation problem and validated them using cross-validation. The results based on 3D-based UNet deep learning approaches did not provide satisfactory performance for the LA segmentation problem.

Therefore, it is desired to develop LA LGE MRI efficient models with effective generalization abilities for multi-center and multi-vendor data. We proposed a semi-supervised solution to tackle the model generalization problem using this challenging dataset. The results showed that the performance of our proposed solution is optimal using a multi-center and multi-vendor challenge dataset. The proposed solution may tackle an unknown domain for the LA segmentation on an unseen test dataset. There exists substantial scope for algorithmic improvement in terms of helping the generalization capability of the model for the automatic LA LGE MRI-based segmentation problem.

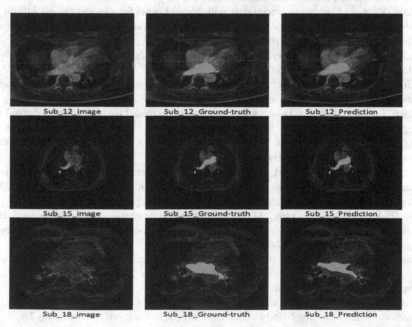

Fig. 3. Qualitative analysis of prediction using validation cases (sub_12, sub_15, sub_18).

4 Conclusion and Future Work

In this paper, the semi-supervised method has been proposed for LA segmentation. The two-stage solution is used to get the optimal performance. In the first stage, the proposed 3DResUNet with deep supervision was used to get the pseudo label and further modified nnUNet was used to obtain the final prediction. Our proposed solution would be used to predict the LA segmentation in clinically sitting. In the pseudo labeling approach, we cater to the validation sample distribution and may be helpful for the generalization of LA segmentation using multi-domain datasets. In the future, we will explore other semi-supervised or super-vised methods to further enhance the performance of the LA and scar segmentation.

Acknowledgment. The authors of this paper declare that the segmentation method they implemented for participation in the LAScarQS 2022 challenge has not used any pre-trained models or additional datasets other than those provided by the organizers. We thank the LAScarQS 2022 challenge organizer teams who provided the dataset and platform to validate our proposed solution.

References

1. Njoku, A., et al.: Left atrial volume predicts atrial fibrillation recurrence after radiofrequency ablation: a meta-analysis. Ep Europace **20**(1), 33–42 (2018)
2. Tobon-Gomez, C., et al.: Benchmark for algorithms segmenting the left atrium from 3D CT and MRI datasets. IEEE Trans. Med. Imaging **34**(7), 1460–1473 (2015)
3. Yang, X., et al.: Combating Uncertainty with Novel Losses for Automatic Left Atrium Segmentation. In: Pop, M., et al. (eds.) STACOM 2018. LNCS, vol. 11395, pp. 246–254. Springer, Cham (2019). https://doi.org/10.1007/978-3-030-12029-0_27
4. Li, L., et al.: Atrial scar quantification via multi-scale CNN in the graph–cuts framework. Med. Image Anal. **60**, 101595 (2020)
5. Xiong, Z., et al.: A global benchmark of algorithms for segmenting late gadolinium-enhanced cardiac magnetic resonance imaging. arXiv preprint arXiv:2004.12314 (2020)
6. Chen, J., et al.: Multiview two-task recursive attention model for left atrium and atrial scars segmentation. In: Frangi, A.F., Schnabel, J.A., Davatzikos, C., Alberola López, C., Fichtinger, G. (eds.) MICCAI 2018. LNCS, vol. 11071, pp. 455–463. Springer, Cham (2018). https://doi.org/10.1007/978-3-030-00934-2_51
7. Vu, T.-H., Jain, H., Bucher, M., Cord, M., Pérez, P.: Advent: adversarial entropy minimization for domain adaptation in semantic segmentation. In: Proceedings of the IEEE/CVF Conference on Computer Vision and Pattern Recognition, pp. 2517–2526 (2019)
8. Ouali, Y., Hudelot, C., Tami, M.: Semi-supervised semantic segmentation with cross-consistency training. In: Proceedings of the IEEE/CVF Conference on Computer Vision and Pattern Recognition, pp. 12674–12684 (2020)
9. Tarvainen, A., Valpola, H.: Mean teachers are better role models: weight-averaged consistency targets improve semi-supervised deep learning results. In: Advances in Neural Information Processing Systems, vol. 30 (2017)
10. Isensee, F., Jaeger, P.F., Kohl, S.A., Petersen, J., Maier-Hein, K.H.: nnu-net: A selfconfiguring method for deep learning-based biomedical image segmentation. Nat. Methods **18**(2), 203–211 (2021)
11. Lalande, A., et al.: Deep learning methods for automatic evaluation of delayed enhancement-MRI. The results of the EMIDEC challenge. Med. Image Anal, vol. 79, p. 102428 (2022)

12. Chen, Z., et al.: Automatic deep learning-based myocardial infarction segmentation from delayed enhancement MRI. Comput. Med. Imaging Graph. **95**, 102014 (2022)
13. Li, L., Zimmer, V.A., Schnabel, J.A., Zhuang, X.: AtrialJSQnet: a new framework for joint segmentation and quantification of left atrium and scars incorporating spatial and shape information. Med. Image Anal. **76**, 102303 (2022)
14. Li, L., Zimmer, V.A., Schnabel, J.A., Zhuang, X.: Medical image analysis on left atrial LGE MRI for atrial fibrillation studies: a review. Med. Image Anal. **77**, 102360 (2022)
15. Li, L., Zimmer, V.A., Schnabel, J.A., Zhuang, X.: AtrialGeneral: domain generalization for left atrial segmentation of multi-center LGE MRIs. In: de Bruijne, M., et al. (eds.) MICCAI 2021. LNCS, vol. 12906, pp. 557–566. Springer, Cham (2021). https://doi.org/10.1007/978-3-030-87231-1_54

Author Index

X. Zhuang et al. (Eds.): LAScarQS 2022, LNCS 13586, pp. 163–164, 2023.
https://doi.org/10.1007/978-3-031-31778-1

Printed in the United States
by Baker & Taylor Publisher Services